CAROLINA CUISINE

A COLLECTION OF RECIPES

Compiled and Edited

By

THE JUNIOR ASSEMBLY

OF

ANDERSON, SOUTH CAROLINA

1969

Published by
Hallux, Inc.
Publishers of Books
Anderson, S. C.

For Additional Copies of

CAROLINA CUISINE

Send $4.50 per copy (plus 40-cents postage)

To: The Junior Assembly of Anderson, S. C.
P. O. Box 931
Anderson, S. C. 29621

CONTENTS

ACKNOWLEDGMENTS

The creation of *CAROLINA CUISINE* has truly been a labor of love for those who have shared in its preparation. It has been made possible only through the co-operation of each of you who has so generously contributed your time and culinary skills in compiling this fine collection of recipes.

The contributions in this book have been submitted by ladies of all ages and walks of life, and to everyone who has aided in its publication, the Junior Assembly wishes to express its appreciation for your interest and support.

For the Junior Assembly members, the realization that through the proceeds from this book Anderson children will find life a richer and more satisfying experience is ample reward for their labors.

As the 1969 President of the Junior Assembly I wish to thank each member personally for the time, talent, and devotion you have shared in compiling *CAROLINA CUISINE*.

And to the Junior Assembly I wish the greatest success in this and all future endeavors.

Harriet T. Yarbrough

CO-EDITORS
Mrs. Neil Chamblee   Mrs. Michael Little

Art Director .... Mrs. Walter Duffie
Editorial Director .... Mrs. Thomas B. Phillips, Jr.
Research Director .... Mrs. Robert L. Waldrep
Recipe Director .... Mrs. Richard Christopher III
Promotional Director .... Mrs. Bruce Salley
Distribution Director .... Mrs. William M. Dillard, Jr.
Features Director .... Mrs. Gerald Welborn
Composition Directors .... Mrs. Richard Anderson
                                        Mrs. Allan P. Sloan, Jr.

STAFF

Mrs. Julian Bannister, Mrs. William F. Bolt, Mrs. Stuart Brown, Mrs. Dan Chamblee, Mrs. James P. Clamp, Mrs. Paul L. Embler, Mrs. Raymond B. Fretwell, Mrs. Sam Fretwell, Jr., Mrs. William P. Fretwell, Mrs. Ernest W. Garrison, Jr., Mrs. Gerald D. Gillespie, Mrs. Michael D. Glenn, Mrs. John M. Greene, Mrs. William Hendrix, Mrs. Robert C. Herndon, Mrs. T. P. Hughes, Mrs. C. Patrick Killen, Mrs. Larry King, Mrs. Larry Kowalski, Mrs. Marshall Kowalski, Mrs. Robert Mayfield, Mrs. Walter A. Mayfield, Jr., Mrs. Douglas C. McDougald, Jr., Mrs. Everett H. Newman, Mrs. John P. Noury, Mrs. Carl G. Oehmig, Mrs. David Owen, Mrs. Robert S. Owens, Jr., Mrs. Robert E. Padgett, Jr., Mrs. John Parasho, Mrs. Joe Prevost, Jr., Mrs. James B. Pruitt, Jr., Mrs. F. Smith Pruitt, Mrs. Richard Shawn, Mrs. F. Spencer Shirley, Mrs. Ben J. Smith, Mrs. James Smith, Mrs. Robert Speakman, Mrs. Wesley R. Strong, Mrs. T. Averette Taylor, Jr., Mrs. William L. Thompson, Mrs. Douglas Thrasher, Mrs. Fritz Waidner, Mrs. Furman K. Walter, Mrs. Warren White.

1969 JUNIOR ASSEMBLY OFFICERS

Mrs. Joseph Yarbrough, Jr......................... President
Mrs. Newton Newell .... Vice-President
Mrs. Cliff Bryant .... Secretary
Mrs. Carroll Smith .... Corresponding Secretary
Mrs. Bruce Salley .... Treasurer

PREFACE

The Junior Assembly of Anderson, South Carolina, presents *CAROLINA CUISINE* as more than a collection of recipes. Within the following pages will be found menus, recipes, illustrations and features that are a part of the tradition of hospitality in the South. The heirloom recipes that open each section are reminiscent of a bygone era. We invite you to read and to try these antiques which we have presented in their original form. While these old recipes are an important part of *CAROLINA CUISINE,* modern recipes do form the main body of the cookbook. Every feature within the following pages is significant to the Junior Assembly as representing the contributions of members, friends, relatives, and of outstanding local and state leaders as well. Through *CAROLINA CUISINE* we hope to continue the traditions of fine foods and hospitality in the South for many years to come.

THE JUNIOR ASSEMBLY STORY

On a brisk winter afternoon in 1935, a group of enterprising young Andersonians met at the home of Flora Young to organize a club for young women. As a result of the ideas and efforts of these young ladies, the Junior Assembly of Anderson, South Carolina, came into being. From this beginning the Junior Assembly has developed into an organization devoted to the enhancing of civic, cultural, charitable, and social life in the city of Anderson.

Through the years numbers of young ladies have devoted their time and energy to this blend of work and fun, and have succeeded in making the Junior Assembly one of the most successful clubs in the state.

Most of the civic and charitable organizations in the city have benefited from the activities of the Junior Assembly, either through financial contributions or the personal assistance of the members. Perhaps the most valuable contributions made by Assembly members have been gifts of their time and varied talents.

A major goal of every adult is the encouragement of the welfare and education of our youth, and it is in this field that the Junior Assembly members have concentrated their efforts to provide as many services as possible to aid Anderson's children.

MENUS

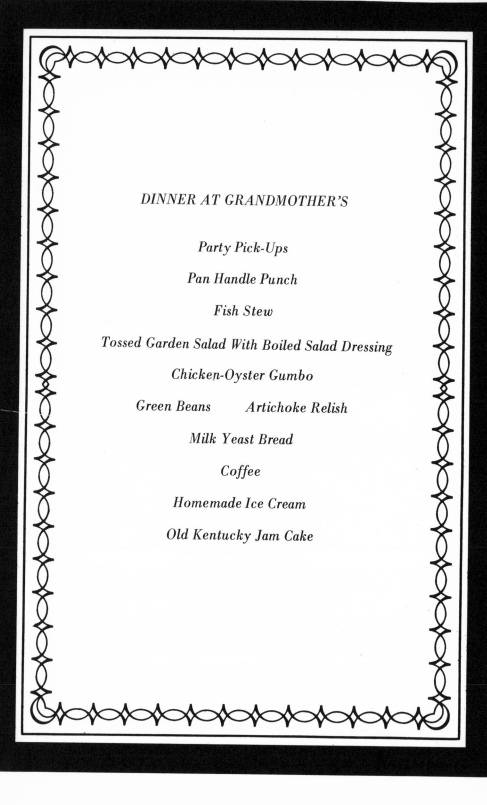

DINNER AT GRANDMOTHER'S

Party Pick-Ups

Pan Handle Punch

Fish Stew

Tossed Garden Salad With Boiled Salad Dressing

Chicken-Oyster Gumbo

Green Beans   Artichoke Relish

Milk Yeast Bread

Coffee

Homemade Ice Cream

Old Kentucky Jam Cake

CAROLINA CUISINE invites you into the homes of the members of the Junior Assembly of Anderson, South Carolina. Our hospitality begins with menus for entertaining submitted by Assembly members and their friends. The menus are followed by recipes collected from all over the world, each representing an Assembly member, either as her own or as one from a friend or member of her family. Every entry in CAROLINA CUISINE speaks of the hospitality for which Carolina is famous, both yesterday and today.

BREAKFAST

Mrs. Samuel R. Moorhead, Junior

Hot Tomato Cocktail or Pink Grapefruit with Lime Sherbet

Appleyard Scrambled Eggs   Broiled Tomatoes

Mushroom Baked Ham

Spoonbread or Creole Corn Muffins

Whipped Unsalted Butter

Assorted Sweet Rolls   Sour Cream Coffee Cake

Coffee

INFORMAL MORNING COFFEE

Mrs. Bruce Salley

Sausage Balls

Doughnut Holes (Bakery)

Mock Chicken Salad Sandwiches

Cheese Favors

Perked Cranberry Punch

Coffee

BRUNCH

Mrs. J. Gary Early

Ginger Ale Melon Cup

Poached Eggs a la Bearnaise   Buttered Asparagus Spears

Canadian Bacon / Garnish with Crab Apples

Spoon Bread / Butter Curls

Coffee

BRIDGE LUNCHEON

Mrs. Richard G. Christopher III

Melon Balls

Ham Tetrazzini

Tomato-Asparagus Bake

Peach Pickle   Onion Bread

Meringue Angel Pie

Coffee

LUNCHEON

Mrs. Virginia Sloan

Creamed Shrimp and Peas in Timbales

Tomato Aspic on Lettuce   Pickled Crabapples

Parsley Potatoes

Hot Rolls

Strawberry Parfait

Coffee

BRIDAL LUNCHEON

Mrs. Beaty Jackson

Barbeque Chicken with Mushrooms

Asparagus Souffle   Orange Sherbet in Orange Halves

Cucumber Aspic on Lettuce

Olive Muffins

Angel Cake with Coffee Ice Cream   Butterscotch Sauce

AFTERNOON TEA

Mrs. M. L. Propp

Sparkle Punch

Cream and Tuna Sandwiches

Snappy Cheese and Ham Pinwheels

Pineapple-Walnut Bread

Chocolate-Coconut Cookies

Snickerdoodles

Stuffed Ripe Olives

Mints

FORMAL DINNER

Mrs. Fritz Waidner

Onion Soup

Roast Wild Duck with Apricot Sauce

Casserole Green Beans   Squash Casserole

Flaming Peaches   Hard Rolls

Baked Alaska

Dry Red Wine

HOLIDAY DINNER

Mrs. Ted Owen

Celery Hearts   Olives   Pickled Peaches

Cranberry Salad with Sour Cream Dressing

Rock Cornish Hen
on bed of
Wild Rice and Mushrooms

Broccoli with Lemon Butter

Orange Halves Stuffed with Sweet Potatoes

Whole Wheat Biscuits

Muscatel Rum Pie

Coffee

DINNER BUFFET

Mrs. Walter C. Duffie

Lime Congealed Salad on Lettuce

Whole Crabapples and Sweet Gherkins

Sliced Baked Ham   **Parsley Buttered Chicken Breasts**

Carolina Rice   **Asparagus Souffle**

Party Yeast Rolls

Cherries Jubilee

Coffee

GOURMET COOK-OUT

Mrs. Neil Chamblee

Spiced Tomato Juice

Cheese Log with Crackers

Stuffed Club Steaks   or   **Stuffed Lamb Chops**

Corn on the Cob

Relish Tray   **Cottage Bread**

Lemonade or Iced Tea

Pineapple and Raspberry Sherbet with Stemmed Cherry

APPETIZERS & HORS d'OEUVRES

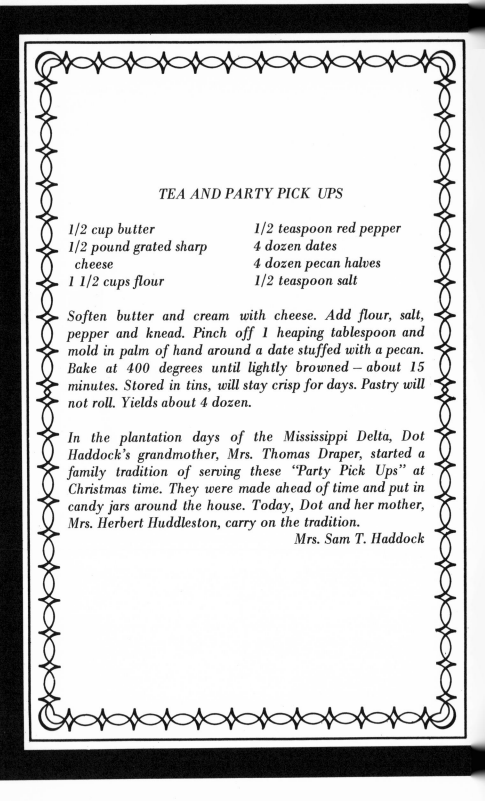

TEA AND PARTY PICK UPS

1/2 cup butter
1/2 pound grated sharp
  cheese
1 1/2 cups flour

1/2 teaspoon red pepper
4 dozen dates
4 dozen pecan halves
1/2 teaspoon salt

Soften butter and cream with cheese. Add flour, salt, pepper and knead. Pinch off 1 heaping tablespoon and mold in palm of hand around a date stuffed with a pecan. Bake at 400 degrees until lightly browned — about 15 minutes. Stored in tins, will stay crisp for days. Pastry will not roll. Yields about 4 dozen.

In the plantation days of the Mississippi Delta, Dot Haddock's grandmother, Mrs. Thomas Draper, started a family tradition of serving these "Party Pick Ups" at Christmas time. They were made ahead of time and put in candy jars around the house. Today, Dot and her mother, Mrs. Herbert Huddleston, carry on the tradition.

Mrs. Sam T. Haddock

BACON CRISPS

24 Waverly Wafers   6 strips raw bacon
quartered

Wrap a quarter of raw bacon around each Waverly Wafer. Place on a broiler pan and place in 225 degree oven for 25 minutes on each side. Serves 8.

Mrs. Richard L. Cromer

BOLOGNA ROLL

1 4-ounce package cream cheese   1 package bologna

Soften cream cheese with milk. Spread cream cheese on thinly sliced bologna. Roll bologna and fasten with toothpick. Chill. Cut into 1/4 or 1/2 slices.

Mrs. Warren F. Harris

GINGERALE MELON CUP

1 quart mixed melon balls   1/4 cup sugar
Cantaloupe   1/4 cup lemon juice
Watermelon   1 1/2 cups chilled gingerale
Honeydew   Mint sprigs
Strawberries

Marinate melon balls with mixture of sugar and lemon juice – chill for several hours. Spoon melon balls and syrup into individual containers. Pour gingerale over them and garnish with mint sprigs. Serves 6.

Mrs. J. Gary Early

ORANGE COATING FOR NUTS

1 1/2 cups sugar
1/2 cup orange juice
1 teaspoon white Karo

1/4 teaspoon salt
2 or 3 cups nut halves

Cook first four ingredients to soft ball stage. Remove from heat and add nuts. Stir until creamy. Turn on foil and separate.

Mrs. Mark Warren

HI! PENNY SNACKS

1 cup flour
1/2 cup margarine

1 cup grated sharp cheese
1/2 envelope onion soup mix

Mix above ingredients together well. Make into roll. Wrap in foil. Chill, for approximately 2 hours. Slice 3/8 inch thick and bake at 350 degrees for 20 minutes.

Mrs. Jones Chamblee

STUFFED ARTICHOKE HEARTS

24 artichoke hearts
1/4 pound smoked ham (ground)
2 tablespoons sour cream
2 tablespoons mayonnaise
1 tablespoon lemon juice

Dash of salt and pepper
1/8 teaspoon dry mustard
1/8 teaspoon coriander seed
24 capers

Wash and drain artichoke hearts. Mix remaining ingredients except capers. Stuff artichoke hearts. Top each with one caper. Yields 24.

Mrs. Joseph C. Yarbrough, Jr.

CAULIFLOWER BUDS AND COCKTAIL SAUCE

1 medium cauliflower

SAUCE

6 teaspoons horseradish	9 tablespoons tomato catsup
1 teaspoon salt	6 tablespoons vinegar
1/2 teaspoon Tabasco	6 tablespoons lemon juice

Cut cauliflower and separate into buds. Serve with sauce as dip.

Mrs. Fritz Waidner

STUFFED RIPE OLIVES

Stuff pitted ripe olives with one large dry roasted peanut in each olive.

Mrs. M. L. Propp

TUNA PINWHEELS

1 small can tuna, drained	1 teaspoon prepared mustard
1/2 cup mayonnaise	20 slices sandwich bread
1/2 cup finely chopped celery	(crusts removed)
2 tablespoons chopped pickle	

Combine first 5 ingredients and spread thinly on buttered bread. Roll like jelly roll. Cut each slice into 3 pinwheels. Fasten with toothpick. When ready to serve, brush with melted butter, sprinkle lightly with paprika and broil until slightly toasted. Yields around 60.

Mrs. Joe Metz, Jr.
Hilliard, Ohio

23

PARTY MEAT BALLS

2 pounds ground chuck
2 eggs
1/2 teaspoon salt
1/4 teaspoon pepper

1 jar chili sauce (12-ounce)
1 jar grape jelly (10-ounce)
1 tablespoon lemon juice

Mix first four ingredients and shape into tiny balls. Combine last three ingredients and place in large baking dish or pan. Add uncooked meat balls and bake at 350 degrees for 1 1/2 hours. Serve warm with toothpicks. Yields 25-30 meatballs.

Mrs. John M. Greene

MARINATED HOT DOGS

1 pound hot dogs
1 can of beer

1 teaspoon Worcestershire
Shake of hot sauce

Cut hot dogs in bite-size pieces. Add Worcestershire sauce and hot sauce to beer. Heat hot dogs in beer mixture until they absorb most of the liquid. Serve hot in chafing dish. Men especially like this. Serves 8-10.

Mrs. W. R. Phillips, Jr.

BROILED STUFFED MUSHROOMS

16 mushrooms (medium)
Olive oil (or melted butter)
1/4 cup finely chopped nuts
1/4 cup fine bread crumbs
Salt and fresh ground pepper

1 teaspoon chopped chives
 (or parsley)
1/4 teaspoon garlic powder
3 tablespoons light cream
1 1/2 tablespoons butter

Remove stems. Peel the mushrooms and place them cap side up, in a shallow, lightly-buttered casserole or copper pan. Brush the tops with oil (or melted butter) and broil for 2-3 minutes. Combine the remaining ingredients, except butter. Turn the caps over and pile high with mixture. Dot well with butter and bake at 350 degrees for 15 minutes. Put aside, when ready to serve, run under hot broiler for 3-4 minutes. Serves 6.

Mrs. Robert T. James

CHEESE BUTTONS

2 sticks margarine
2 cups grated sharp cheese

2 cups sifted flour
2 cups Rice Krispies

Allow margarine to soften at room temperature. Combine with other ingredients, mixing thoroughly. Roll into small balls (size of a small marble), then place on ungreased cooky sheet and flatten with a fork. (Will be about the size of a quarter.) Bake at 325 degrees until light tan, about 18 minutes. One recipe makes 100 plus "buttons".

Mrs. James H. Young

CHEESE FAVORS

1 cup grated sharp cheese
1 cup flour
1 stick margarine

1/8 teaspoon salt
2 tablespoons milk or cream
1 jar apple jelly

Cream margarine and cheese together. Add flour and salt, and mix well. Knead and roll on flour board. Cut with biscuit cutter. Add 1/4 teaspoon of apple jelly and fold over. Crimp edges. For variety, add dates and nuts to apple jelly or fig preserves as filling. Cook at 350 degrees for 15 minutes. Yields 36.

Mrs. D. Bruce Salley

CHEESE PUFFS

1/4 pound grated natural
   sharp cheddar cheese
1/4 cup soft butter
1/2 cup sifted regular
   all purpose flour

1/4 teaspoon salt
1/2 teaspoon paprika
24 stuffed olives

At least 5 hours before serving: Blend cheese and butter — stir in flour, salt and paprika and mix well. Wrap 1 teaspoonful of dough around each olive, covering completely. Arrange on ungreased baking sheet and refrigerate. About 1/2 hour before serving, bake in 400 degree oven for 10-15 minutes. Serve warm. Yields 24.

Mrs. William York

CHEESE WAFERS

1 large can Parmesan cheese
2 1/2 cups plain flour
2 sticks soft margarine

1/2 teaspoon red pepper
1 tablespoon Worcestershire

Mix all ingredients. Form small balls and place on ungreased cookie sheet two inches apart. Press flat with fork. Bake 6-10 minutes at 350 degrees. Yields 40 wafers.

Mrs. George B. Salley, Jr.
Spartanburg, S. C.

CHEESE WAFERS

1 stick margarine
1/4 pound medium sharp
   cheddar cheese

1 cup flour
Salt
White of one egg

Grate cheese and mix with soft margarine. Sift flour into mixture. Roll out and cut with small cutter. (Dough is rolled as thick as a thick cookie.) Brush each with white of egg and sprinkle with salt lightly. Bake at 350 degrees for about 10 minutes on ungreased cookie sheet. Dash on paprika. Yields 30 wafers.

Mrs. William P. Lowe
Louisville, Kentucky

CAVIAR CHEESEBALL

16 ounces extra sharp cheese
1 8-ounce cream cheese
1 tablespoon mayonnaise
1 tablespoon of Worcestershire

1 teaspoon dry mustard
Dash of Tabasco
Garlic salt
Small jar red or black caviar

Grate cheese at room temperature, and add cream cheese, mayonnaise, Worcestershire, Tabasco and garlic salt to taste. Place into double boiler until melted and then pour into desired mold. Mold should be greased generously with cooking oil. Refrigerate. Before serving, spoon caviar on cheeseball.

Mrs. Ted Owen

CHRISTMAS CHEESE LOG

1/2 pound grated sharp cheese
2 tablespoons minced onion
3 tablespoons minced bell
   pepper
3 chopped olives
1 tablespoon chopped pimento

2 tablespoons chopped pickles
1 hard boiled egg
1/2 cup crushed saltine
   crackers
1/4 cup mayonnaise
1/2 teaspoon salt

Mix all ingredients. Roll and shape into log on waxed paper. Chill until firm. Serves 20.

Mrs. Bobby McAlister

CHEESE BALLS

1/2 pound American cheese
Small wedge of blue cheese
1 tube garlic cheese

1 tube smoky or nippy cheese
2 8-ounce packages cream
cheese with chives

Grind up. Mix well. Make into balls. Chill, then roll in ground nuts.

Mrs. William L. Thompson

CHILI CHEESE LOG

3/4 pound cheese (sharp)
1 3-ounce cream cheese
1/4 teaspoon salt

1/8 teaspoon garlic salt'
1 1/2 teaspoon Worcestershire
1/8 teaspoon pepper

Blend ingredients well and roll into two logs on wax pepper. Roll logs in chili powder and chill before serving on crackers.

Mrs. James H. Barton

SNAPPY CHEESE AND HAM PINWHEELS

2 3-ounce packages cream cheese
1 5-ounce jar blue cheese spread

1/2 teaspoon onion juice
5 slices boiled ham

This recipe can be prepared up to 6 weeks ahead. Soften cream cheese and blue cheese spread at room temperature. Beat cream cheese until soft and fluffy, gradually add blue cheese; stir in onion juice. Spread mixture on ham slices and roll each slice in jelly-roll fashion. Wrap in foil. Freeze.

TO SERVE
Slice frozen rolls into pinwheels 3/4 inch thick, place on serving dish. Makes 30.

Mrs. M. L. Propp

COCKTAIL NIBBLES

2 boxes plain pretzel sticks
1 box cheese pretzel sticks
2 boxes Rice Chex cereal
1 box Wheat Chex cereal
2 boxes Cheerios cereal
1 box Alphabets cereal
1 box Life cereal
Planters Peanuts (small can)

Spanish Peanuts (small can)
Pecan halves (about 1 quart)
1 pound margarine
3/4 cup Wesson oil
1/2 cup Worcestershire
3 tablespoons garlic salt
2 tablespoons onion salt
2 tablespoons celery salt

Mix the above cereals in a large roaster pan (two if needed). Add the peanuts and pecans, and mix well. Heat the remaining ingredients until mixed well. Pour over mixture, cover with foil or lid, and bake for 45 minutes at 300 degrees. Remove cover and continue baking until brown. Stir frequently and add more salt, any or all types listed, if needed. Omit any types of cereal not desired. Recipe will half and is still quite good.

Mrs. Thomas B. Phillips, Jr.

DEVILED HAM PASTRIES

1 3-ounce can deviled ham
2 teaspoons tomato pickle
  relish

1/2 teaspoon mustard
Piecrust mix

Combine the deviled ham, tomato pickle relish and prepared mustard in a small bowl. Prepare 1/2 package (1 stick) piecrust mix. Roll out on floured board to 1/8 inch thickness. Cut out 30 2-inch rounds. Arrange half on ungreased cookie sheet. Spoon 1 level teaspoon ham mixture in center of each. Moisten edges. Cut out center of remaining rounds with small cutter or thimble. Place rings over filled rounds. Seal edges. Bake for 15 minutes at 425 degrees. Serve warm. Yields 15.

Mrs. Curtis Gillespie

CHILI-CON-QUESO DIP

2 1-pound cans tomatoes
1 large green chili pepper
1/8 teaspoon garlic powder
1/8 teaspoon salt

1/8 teaspoon pepper
4 medium onions (chopped)
1 1/2-pound Velvetta cheese

Melt cheese. Drain tomatoes. Dice pepper. Add other ingredients. Stir constantly. Heat 15 minutes; serve hot. Eat on Fritos Corn Chips.

Mrs. Richard Anderson

CLAM DIP

3 tablespoons butter
1 chopped onion
1/2 chopped green pepper
1 10 1/2-ounce can minced clam
1/4 pound Velvetta cheese

4 tablespoons catsup
1 tablespoon Worcestershire
1 tablespoon sherry
1/4 teaspoon red pepper

Saute' onion and green pepper in butter. Drain clams and add cheese, catsup , Worcestershire, sherry and red pepper. Cook in chafing dish or casserole until mixed. Serve hot.

Mrs. Robert Herstine

HOT ROLL SNACKS

1 can Crescent Rolls
Sour cream
Onion salt
Crisp fried bacon

Sliced cheese
Olives
Deviled ham
Cream cheese with horseradish

Roll the dough thin. Cut into 2-inch squares. Spread each square with one of the following: sour cream, onion salt and bacon; sliced cheese and an olive; deviled ham; cream cheese with horseradish. Pinch corners of squares together and bake at 375 degrees for 10 minutes. Yields 16 to 20.

Mrs. Michael L. Little
Mrs. Thomas B. Phillips, Jr.

HOT CRAB DIP

1 can cream of celery soup
1 can cream of asparagus soup
1 stick butter or margarine

1 pound crab meat
2 teaspoons sherry

Heat soup and butter in heavy pan, stirring often to keep from burning. When mixture begins to boil, add carefully picked crab meat and continue stirring intermittently until it again boils. Add sherry, and when thoroughly mixed, pour into heated chafing dish and with ice-teaspoon serve onto crisp crackers or very thin small biscuits. Serves 20-30.

Mrs. C. Edwin Roberts
Charleston, S. C.

HOT CRAB COCKTAIL SPREAD

1 8-ounce cream cheese
1 tablespoon milk
2 teaspoons Worcestershire
1 7 1/2-ounce can crabmeat
drained and flaked

2 tablespoons chopped green
onion
2 tablespoons toasted slivered
almonds

Thoroughly combine cream cheese with milk and Worcestershire sauce. Add crabmeat and onion. Spread into small, shallow baking dish, greased. Top with almonds. Bake in 350 degree oven 15 minutes or until heated through. Keep warm over candle warmer. Serve with assorted crackers. Have spreaders handy.

Mrs. Calvin Kinard
Greenwood, S. C.
Mrs. Wilburn Gable

LOBSTER SPREAD

1 pound lobster meat
finely chopped
1 tablespoon minced onion
1 tablespoon minced celery
2 teaspoons fresh lemon juice

1/2 teaspoon grated lemon rind
1/4 teaspoon salt
4 or 5 drops Tabasco
3/4 cup mayonnaise
1/8 teaspoon black pepper

Mix all ingredients together and adjust seasonings to suit taste.

Mrs. Fritz Waidner

HOT LOBSTER (OR CRABMEAT) CANAPES

14 1 1/2-inch bread rounds
1/2 cup mayonnaise
1 teaspoon fresh lemon juice
1/4 teaspoon curry powder

1 cup chopped lobster or crab-
meat (fresh or canned)
Grated Parmesan cheese
Paprika

Toast bread rounds on one side, remove from stove; turn, and spread lightly with a blend of mayonnaise, lemon juice and curry powder. Cover with chopped lobster, salt to taste and spread with balance of seasoned mayonnaise. Sprinkle each round with Parmesan cheese and a shake of paprika. Place under broiler until hot and bubbly (3-4 minutes). Serves 6.

Mrs. Robert T. James

SHRIMP DIP

1 1/2-pounds frozen or fresh
green shrimp (boiled)
2 8-ounce packages cream
cheese
1 medium onion, grated

1 1/2 teaspoons celery salt
1 teaspoon Texas Pete's
Hot Sauce
1 teaspoon lemon juice
1 1/2 teaspoons A-1 Sauce

Grind boiled shrimp and onion (very finely). Whip cream cheese with beater until fluffy. Mix all ingredients together. Add more of A-1 or hot sauce to taste if desired. Serves 100-150 for a drop-in (small servings). Can be halved.

Mrs. Cary Doyle

SHRIMP DIP

1 can frozen cream of shrimp
soup
6 ounces cream cheese, cubed

3 tablespoons chili sauce
1/8 teaspoon Tabasco

Place all ingredients in blender. Cover and blend just until smooth. Chill. Serve with potato chips, crackers, raw vegetables or cooked shrimp. Makes 1 1/2 cups.

Mrs. John Parasho

SHRIMP SANDWICH SPREAD

2 3-ounce packages cream
  cheese
4 tablespoons mayonnaise
3 tablespoons catsup
1/2 teaspoon mustard

1/4 teaspoon garlic powder
1 can shrimp (finely chopped)
1/2 cup celery (finely chopped)
3 teaspoons onion (grated)

Mash cream cheese well. Blend all remaining ingredients except celery and onion and then combine with the celery and onion. Combine this mixture with cream cheese mixture and mix well. Spread on bread cut in desired shapes.

Mrs. W. Ray Thompson

*There is nothing better for a man, than
that he should eat and drink, and that
he should make his soul enjoy good in
his labor. — Ecclesiastes 11:24*

SHRIMP BALLS

1 pound chopped cooked shrimp
2 3-ounce packages soft
  cream cheese
1/4 cup finely cut celery
1 tablespoon chili sauce
1 hard cooked egg, chopped

2 tablespoons diced green
  pepper
1 tablespoon grated onion
1 teaspoon Worcestershire
2 teaspoons horseradish
Salt and pepper to taste

Mix the above ingredients well and shape into small balls. Roll in chopped parsley. Chill until serving time.

Mrs. Fred E. Green

SHRIMP DIP

1 pound shrimp (peeled)
1 cup mayonnaise
1 medium onion, grated
Juice of one lemon

1 stick margarine
1/8 teaspoon red pepper
1/4 teaspoon Tabasco
1/2 teaspoon Worcestershire

Prepare dip 24 hours in advance. Mix dip ingredients together. Use with one pound of peeled shrimp.

Mrs. Alfred Ellison
Greenville, S. C.

MARINATED SHRIMP

1 cup oil
1/2 cup vinegar
1 jar horseradish mustard
1 cup chopped celery

1 or 2 onions in rings
2 pounds cooked shrimp
Salt and pepper to taste

Put first 3 ingredients in blender and blend with salt and pepper. Then add chopped celery. Layer shrimp and onions in bowl. Pour marinade over shrimp and let stand in refrigerator 24 hours. I use this as an appetizer with crackers or as a salad for luncheon.

Mrs. Charles Bauknight

PICKLED SHRIMP

3/4 cup vinegar
1/2 pound cooked shrimp
1/4 teaspoon salt
1/4 teaspoon freshly ground
  pepper

1/2 teaspoon dry mustard
1/8 stick butter
1/2 cup water
Pinch of sugar

Boil vinegar, salt, pepper, mustard, butter, water and sugar and pour over cooked shrimp; chill overnight.

Mrs. Raymond B. Fretwell

34

MOCK CHICKEN SALAD SANDWICHES

1 cup chopped nuts
1 hard cooked egg
1 small bottle olives

1 small onion
1 pint mayonnaise

Chop all ingredients fine and mix together. Add one pint mayonnaise. Keep in refrigerator. Spread on small squares of whole wheat or sandwich bread. Makes 2 cups spread.

Mrs. D. Bruce Salley
Mrs. Furman Walter

And now: "Let the mistress of the house see to it that the coffee is excellent." — Brillat-Savarin

SANDWICH CAKE

2 8-ounce packages cream cheese
1 can beef consommé
1/2 stick of butter
2 tablespoons mayonnaise
1 can deviled ham

1 can deviled chicken
1 can chicken liver pate
Garlic salt
3 loaves sliced sandwich
    bread, decrusted

Allow cream cheese to soften at room temperature. Add enough consommé a little at a time to make it easy to spread. Add 1/2 stick of butter, 2 tablespoons mayonnaise and 1/8 teaspoon garlic salt. Place bread on tray. Spread each slice with 1 of the 3 fillings (chicken, ham or chicken liver pate) and place face down. Spread the other side of the bread with cream cheese mixture. Frost with remaining cheese spread and decorate with radishes, carrots, olives and parsley to resemble a bouquet of flowers. Place in refrigerator 2 hours before serving.

Mrs. George Campbell
Greenville, S. C.

HAM-PEANUT SANDWICH FILLING

1 pound lean ham, in chunks
1 small onion, quartered
1/2 cup Spanish peanuts
  with husks

1/2 cup drained pickle relish
1/2 cup mayonnaise

Alternate ham, onion, and peanuts through food grinder. Mix with relish and mayonnaise and refrigerate. Use as desired for sandwiches. Yields about 3 cups.

Mrs. Ken Monson
Crosby, North Dakota

PIMENTO-CHEESE SANDWICH SPREAD

1/2 pound sharp cheese
1 teaspoon grated onion
1 teaspoon prepared mustard
1 small jar pimento

1/8 teaspoon freshly ground
  pepper
2 teaspoons sugar

Mix above ingredients and add enough salad dressing to spread.

Mrs. Warren White

SANDWICH SPREAD

1 small onion, chopped
1 green pepper, chopped
9 ripe olives, chopped

1 sour pickle, chopped
1 cup grated sharp cheese

Add mayonnaise to make spreading consistency.

Mrs. Theo L. Burriss

SWEET SANDWICHES

1 lemon, all grated
1 cup sugar
1 egg
1 tablespoon butter

1 cup mayonnaise
1 cup chopped pecans
1 cup raisins

Cook first 4 ingredients on stove until thick. Add mayonnaise,pecans and raisins. Cool and spread on sandwich bread. This mixture can be refrigerated for future use. Sandwiches add a touch of sweet on a picnic (men love them!).

Mrs. James B. Cox
Columbia, S. C.

TUNA PUFF SANDWICHES

1 7-ounce can tuna, drained and flaked	2 tablespoons chopped green pepper
1 1/2 teaspoons mustard	3 hamburger buns, split
1/4 teaspoon Worcestershire	6 tomato slices
1/4 cup mayonnaise	1/2 cup mayonnaise
1 1/2 teaspoons grated onion	1/4 cup grated American cheese

Blend first six ingredients. Pile onto bun halves. Top each with tomato slice. Blend 1/2 cup mayonnaise with cheese. Spread on tomato slices. Broil 4 inches from heat until topping puffs and browns. Serves 6.

Mrs. George Marianos

CREAM AND TUNA SANDWICHES

2 3-ounce packages cream cheese	3 tablespoons mayonnaise
1/4 teaspoon Tabasco	1 6 1/2-ounce can tuna
	1 tablespoon lemon juice

Have cream cheese at room temperature. Rinse tuna in a strainer in hot water to remove all oil and juice. Add tuna and remaining ingredients to cream cheese. Mix well with mixer or in blender. Spread on white bread and cut in any desired shape.

Mrs. M. L. Propp

SAUSAGE BALLS

1 pound hot or mild sausage   1 small package biscuit mix

Blend together and make out into balls on a cookie sheet (around 50 balls). Cook in 350 degree oven for 20 minutes. Let cool and place toothpicks in each ball. Serves 8-10.

Mrs. Ben J. Smith
Mrs. Bruce Salley

SAUCY SAUSAGE MUFFINS

2 cups self rising corn meal
1 tablespoon sugar
2 eggs, beaten
1 cup milk
1/4 cup oil
1 tablespoon barbecue sauce

6 links ready-to-serve sausage
 (cut in small pieces)
2 tablespoons barbecue sauce
 (reserve for brushing hot
 muffins)

Blend eggs, milk, oil and 1 tablespoon barbecue sauce. Add liquid to corn meal mix, stirring only until corn meal is moistened. Fold in sausage pieces. Fill greased muffin pans 2/3 full. Bake in 425 degree oven for 15-20 minutes for large muffins, 10 minutes for small muffins. Yields 12 large muffins or 24 small.

Mrs. Bruce Salley

SAUSAGE ROLL-UPS

2 pounds hot pork sausage   1 loaf thin sliced bread

Make sausage into small oval balls. Cook slowly until done, but not brown. Trim the crust from bread. Cut each slice into 4 strips. Wrap the strips around the sausage balls. Secure with toothpick. Run in a 350 degree oven for about 10 minutes or until sausage is heated and bread toasted. Yields 5 dozen.

Mrs. Douglas McDougald

SEAFOODS

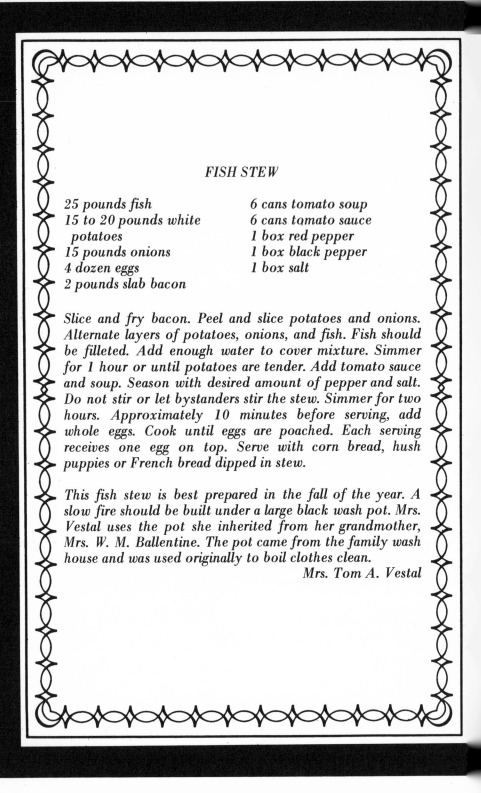

FISH STEW

25 pounds fish
15 to 20 pounds white
  potatoes
15 pounds onions
4 dozen eggs
2 pounds slab bacon

6 cans tomato soup
6 cans tomato sauce
1 box red pepper
1 box black pepper
1 box salt

Slice and fry bacon. Peel and slice potatoes and onions. Alternate layers of potatoes, onions, and fish. Fish should be filleted. Add enough water to cover mixture. Simmer for 1 hour or until potatoes are tender. Add tomato sauce and soup. Season with desired amount of pepper and salt. Do not stir or let bystanders stir the stew. Simmer for two hours. Approximately 10 minutes before serving, add whole eggs. Cook until eggs are poached. Each serving receives one egg on top. Serve with corn bread, hush puppies or French bread dipped in stew.

This fish stew is best prepared in the fall of the year. A slow fire should be built under a large black wash pot. Mrs. Vestal uses the pot she inherited from her grandmother, Mrs. W. M. Ballentine. The pot came from the family wash house and was used originally to boil clothes clean.

                                      Mrs. Tom A. Vestal

SHRIMP PIE

2 cups cooked shrimp
3 slices of bread, cubed
1 cup milk
3 eggs well beaten
2 tablespoons melted butter

1/2 teaspoon salt
1/4 teaspoon pepper
1 cup chopped green pepper
 and celery mixed

Soak bread in milk and mash with fork. Add shrimp, butter, seasonings and other ingredients. Turn into buttered casserole and bake at 350 degrees for 20 minutes.

Mrs. James F. Byrnes
Columbia, S. C.

SHRIMP CURRY

2 pounds shrimp
1 medium onion, sliced
3 tablespoons oil
2 cans condensed tomato soup
1 teaspoon sugar
1/8 teaspoon salt

1 tablespoon Worcestershire
1 teaspoon vinegar
3 1/2 teaspoons curry powder
1 tablespoon butter
3/4 can water (soup can)

Simmer shrimp until pink. Shell and devein. Saute onion slices slowly in oil until golden and tender, but not brown. Add other ingredients except shrimp. Mix well and simmer uncovered for 10 minutes. Add shrimp, reheat and serve. This is even better made in advance, but do not overcook shrimp, or they will be tough. Serve with steamed rice and any or all of the following condiments. Serves 4.

CONDIMENTS

Chopped nuts
Sieved hard-boiled egg yolks
Sieved hard-boiled egg whites
Raisins, plumped in warm water
Chutney

Chopped crumbled bacon
Chopped green onions
Fresh pineapple chunks
Banana slices
Fresh grated coconut

Mrs. William Jennings Bryan Dorn
Greenwood, S. C.

BAKED FISH CASSEROLE

1 package frozen fish fillets
1 can frozen shrimp soup

1 cup bread crumbs
1/4 cup melted margarine

Place thawed fish in greased casserole. Pour thawed shrimp soup over fish. Put crumbs over top and pour melted margarine over crumbs. Bake at 350 degrees for 35 minutes.

Mrs. Martha Bleckley Barnes
Clemson, S. C.

He who does not mind his belly will
hardly mind anything else. — Samuel Johnson

BAKED STUFFED RED SNAPPER WITH CREOLE SAUCE

CREOLE SAUCE

2 tablespoons margarine
3/4 cup sliced celery
1/2 cup chopped onion
1/4 cup bell pepper
1 clove garlic (crushed)
1 (1-pound) can tomatoes

1 bay leaf
1 teaspoon salt
1/2 teaspoon sugar
1/2 teaspoon thyme
1/4 teaspoon pepper

In margarine sauté celery, onion, pepper and garlic until onions are golden brown, about 5 minutes. Add tomatoes and remaining ingredients. Bring to a boil, reduce heat and simmer about 40 minutes.

STUFFING

1/4 cup margarine
1 cup chopped onion
4 slices bread

2 tablespoon chopped parsley
1/2 teaspoon salt
1/2 teaspoon pepper

Sauté onion in margarine for 5 minutes. Soak bread in water until softened. Squeeze water from bread. Add bread to onion. Salt and pepper. Stir until well blended.

PREPARATION

3 to 5 pound red snapper   1 teaspoon salt
2 tablespoons margarine   1/4 teaspoon pepper

Brush inside and outside of fish with margarine, salt and pepper. Put stuffing in fish. Bake uncovered for 30 minutes at 450 degrees. Then reduce heat to 350 degrees. Pour sauce over fish. Baste often with sauce. Cook for 30 minutes or until fish will flake. Serves 6 to 8.

Mrs. W. B. Betsworth
Pensacola, Fla.

After a good dinner, one can forgive anybody,
even one's own relatives. — Oscar Wilde

CURRIED FISH FILLETS AMANDINE

1 pound frozen fish fillets   1/2 cup margarine
2 teaspoons curry powder   1/2 cup blanched almonds
1/4 teaspoon salt   Chutney
1/2 cup flour

Combine flour, curry powder and salt. Roll fillets in this mixture, coating thoroughly. Heat butter in large skillet. Add floured fillets and cook over moderate heat until browned (about 4 minutes). Turn and brown other side, cooking until fish flakes easily with a fork (about 3 minutes more). Remove to heated platter. To butter remaining in pan, add chopped almonds and stir over moderate heat until browned. Pour over fish.

Mrs. James H. Barton

FISH RICE DRESSING

1/2 cup melted margarine
1 1/2 cups chopped onion
1 1/2 cups diced celery
2 2/3 cups cooked rice
1/2 teaspoon pepper

1/2 teaspoon sage or thyme
1 cup chopped stuffed olives
1 cup chopped dill pickles
1 fish (6 to 8 pounds)
Lemon juice

Saute' onion and celery in margarine for 5 minutes (until tender). Add remaining ingredients (except lemon juice) and mix well. Use to stuff fish. Prior to stuffing fish, rub inside and out with lemon juice. Bake at 350 degrees until fish flakes easily. Serves 6.

Miss May Dell Byars

The day has the color and the sound of winter.
Thoughts turn to chowder. Chowder breathes
reassurance. It steams consolation,
— Clemetine Paddleford

LOBSTER CASSEROLE

1/2 pound mushrooms
1/4 cup butter
4 tablespoons flour
2 teaspoons curry powder
2 cups light cream

Salt and pepper to taste
1 large peeled, diced tomato
2 cups cooked diced lobster
1 cup hot mashed potatoes

Peel and slice mushrooms. Saute in butter 5 minutes. Add flour and curry powder and stir until smoothly mixed. Add cream and cook, stirring constantly, until thickened. Season to taste. Add tomato and lobster and heat well. Pour into a shallow 2 quart casserole and pipe a border of mashed potatoes around the edge. Run under the broiler to brown lightly. Serves 4.

Mrs. C. L. Mayo

STUFFED LOBSTER SUPREME

8 frozen lobster tails (small)
1/4 pound butter
4 tablespoons flour
1 teaspoon salt
1 teaspoon paprika
Few grains cayenne pepper

2 cups light cream
2 tablespoons lemon juice
1/4 cup cracker crumbs
1/4 cup grated Parmesan Cheese
1 tablespoon melted butter
(for topping)

Cook lobster in boiling salted water, following directions on label; drain. Cut meat away from shell with scissors. Dice meat. Save shell. Saute lobster in butter. Remove from heat; blend in flour, salt, paprika and cayenne. Stir in cream. Cook, stirring until mixture thickens. Stir in lemon juice. Spoon filling into shells. Sprinkle with mixture of crumbs, cheese and butter. Arrange shells in shallow pan. Bake at 450 degrees for 10-12 minutes. Serves 8.

Mrs. Curtis Gillespie

STUFFED LOBSTER TAILS

6 large Rock Lobster Tails
2 tablespoons butter
2 tablespoons flour
3/4 cup Half and Half milk
1/4 cup dry white wine
1/4 teaspoon salt
1 cup packaged bread stuffing

3 tablespoons water
1/2 cup flaked crabmeat
1 tablespoon chopped parsley
1/8 teaspoon garlic salt
Few grains pepper
1/4 cup grated Parmesan cheese
2 tablespoons chopped onion

Cook lobster tails in boiling salted water 6 to 8 minutes or until tender. Drain and cool. Melt butter in saucepan. Remove from heat and blend in flour. Gradually add Half & Half stirring constantly until thickened. Stir wine into sauce. Add salt. Cut and remove along both edges of lobster tails. Lift meat out of shells and reserve shells. Cut lobster meat into bite size pieces. Mix bread stuffing and water. Combine stuffing, lobster, crabmeat, onion, parsley, garlic salt and pepper. Mix in white sauce. Spoon lobster mixture into shell. Sprinkle with Parmesan cheese. Bake at 375 degrees for 20 to 30 minutes. Serves 6.

Mrs. Robert James

OYSTERS BIENVILLE

1/4 cup butter
3 tablespoons flour
1 clove garlic
1 tablespoon onion juice
1 tablespoon Worcestershire
1/4 teaspoon celery seed
Salt to taste
1 2-ounce can mushrooms

3/4 cup liquid (juice from
   mushrooms and shrimp)
1 dozen cooked, chopped shrimp
1 tablespoon sherry
1 1/2 pints oysters
Parmesan cheese
Paprika

Make sauce of butter, flour, garlic, onion, salt, Worcestershire, celery seed and liquid. Add mushrooms, shrimp and sherry. Slide oysters under broiler until edges just curl. Pour off liquid. Sprinkle liberally with Parmesan cheese. Cover with sauce. Sprinkle with paprika. Slide back under broiler for 5 to 8 minutes until bubbly.

Mrs. Sam T. Haddock

It is unseasonable and unwholesome in all
months that have not an R in their name
to eat an oyster. — Henry Buttes

OYSTER PIE

2 cups milk
1 quart standard oysters
24 saltine crackers

1 stick butter
1/2 teaspoon salt
1/4 teaspoon pepper

Grease a 3 quart baking dish with butter. Crumble a layer of saltine crackers; top with a layer of oysters, and dot with butter. Sprinkle salt and pepper. Continue with layers of crackers and oysters, ending with crackers, topped with butter. Add whole sweet milk to come to top of pie. Refrigerate for 2 hours; then bake for 1 hour at 350 degrees. Serves 12.

Mrs. Fred Bolt

SEAFOOD CASSEROLE

2/3 cup rice
1 pound shrimp
1/2 teaspoon curry powder
1 teaspoon Worcestershire
3/4 teaspoon salt
1/8 teaspoon pepper
1 cup mayonnaise

1 pound crabmeat
1 cup English peas
3 tablespoons chopped onion
1/2 cup chopped green pepper
1 cup chopped celery
1 cup buttered bread crumbs

Cook rice and drain. Cook shrimp and cut lengthwise. Combine rice and shrimp with curry powder, Worcestershire, salt, pepper, mayonnaise and mix all together. Add crabmeat, drained English peas, onion, green pepper and celery. Toss together well and place in 2 quart casserole. Top with buttered bread crumbs. Bake at 350 degrees for 45 minutes. Serves 6.

Mrs. H. Randolph Wilson

A hungry people is unreasonable, unjust,
and unmerciful. — Seneca

SCANDINAVIAN SUPPER DISH

1 can (10 1/4-ounce) frozen
  condensed cream of shrimp
  soup
1 can (15-ounce) fish balls in
  bouillon

2 tablespoons butter
1/4 cup milk
1 can potatoes (1 pound)
  drained

Heat thawed shrimp soup, butter, and milk in a saucepan about 5 minutes or until butter is melted. Add the drained fish balls and potatoes. Cover and simmer until mixture is thoroughly heated (about 10 minutes). Serve garnished with chopped parsley. Serves 4.

Mrs. Jim Gray Watson

SHRIMP AU GRATIN

2 to 3 pounds shrimp
Dash of lemon juice
1/2 cup butter
1 cup flour
Liquid from cooking shrimp
1/4 teaspoon pepper

1 teaspoon salt
3 egg yolks
2 tablespoons cooking sherry
2 tablespoons grated cheese
1 cup buttered bread crumbs

Clean and wash shrimp. Place in saucepan with 1 quart water and dash lemon juice. Cook 10 minutes and reserve liquid. In another pan, melt butter; then add flour and stir to a smooth paste. Add shrimp stock a little at a time stirring constantly. Add seasonings, egg yolks, sherry, cheese, and shrimp. Place in a buttered shallow casserole. Top with crumbs. Bake 350 degrees about 15 minutes. Serves 6 to 8.

Mrs. Mitchell Sutherland

SHRIMP CASSEROLE

2 cans frozen Cream of Shrimp
  Soup, thawed
1 (6 1/2-ounce) can tuna fish
1 cup sour cream
1 jar sliced pimento (4-ounce)
1 small can water chestnuts

1 small can tiny English peas
  drained
2 tablespoons Parmesan cheese
1/2 teaspoon paprika
2 cans Chinese noodles

Preheat oven to 400 degrees. In a deep casserole dish mix shrimp soup, tuna, sour cream, pimento, water chestnuts, English peas. Sprinkle top with Parmesan cheese and paprika. Heat in oven until it bubbles, about 15 minutes. Serve over heated Chinese noodles. Serves 6.

Mrs. Fred Auld
Columbia, S. C.

A hungry man is not a free man. — Adlai Stevenson

CURRIED SHRIMP

3 tablespoons butter
1/2 medium onion chopped
2 stalks celery chopped
1/2 apple chopped
1 teaspoon curry powder

2 tablespoons flour
1/2 teaspoon salt
Pepper to taste
1 cup milk
1 1/2 cups boiled shrimp

Sauté onion, celery and apple in butter. Do not brown. Add curry powder, salt and pepper to flour. Then add to butter mixture. Mix well. Add 1 cup milk. Stir until thick. Add shrimp and simmer 10 minutes. Serve hot with Chinese noodles or steamed rice. Side dishes may include crushed peanuts, chutney, shredded coconut, raisins soaked in sherry, chopped chili peppers. Variations in the shrimp dish: Use Thomson seedless grapes or firm banana instead of apple. Serves 4.

Miss Carolyn Hodges

SHRIMP ISOBEL

1 cup diced celery
1/2 cup diced green pepper
1/2 cup diced onion
3 tablespoons butter
1 can mushroom soup
2/3 cup milk

Salt and pepper to taste
1 1/2 pounds shrimp, cooked
1 teaspoon lemon juice
1/2 cup chopped parsley
1/4 pound sharp cheese, grated
Toasted slivered almonds

Sauté celery, onion, and pepper in butter. Add soup, milk, cooked shrimp, salt and pepper to taste. Bring to boil. Add lemon juice and simmer. Add parsley and cheese. Stir. Garnish with toasted slivered almonds. Serve on rice. Serves 6.

Mrs. Tom Temple
Columbia, S. C.

SHRIMP MARINANA

2 tablespoons olive oil
1 chopped medium onion
2 cloves garlic, chopped
1 large can plum tomatoes
1 small can tomato paste
1 small can water
1 tablespoon chopped parsley

1 teaspoon salt
1/4 teaspoon pepper
1 teaspoon oregano
1 tablespoon sugar
2 pounds fresh shrimp, cleaned
1/4 cup sherry
1 package thin spaghetti

Brown garlic and onion in olive oil. Add tomatoes, tomato paste, water, parsley, salt, pepper, oregano and sugar. Simmer 15 minutes. Add raw, cleaned shrimp, and cook until shrimp turns pink. Add sherry 10 minutes before serving. Serve over spaghetti. Good in a chafing dish. Serves 6-8.

Mrs. J. Philip Noury

SHRIMP AND PEAS IN TIMBALES

1 1/2 pounds shrimp
1 16-ounce can tiny English
  peas

1 8-ounce can mushrooms
8 pie-crust timbales
1 cup white sauce

Shell raw shrimp. Prepare your favorite cream sauce recipe. Mix drained peas, drained sliced mushrooms, cream sauce, and shrimp and cook slowly for 10 minutes or until shrimp are tender and pink. Season to taste and pour into individual pie-crust timbales. Serves 8.

Mrs. Virginia Sloan

PLANTATION SHRIMP PILAU

4 slices bacon
1 cup raw rice, cooked
1/2 cup chopped celery
2 tablespoons bell pepper
2 tablespoons butter

2 cups small shrimp
1 teaspoon Worcestershire
1 tablespoon flour
Salt and pepper to taste

Fry bacon until crisp. Save to use later. Add bacon grease to water in which rice will be cooked. In frying pan melt butter, add celery and chopped bell pepper. Cook a few minutes; add shrimp sprinkled in Worcestershire and dredged in flour. Stir and simmer until flour is cooked. Season with salt and pepper and add rice and mix. More butter may be added. Stir in crumbled bacon and serve.

Mrs. Joe Dent
Lexington, N. C.

SHRIMP RICE

1 stick butter	1 1/2 cans water
2 cups uncooked rice	2 teaspoons salt
1 can beef bouillon soup	2 pounds shrimp, cooked
1 can onion soup	

Melt butter in 2 quart casserole. Add rice, soups, water, salt, and shrimp. Cover casserole. Bake for 1 hour at 350 degrees.

Mrs. Julian M. Smith, Jr.
Charleston, S. C.

SHRIMP SOUFFLE

6 tablespoons butter	1/4 cup minced onions
6 tablespoons flour	6 eggs (separated)
2 cups light cream	3/4 teaspoon salt
2 cups chopped cooked shrimp	2 tablespoons lemon juice
1/4 cup finely chopped celery	2 tablespoons Worcestershire
1/4 cup finely chopped parsley	1 teaspoon curry powder

To prepare cream sauce, melt butter, add flour and blend over low heat 5 to 10 minutes. Slowly stir in light cream. When mixture is smooth and boiling, stir in shrimp, celery, parsley and onions. When these ingredients are hot, reduce heat and stir in beaten egg yolks. Cook and stir a little longer to allow yolks to thicken. Season with salt, lemon juice, Worcestershire, and curry powder. Cool slightly. Whip 6 egg whites until stiff. Fold the hot mixture carefully into the egg whites. Bake in an ungreased 2 quart baking dish at 325 degrees until firm (about 1 hour). Serves 12.

Mrs. James Halford, Jr.

SHRIMP TOAST

8 slices white bread
1 pound peeled shrimp
1/3 cup minced water chestnuts
1 tablespoon cornstarch

2 egg whites
1 teaspoon dry wine
1 teaspoon salt
1 teaspoon minced scallion

Remove crusts from bread and cut in half diagonally. Mince the shrimp fine. Mix with remaining ingredients and heap onto each triangle of bread. Refrigerate until ready to cook. Heat deep oil to 350 degrees, slide triangles, shrimp side down, into oil, one or two at a time. Fry until bread side is golden, turn and fry for about a minute longer. Drain on absorbent paper and keep in a warm oven until all pieces are done. Serve two triangles to each person. Serves 8.

Mrs. C. L. Mayo

*Their sole reason for living lies in
their palate. — Juvenal*

SHRIMP WIGGLE

1 pound shrimp
1/4 cup butter
1/4 cup flour
2 cups milk
1 can shoestring
 potatoes

1/4 teaspoon Worcestershire
1/4 teaspoon dry mustard
1 teaspoon salt
Dash pepper
1 package frozen peas, cooked

Clean and cook shrimp for 3 or 4 minutes in salted water. Drain. Melt butter in sauce pan. Remove pan from heat. Stir in flour until well blended. Add milk, stir until smooth. Return to heat and cook until thickened. Add Worcestershire, mustard, salt, pepper, shrimp and peas. Continue cooking until shrimp and peas are heated through. Serve over shoestring potatoes. Serves 4.

*Mrs. Wes Williams
St. Petersburg, Fla.*

SHRIMP AND WILD RICE SALAD

2 pounds cooked cleaned shrimp
1 1/2 cups cooked wild rice
1/2 cup thinly sliced radishes

1/2 cup finely chopped celery
A sprinkling of curry powder

Combine all ingredients and chill.
Before serving add dressing.

DRESSING

1 pint French dressing
1 tablespoon onion juice
1 teaspoon paprika

Dash of Tabasco
Salt and pepper to taste

Serve on crisp lettuce. Garnish with slices of avocado or tomatoes.
Serves 6.

Mrs. J. S. Ezelle

SHRIMP QUICHE

1 pound peeled, cleaned shrimp
1/4 pound Swiss cheese
1/4 pound Gruyere cheese
1 tablespoon flour
3 eggs
Dash of Tabasco

1 cup light cream
1/4 teaspoon salt
Dash of pepper
1/4 teaspoon Worcestershire
9-inch unbaked pastry shell.

Cut up shrimp if large. Grate cheese and toss with flour. Beat eggs, cream, salt, pepper and sauces. Line pastry shell with 3/4 of cheese. Add shrimp and cover with remaining cheese. Pour egg mixture over all. Bake in 400 degree preheated oven for 10 minutes. Reduce heat to 325 degrees and bake 40 minutes until silver knife comes clean. Let stand 10 minutes before cutting into wedges. Serve warm. Serves 6. Substitute crabmeat for shrimp, if desired.

Miss Carolyn Hodges

HOT SHRIMP SAUCE

1 stick butter
6 tablespoons Worcestershire
6 tablespoons tomato catsup

Juice of 1 lemon
Dash of Tabasco
Salt and pepper to taste

Mix and bring to a boil. Serve hot over boiled shrimp.

Mrs. Charles Bauknight

SHRIMP COCKTAIL SAUCE

1 cup catsup
1 tablespoon lemon juice
1 tablespoon Worcestershire
1 tablespoon vinegar
1/2 teaspoon salt
1/2 teaspoon pepper

2 to 3 drops Tabasco sauce
1/2 cup chopped celery
1/2 cup diced salad pickles
   with juice
1/2 cup chopped radishes

Combine all ingredients and chill. Serves 6-8.

Mrs. L. A. McCrary

QUICK TARTAR SAUCE

1/2 cup mayonnaise
1 tablespoon chopped pickles
1 tablespoon chopped olives

1 tablespoon lemon juice
1/4 teaspoon Worcestershire
1/2 teaspoon grated onion

Combine and mix well. Chill. Serves 4 to 6.

Mrs. Marshall Kowalski

WHITE SAUCE

2 tablespoons butter
2 tablespoons flour

1 cup milk

Melt butter over low heat. Blend in flour. Gradually add milk. Stir until smooth.

Recipe Committee

SALMON CROQUETTES

1 pound can of salmon (remove
  juice and bones and flake)
1 cup creamed Irish potatoes
1 egg
1 teaspoon tomato catsup

1/2 teaspoon hot sauce
1/8 teaspoon black pepper
2 well beaten eggs
1 1/2 cups of cracker crumbs

Mix well first 6 ingredients and shape into croquettes the size of a small egg. Roll each in well beaten eggs and then in cracker crumbs. Heat enough grease in skillet to boiling point to cover croquettes. Drop croquettes in skillet and reduce heat. Fry until golden brown and drain on paper towels. Yields 16.

Mrs. Fred Felkel

"The discovery of a new dish
does more for the happiness of mankind
that the discovery of a star." — Brillat-Savarin

TUNA CASSEROLE

1 can of tuna
5 carrots
1 large can English peas

1/2 package noodles
1 can mushroom or celery soup

Chop, cook and drain carrots. Cook and drain noodles. Drain tuna and mix with carrots, peas and soup. Place in casserole and top with grated cheese. Bake 30 minutes in 350 degree oven.

Mrs. Theo L. Burriss

CRAB-BROCCOLI CASSEROLE

1 package frozen broccoli
1 cup grated sharp cheese
1/2 stick butter
2 tablespoons minced onion
2 tablespoons flour
1/8 teaspoon curry powder
1/2 teaspoon salt

1 cup milk
1 tablespoon lemon juice
2 6-ounce packages frozen king
  crab, thawed and drained
2 tablespoons melted butter
1/2 cup bread crumbs

Arrange cooked broccoli spears on bottom of buttered casserole. Sprinkle cheese over broccoli. Saute onion in 1/2 stick butter until tender. Add flour, curry powder, salt and milk. Cook until thick. Add lemon juice and drained crabmeat. Pour this on top of broccoli and cheese. If it doesn't cover properly pour a little milk over it. Melt 2 tablespoons butter and add bread crumbs. Mix until butter is absorbed and sprinkle over casserole. Bake at 350 degrees for 30 minutes. Serves 4.

Mrs. Robert James

A man seldom thinks with more earnestness
of anything than he does of his dinner.
—Samuel Johnson

CRAB MEAT CASSEROLE

2 packages frozen king crab
2 hard boiled eggs
1 green pepper, chopped
2 small cans mushrooms

4 cups medium white sauce
1/2 pound sharp cheese, grated
1 or 2 tablespoons sherry
1/4 teaspoon garlic salt

Mix ingredients well. Place in a casserole dish. Cover with cracker crumbs. Bake at 350 degrees for 25 minutes. Serves 8.

Mrs. Donald C. Roberts

CRAB MEAT CASSEROLE

2 cans white claw crab meat
2 tablespoons butter
2 tablespoons flour
2 cups milk
3 hard boiled eggs

1/2 cup sharp
  grated cheese
1 small jar chopped pimento
1 large can mushrooms
Crushed saltine crackers

Melt butter in saucepan over low heat. Blend in flour. Add milk. Stir in cheese and pimento. Alternate layers of crab meat, eggs and mushrooms. Top with sauce. Top with crushed saltine crackers and dot with butter. Cook at 350 degrees for 30 minutes. Serves 4 to 6.

Mrs. William G. Albergotti

*No one can worship God or love his neighbor
on an empty stomach. — Woodrow Wilson*

DEVILED CRAB

1 small onion, minced
1 small bell pepper, minced
1/2 stick margarine
1 can Harris Fancy White
  Crabmeat
1 egg

1 teaspoon Worcestershire
1 teaspoon mustard
1 teaspoon lemon juice
1 teaspoon mayonnaise
8 to 12 crumbled Ritz crackers

Mince onions and pepper and brown in margarine. Combine all ingredients well. Chill in refrigerator for 1 hour or more. Spoon into individual shells or in casserole. Brown in 350 degree oven for 20 to 30 minutes. Serves 4.

Mrs. Newton Newell, Jr.

*The way to a man's heart is through
his stomach — Sara Payson*

CRABMEAT SNUG HARBOR

2 1/2 pounds crabmeat
  shredded and drained
1 cup medium white sauce
1 cup mayonnaise
Juice of 1 1/2 lemons
1 1/2 tablespoons onion juice

1 tablespoon Worcestershire
1 cup small toasted bread cubes
2/3 cup bread crumbs
Melted butter
Paprika
Chopped parsley

Make white sauce by usual method of 2 tablespoons butter and 2 tablespoons flour to 1 cup milk. Fold in mayonnaise, lemon juice, onion juice, Worcestershire, bread cubes and crabmeat. Pour into greased casserole. Mix parsley and paprika with buttered bread crumbs. Spread on casserole. Bake at 350 degrees 45 minutes. If using individual shells or ramekins, bake 15 minutes. Serves 12.

Mrs. Robert E. Padgett, Jr.

MEATS

CHICKEN, OYSTER GUMBO
(over 100 Years Old)

1 large hen cut in serving pieces	2 quarts warm water
7 large kitchen spoons of flour	Salt and pepper (black and red to taste)
7 large kitchen spoons of fat	Filé powder
1 large onion chopped	One pint oysters
	Garlic to taste

Salt and pepper chicken pieces. Heat fat, add flour and brown. Add garlic and onion. Add pieces of chicken into brown flour mixture (roux). Fry slowly until fat comes out around edges. Add warm water and simmer until chicken is tender. Add oysters about 10 minutes before serving. Dish Gumbo into large tureen. Add filé. Serve with rice, French bread and, of course, traditional red wine. Serve 8.

This recipe was given to Mrs. Douglas Thrasher by her father's sister, Mrs. Margaret Erskine Betsworth from Pensecola, Florida. Mrs. Betsworth received the recipe from her husband's family who originally obtained it from New Orleans.

BEEF

BARBECUE HAMBURGER

2 large onions
3 pounds hamburger
1 large can tomatoes
1/3 bottle Worcestershire
1/2 cup vinegar

1 teaspoon sugar
1 teaspoon salt
1 teaspoon black pepper
1 teaspoon red pepper

Chop onions and brown; add hamburger meat; then add tomatoes, Worcestershire, vinegar, sugar, salt and pepper. Cook at least 1 hour. Serve on toasted hamburger buns topped with slaw. Serves 12.

Mrs. Larry King

HAMBURGER SANDWICH

1/4 cup chopped celery
1/4 cup chopped green pepper
1/4 cup chopped onion
1 pound hamburger
2 tablespoons oil

1/2 cup catsup
1 teaspoon salt
1/4 teaspoon pepper
1 tablespoon Worcestershire

Simmer the first three ingredients for 5 minutes in oil. Add 1 pound hamburger and cook until redness is gone. Add the remaining ingredients. Heat and serve on buns. Serves 4.

Mrs. William V. McAbee

SLOPPY JOE HAMBURGERS

1 1/2 pounds hamburger
1/4 cup chopped onions
1/2 cup chopped celery
1/2 teaspoon salt
Dash of pepper

1 tablespoon brown sugar
1 teaspoon mustard
1 cup catsup
1/2 cup water
2 tablespoons vinegar
2 tablespoons Worcestershire

Brown together ground beef and onion. Add remaining ingredients and simmer for 30 minutes. Serve on heated hamburger buns. Serves six.

Mrs. Robert Herstine

BEEF PORCUPINES

1 pound ground beef
1/2 cup raw rice
1/2 cup chopped onion
1/2 teaspoon garlic salt

1/4 teaspoon pepper
2 tablespoons oil
1 8-ounce can tomato sauce
1 can water

Mix beef, rice, onion and seasonings. Shape into 12 balls. Brown in oil. Pour in tomato sauce and water. Simmer for 45 minutes. Serves six.

Mrs. Charles A. Brown

CHILI AND BEANS

2 pounds ground beef
1 medium onion, chopped
1 green pepper, chopped
2 garlic cloves, minced
3 1/2 cups tomatoes
2 teaspoons salt
2 bay leaves

3 tablespoons chili powder
1/4 teaspoon cayenne pepper
4 whole cloves
1/2 teaspoon celery seed
1/4 teaspoon basil
1 cup water
2 cans chili beans

Brown the beef, onion, green pepper, garlic. Add tomatoes, salt, spices, and water. Simmer for 2 1/2 hours. Add chili beans the last 20 minutes of cooking time. Serves 8 to 10.

Mrs. Bill Porter
Charlottesville, Virginia

CHILI CON CARNE

2 pounds ground round steak
2 tablespoons butter
1 green pepper, chopped
3 medium onions, sliced
2 cans kidney beans, drained

1 large can tomatoes
1 8-ounce can tomato sauce
2 tablespoons chili powder
1 teaspoon salt
1/2 teaspoon pepper

Brown meat in butter. Add pepper and onions, cooking until onions are soft. Add beans, tomatoes and seasoning. Simmer 30 minutes. Serve while hot with garlic bread and salad. Serves 8 to 10.

Mrs. Larry Kowalski

CHINESE HAMBURGER CASSEROLE

1 pound ground beef
2 tablespoons cooking oil
2 onions, chopped
1 can cream of mushroom soup
1 can cream of chicken soup

1 1/2 cups warm water
1/2 cup uncooked rice
1/8 cup soy sauce
1/4 teaspoon pepper
1 can chow mein noodles

Brown meat in oil, add onions. Then add soups. Fill cans with warm water and add to mixture. Stir in uncooked rice, soy sauce, and pepper. Turn into large (lightly greased) casserole. Cover and bake in moderate oven 350° for 30 minutes. Remove cover and continue baking 30 minutes longer. Cover mixture with chow mein noodles 10 minutes before removing from oven. Serves 6.

Mrs. C. Patrick Killen

GROUND BEEF CASSEROLE

1 pound ground beef
1/2 cup chopped onion
1 clove garlic
1 cup uncooked rice
1 cup sliced ripe olives

1 4-ounce can mushrooms
1 Number 303 can of tomatoes
1/2 cup sherry
1 cup grated cheese
1 teaspoon salt

Brown beef, add onions and then add all ingredients except cheese. Bake at 350° for 30 minutes. Add cheese and cook for 15 minutes more. Serves 6 to 8.

Mrs. Hugh Croxton

"JOHNNY MARZETTI"

8 chopped medium onions
1/2 teaspoon garlic salt
3 pounds ground chuck
1/4 teaspoon pepper
2 teaspoons salt
1/2 stick margarine
1/4 cup Burgundy wine

1 8-ounce can tomato sauce
8 cups shell macaroni
1/4 cup margarine
4 cups grated sharp cheese
2 8-ounce cans tomato sauce
2 4-ounce cans chopped
    mushrooms, undrained

In advance, sauté in skillet the first five ingredients in 1/2 stick oleo about 15 minutes. Cook macaroni as directed on package, until barely tender and drain. Add 1/4 cup oleo. Place in 2 quart casserole; add 2/3 of cheese to meat mixture. Let cheese melt. Add 1 1/2 cans tomato sauce, mushrooms and pour over macaroni. Top with 1 1/2 cans of tomato sauce. Sprinkle with remaining cheese. Cool quickly and wrap for freezing. The day before serving, remove casserole and thaw in refrigerator. Cook at 325° for 1 hour, 40 minutes or until hot and bubbling. Pour on wine. Serves 14 to 16.

Mrs. Jack Ross, Jr.

64

LASAGNE

1 pound ground beef
1 large onion, chopped
1 garlic bud, minced
2 cans tomato paste
8 cans water

2 small cans tomato sauce
8 bay leaves
1/2 teaspoon oregano
1 teaspoon salt
1 teaspoon pepper

Brown beef, onion and garlic. Add remaining ingredients. Simmer for 2 1/2 hours, stirring frequently.

CHEESE MIXTURE

1/2 cup Parmesan cheese
1 pound Mozzarella cheese, grated

2 eggs
1 small carton cottage cheese
6 to 8 Lasagne noodles

Cook noodles according to directions on box. Combine other ingredients in large bowl. Place 1 layer noodles in bottom of greased baking dish. Add 1 layer meat sauce, then 1 layer cheese mixture. Continue layers until all is used. Bake at 350° for 30 minutes. Let cool for 10 minutes. Cut in squares. Serves 6.

Mrs. Ernest Latimer

MAGETTI

3 pounds lean ground meat
2 large onions
2 large bell peppers
2 stalks celery
1 1/2 teaspoons chili powder

3 small cans tomato sauce
3 cans tomato soup
3 cans mushroom soup
2 large packages egg noodles

Brown onions, pepper, and celery in 2 tablespoons cooking oil. Add meat and cook until browned. Continue cooking for about 15 minutes. Remove and add tomato sauce, soups, egg noodles, cooked and drained. Mix well. Spread evenly in 2 large pans. Cover with squares of sharp cheese. Cover with foil and cook for 45 minutes at 325°. Cut into squares and serve. Good with green salad and French bread. Serves 25.

Mrs. J. Frank Parnell

FANCY, TASTY MEATBALLS

3/4-pound ground beef
1/2-pound ground veal
1/4-pound ground pork
2 cups bread crumbs
1 can beef consommé
1 cup evaporated milk
1/2 can tomato soup
  (soak bread crumbs in soup)

1 tablespoon butter
1/2 cup chopped onion
1 egg
1/4 cup chopped parsley
2 teaspoons salt
Dash pepper
Dash ground ginger
Dash ground nutmeg

Sauté onions in butter. Mix all ingredients and beat 5 minutes with mixer at medium speed. Shape into 1 1/2 inch balls. Brown meatballs in 2 tablespoons butter. Remove from skillet and continue with directions given with sauce preparation.

SAUCE

Melt 2 tablespoons butter in skillet with drippings from browning meatballs. Stir in 2 tablespoons corn starch — add 2 beef bouillon cubes which have been dissolved in 2 cups of boiling water. Add meatballs and cook about 30 minutes. Serves 8.

Mrs. Joe T. Greenway

SWEDISH MEATBALLS

2 eggs, slightly beaten
1 cup milk
1 cup dry bread crumbs
3 tablespoons butter
1/2 cup finely chopped onion
1 pound ground chuck
1/4 pound ground pork
1 3/4 teaspoons salt

3/4 teaspoon dill weed
1/4 teaspoon allspice
1/8 teaspoon nutmeg
1/8 teaspoon cardamom
3 tablespoons flour
1/8 teaspoon pepper
1 can (10 1/2 ounce) beef broth
1/2 cup light cream

In a large bowl combine the eggs, milk, and dry bread crumbs. In large skillet, heat 1 tablespoon butter. Saute' chopped onion until soft – about 5 minutes. Lift out with slotted spoon. Add to bread crumb mixture, along with ground chuck, pork, 1 1/2 teaspoons salt, dill weed, allspice, nutmeg, and cardamom. Combine well with wooden spoon or hands. Refrigerate, covered, for 1 hour. Shape meat mixture into meatballs, each about 1 inch in diameter. In remaining butter, saute' meatballs, until well browned, removing meatballs to a 2-quart casserole as they are browned. If necessary, add more butter to make 2 tablespoons in skillet. Add flour, the remaining 1/4 teaspoon salt and pepper, stirring to make a smooth mixture. Gradually stir in beef broth; bring mixture to boil, stirring constantly. Add cream and remaining 1/2 teaspoon dill weed. Pour over meatballs in casserole. Bake covered, at 325° for 30 minutes. Serves 6.

Mrs. Cliff W. Bryant

Carve to all but just enough,
Let them neither starve nor stuff
And that you may have your due,
Let your neighbor carve for you.
—Jonathan Swift

MEAT LOAF FOR COMPANY

1/2 cup bell pepper, chopped	1 egg
1 medium onion, chopped	1 teaspoon salt
1/2 cup celery, chopped	1/2 teaspoon pepper
3 slices dried bread, crumbled	1 level tablespoon mustard
2 pounds ground beef	1 8-ounce can tomato sauce

Add bell pepper, onion, celery, bread pieces to ground meat. Work in egg, mustard, and tomato sauce along with salt and pepper. Shape and put in greased casserole. Add potatoes and carrots if desired. Cover with foil. Bake at 325° for 1 hour and 30 minutes. Uncover and brown on top. Serves 8.

Mrs. C. A. Evans

MEAT LOAF

3 pounds lean ground beef
1/2 cup catsup
1 teaspoon salt
2 tablespoons mustard
1 egg

1/2 cup bread crumbs
1 large onion
1 tablespoon Worcestershire
1/2 teaspoon pepper

Soak crumbs in milk. Mix all ingredients thoroughly. Shape oblong. Pat brown sugar on top and bake at 350° for 1 to 1 1/2 hours. Serves 6 to 8.

Mrs. Charles H. Browne

MEAT LOAF

1 pound ground beef
1 egg
1 medium onion, chopped
3/4 cup catsup

1 cup cracker crumbs
1 teaspoon salt
1/4 teaspoon pepper
2 slices bacon for top

Mix thoroughly; press into greased baking dish. Bake in 350° oven for 30 to 40 minutes. Serves 4.

Mrs. W. L. Hendrix, Sr.
Greenwood, S. C.

ITALIAN MEAT SAUCE FOR SPAGHETTI

4 pounds ground chuck
4 large onions, chopped
1 stalk celery, chopped
1 teaspoon oregano
1/2 teaspoon garlic powder
4 bay leaves

2 teaspoons Worcestershire
2 cups mushrooms
2 6-ounce cans tomato paste
6 cups tomatoes
1 teaspoon pepper

Sauté chopped onions, celery, and bell pepper in bacon grease. Brown ground beef in a separate container, preferably a dutch oven. Combine onions, celery, bell pepper, ground beef, oregano, garlic powder, Worcestershire, bay leaves, tomato paste, mushroom liquid, tomatoes, and pepper. Cook mushrooms in 3/4 stick margarine in a small saucepan for 10 minutes and then add to rest of ingredients. Cook over low heat for 1 1/2 to 2 hours. Serves 6 to 8.

Mrs. Walter Duffie

Let the stoics say what they please, we do
not eat for the good of living, but because
the meat is savory and the appetite is keen.
— Emerson

MEAT SAUCE FOR SPAGHETTI

1 green pepper, chopped
1 cup celery, chopped
3 medium onions, chopped
1 tablespoon bacon drippings
1 1-pound can tomatoes
3/4 can water
1 1/2 pounds ground beef

1 tablespoon margarine
1/2 cup catsup
1 can tomato paste
1 can water
1/8 teaspoon red pepper
1 teaspoon salt

Sauté pepper, onions and celery in bacon drippings. Mix in tomatoes and water. Cook 45 minutes. On low heat, brown ground meat in margarine. Add catsup, tomato paste and water. Add to pepper mixture and cook one hour. Season with red pepper and salt. Serve over spaghetti. Serves 8.

Mrs. James Barham, Jr.
Aiken, S. C.

Cooking is like love. It should be entered
into with abandon or not at all. — Harriet Van Horne

TEXAS HASH

1 large chopped onion
1 green pepper, minced
3 tablespoons cooking oil
1 pound ground beef
2 cups canned tomatoes

1/2 cup uncooked rice
1 teaspoon chili powder
2 teaspoons salt
1/8 teaspoon pepper

Cook onions and green pepper in oil. Add ground beef. Fry until mixture falls apart. Stir tomatoes, rice, and seasonings. Pour into 2-quart greased casserole, cover. Bake 1 hour at 350°. Remove cover last 15 minutes of cooking time. Serves 8.

Mrs. Richard Anderson
Mrs. James Smith

*Your labouring people think, beyond all
question,
Beef, veal, and mutton, better for digestion.
—Byron*

BEEF STROGANOFF

2 pounds round steak
4 tablespoons bacon grease
1 large chopped onion
2 cans tomato soup
2 cans (large) tomato sauce
1 large can sliced mushrooms
1 tablespoon Worcestershire
6 drops Tabasco

1/2 teaspoon salt
1/4 teaspoon pepper
1/3 teaspoon marjoram
1/4 teaspoon rosemary
1/3 teaspoon basil
1/2 teaspoon oregano
1/4 teaspoon garlic powder
1 pint sour cream

Cut meat in bite size pieces and dredge with flour. Brown in oil. Add onions and other ingredients omitting sour cream. Cook 3 to 4 hours. Add sour cream just before serving. Serve over rice. Serves 6 to 8.

Mrs. Robert Dupre

BEEF STROGANOFF

1 8-ounce can mushrooms
1 medium onion
1 stick butter
2 pounds round steak

Flour
1 teaspoon salt
1 can consommé
1 cup sour cream

Sauté mushrooms and onions in 2 tablespoons butter until golden. Remove from pan and set aside. Cut steak into bite-sized pieces, and coat with flour. Brown on all sides in remaining butter. Add consommé diluted with water to make 2 cups. Add salt. Simmer for 1 hour stirring occasionally. Stir in mushrooms and onions, then sour cream, heating thoroughly. Serve over rice or noodles. Serves 4 to 6.

Mrs. Michael D. Glenn

He that eats till he is sick,
must fast till he is well. — Thomas Fuller

CHUCK WAGON STEAK

2 1/2-pounds round steak
1/3 cup flour
1 teaspoon salt
1/4 teaspoon pepper
3 tablespoons oil
1 14 1/2-ounce can beef broth

1/2 cup water
1/2 cup barbecue sauce
1 teaspoon chili powder
1 green pepper, diced
1/2 cup sliced stuffed olives

Mix flour, salt and pepper together; rub or pound mixture well into both sides of meat. Heat oil in heavy skillet or dutch oven. Brown meat well on both sides. Blend beef broth, water, barbecue sauce, and chili powder; pour over meat. Cover and simmer 1 hour. Add green pepper and olives; simmer 1 hour to 1 1/2 hours longer. Skim any fat from gravy; thicken gravy if desired. Serves 8 to 10.

Mrs. W. Y. Quarles
McCormick, S. C.

GREEN PEPPER STEAK

2 pounds steak
2 tablespoons oil
1 1/2 teaspoons garlic salt
1/4 teaspoon black pepper
1/4 teaspoon ground ginger
1/2 cup soy sauce

1/2 teaspoon sugar
4 tomatoes
2 green peppers
1 1-pound can bean sprouts
1 tablespoon cornstarch
6 tablespoons water

Cut flank steak into thin strips across the grain of the meat. Heat oil in large heavy skillet. Add meat, garlic, salt, pepper and ginger. Brown quickly over high heat. Blend in soy sauce and sugar. Cover and cook slowly 5 minutes. Peel and quarter tomatoes. Chop green peppers. Add tomatoes, peppers and drained bean sprouts. Cover and cook 20 minutes. Blend together the cornstarch and water, add to skillet, stirring constantly until sauce thickens. Serve with fluffy cooked rice. Serves 6 to 8.

Mrs. J. C. Yarbrough, Sr.

Sit down and feed, and welcome to our table.
—Shakespeare

"MEAL 'N ONE CASSEROLE"

2 pounds one inch round steak
3 tablespoons olive oil
1 medium onion
1 large can tomato paste

2 pounds fresh or 2 packages
  frozen green beans
6 medium Irish potatoes
2 cups water

Cut round steak in serving size pieces. Brown in olive oil. Brown a chopped medium onion. Place steak, onion, salt, and pepper in a casserole. Add one can of tomato paste and 2 cups water. Cook for 1 1/2 hours in 350° oven. Add green beans and quartered potatoes and cook covered until meat is tender and vegetables are done. Serves 6.

Mrs. Jack Ross, Jr.

SAUERBRATEN

2 pounds of beef round	5 peppercorns
2 cups wine vinegar	5 cloves
1 teaspoon salt	2 bay leaves
4 cups water	1 large carrot
1 large onion, chopped	2 juniper berries

To prepare marinade, mix all ingredients (except roast) and boil for two minutes, then cool to room temperature. Cover roast completely with marinade and keep in the refrigerator for a week, turning daily. Remove the meat from marinade and let it drip. Brown meat in hot cooking oil. When brown, add a cup of filtered marinade and cook for 90 minutes adding a cup of marinade at regular intervals, keeping about 3 cups in the pan.

SAUCE

2 cups sour cream	1/2 teaspoon salt
1 tablespoon flour	1/4 teaspoon pepper
1/2 teaspoon sugar	

When meat is done, mix sour cream and flour and add to the marinade. Cook again for 10 minutes. Add sugar, salt and pepper. Serve with potato dumplings. Serves 4.

Mrs. Hermann Buchert

SMOTHERED STEAK

1 1/2-pounds cubed steak	1 can mushroom soup
1 large onion	

Brown cubed steak on both sides. Place in casserole dish and cover with onion slices and soup (undiluted). Bake in 400° oven approximately 1 hour. Serves 4.

Mrs. John M. Greene

STEAK a'la MOUTARDE

2 filet mignon
1 stick butter
1/2 cup dry white wine
1 beef bouillon cube, dissolved
 in 1/2 cup boiling water

1/2 teaspoon salt
1/8 teaspoon pepper
1 tablespoon Dijon mustard
1 tablespoon tarragon leaves

Brown steaks in butter. Continue cooking 10 minutes. Remove to platter and keep warm. Add wine to skillet and reduce by 1/2. Add bouillon, salt, pepper. Reduce by 1/2. Spread steak with mustard, sprinkle with tarragon. Pour sauce over steak. Serves 2.

Mrs. Robert E. Jones

STUFFED STEAKS

4 1 1/2 inch thick club steaks

STUFFING
1/2 pound chopped mushrooms
1/4 cup chopped onion
1 clove garlic, minced
2 tablespoons butter

1/2 teaspoon salt
2 teaspoons Worcestershire
3 to 4 drops Tabasco
1 cup dry claret (red wine)

STEP ONE
Arrange with butcher to cut opening (pocket) in 1 1/2-inch thick steak, clear to the bone. (For group use, a sirloin steak can be used.) For individual steaks, club steaks work nicely.

STEP TWO
Saute' onion and garlic in butter. Add mushrooms, salt, Worcestershire, Tabasco, and claret. Simmer in open saucepan for 3 or 4 minutes. Stuff mixture into steak and secure edges with a toothpick.

STEP THREE
Broil steaks three inches from heat in very hot broiler or on charcoal grill. Add extra seasonings at turning point, if desired. Serves 4.

Mrs. Neil Chamblee

SHISH KEBAB

1/2 cup Burgundy or claret	1/2 teaspoon salt
1 teaspoon Worcestershire	1/2 teaspoon monosodium
1 clove garlic	glutamate
1/2 cup salad oil	1 tablespoon vinegar
2 tablespoons catsup	1/2 teaspoon marjoram
1 teaspoon sugar	1/2 teaspoon rosemary
12 large fresh mushrooms	1 pound sirloin steak

Mix all ingredients except mushrooms and steak. Cut meat into 2 inch cubes. Wash mushrooms thoroughly. Marinate steak cubes and mushrooms in wine mixture for 2 hours. Alternate meat and mushrooms on skewers. Broil, turning on all sides, basting frequently. Serves 4.

Mrs. William F. Bolt

At table it becomes no one to be bashful.
—Plautus

ORIENTAL PEPPER STEAK

1/4 stick margarine	1 16-ounce can drained Chinese
6 cups cubed sirloin steak	bean sprouts or vegetables
4 bouillon cubes	1 5-ounce can water chestnuts,
3 1/4 cups hot water	drained and sliced
4 large bell peppers	1/2 teaspoon salt
2 small onions	1/2 teaspoon pepper
1/2 cup celery, chopped	

Brown steak in margarine. Add bouillon cubes dissolved in water to steak. Next add chopped bell peppers, sliced onions, chopped celery, bean sprouts or vegetables and water chestnuts. Cover and let simmer until tender, but do not overcook. Serve over cooked rice. Serves 4.

Mrs. Sam Fretwell, Jr.

CHOP SUEY

3 tablespoons oil
1 1/2-pounds sirloin steak
  (cubed)
1 cup onions
2 cups celery
1 teaspoon salt
1/8 teaspoon pepper
4-ounce can chopped mushrooms

1 teaspoon ginger
2 1/4 cups beef bouillon
3 tablespoons soy sauce
1 can bean sprouts
3 tablespoons cornstarch
1/3 cup cold water
Hot cooked rice
Fried noodles

Preheat skillet to 360 degrees. Brown meat in fat and stir. Add thinly sliced onion and diced celery; brown slightly. Add salt, pepper, mushrooms, ginger and bouillon. Bring to a boil, cover, and simmer at 200° about 40 minutes, or until meat is tender. Add soy sauce and well drained bean sprouts. Bring to a boil and thicken with cornstarch and cold water. Cook until thickened, and simmer 10 minutes longer. Serve over hot cooked rice and sprinkle with fried noodles. Serves 4.

Mrs. Cliff Bryant

BARBECUED POT ROAST

1 chuck roast (4-5 pound)
4 cloves (minced)
Juice of 3 lemons
3/4 cup olive oil

1 teaspoon crushed rosemary
1/2 teaspoon dry mustard
2 tablespoons soy sauce
1 cup California red wine

Marinate meat for 2 days in mixture. Cook until fork-tender over hot coals, basting frequently with mixture. Serves 6 to 8.

Mrs. Henry Castles

ROAST BEEF

1 package onion soup mix   1 can cream of
3 1/2-pound roast   mushroom soup

Place heavy duty foil in pan; sprinkle dry onion soup on bottom. Set meat on top of soup; pour mushroom soup over roast and fold foil tightly around roast. Cook at 300° for 4 hours. Serves 4 to 6.

Mrs. F. Spencer Shirley

A cook is known by his knife. — Thomas Fuller

BRUNSWICK STEW

1 pound roast beef   1 cup catsup
1/2 small fryer, no giblets   1/2 cup evaporated milk
3/4 pound pork shoulder   1 stick butter
1 1/2 cups Irish potatoes   2 1/2 teaspoons salt
3/4 cup white onions   1 tablespoon black pepper
1/2 cup white cabbage   2 tablespoons vinegar
2 cups tomatoes   1 cup hot water
1/2 cup cream style corn

Cook beef, chicken and pork covered with water until meat will slide from bone. Remove meat, saving broth. Remove bones and run meat through food chopper. Add 1 cup hot water to broth and bring to a slow boil; add chopped potatoes, chopped cabbage and chopped onions and cook for 20 minutes, stirring with wooden spoon. Add corn, catsup, tomatoes and cook for 10 minutes longer. Then add 1 teaspoon salt and meat. Stir slowly adding pepper, vinegar and remaining salt and cook 10 minutes longer. Add butter and milk last, pouring milk slowly. Serve hot. Yields 1 gallon.

Mrs. Jack Cobb

BRUNSWICK STEW

1 pound pork
1 pound chicken
1 pound ground beef
1 pound onions
3 pounds potatoes
2 cans tomatoes
2 cans cream-style corn
1 large can English peas

1 1/2 bottles catsup
1/2 bottle Worcestershire
1/4 cup vinegar
3 cups lemon juice
2 teaspoons Tabasco
2 tablespoons salt
1 teaspoon black pepper

Cook meat until well done. Grind and set meat aside. Put onions and potatoes through food grinder and add to broth. Cook until well done. Add meat and other ingredients. Cook on low heat until done and thick (2 to 3 hours). Serve hot. Can freeze. Yields 5-6 quarts.

Mrs. W. Glenn Garrison

A wife who is obliged to shop with the utmost of care and thrift throughout the rest of the year is, in summer, constrained to watch her husband demand the choicest, thickest, juiciest pieces of good red beef so that he might, on weekends, destroy them over an unmanageable charcoal fire and then try to take the curse off with anointments of home-brewed barbecue sauce representing as horrid a concoction to come out of a pot since Macbeth's witches gave up cooking. — Donald Rogers

PORK

HAM BUFFET RING

1 can tomato soup
3/4 cup water
2 tablespoons gelatin
  (softened in 1/2 cup water)
1 3-ounce package cream cheese

2 tablespoons lemon juice
1 tablespoon grated onion
1/2 cup mayonnaise
2 cups ground ham

Combine soup and water, and boil. Then add soft gelatin and cream cheese, and beat. Cool and add other ingredients. Pour into ring mold and refrigerate until set. Garnish with hard boiled eggs and olives. Serves 10 to 12.

Mrs. Joe Crudup, Jr.

HAM CASSEROLE

3 cups diced ham
6 hard cooked eggs sliced
1 6-ounce can mushrooms
  sliced
1 can cream of celery soup

1/2 cup milk
2 cups sharp cheese grated
2 teaspoons Worcestershire
5 to 6 drops Tabasco
3/4 cup dry bread crumbs

Place ham, cheese and eggs in layers in buttered casserole dish. Mix soup, milk, mushrooms, and seasonings. Pour over cheese, ham and eggs. Top with bread crumbs. Dot with butter. Bake at 375º for 30 minutes. Serve over rice. Serves 6.

Mrs. Jerry W. Little, Jr.

MUSHROOM BAKED HAM

1 teaspoon dry mustard
1/2 teaspoon ginger

1/2 cup dry white wine
1 center slice ham
(1 1/2-inch thick)

Mix together and pour over one 1 1/2 inch thick center slice of ham. Marinate for several hours. Reserve marinade. Drain ham, brown in a small amount of fat. Add a little water and place in 325 degree oven to cook for about an hour.

SAUCE
1 medium sized minced onion
3 tablespoons margarine
1/4 cup flour

1 cup milk
1 4 1/2-ounce can mushrooms

Sauté onion in margarine and push to side. Add flour and stir; slowly add milk and mushroom liquid. Heat stirring until smooth and thick. Add mushrooms and reserved marinade. Pour sauce over ham. Bake until bubbly at 350 degrees (about 20 minutes). May be prepared ahead and frozen. Serves 8.

Mrs. Samuel R. Moorhead, Jr.

DRESSING FOR BAKED HAM

1 tablespoon butter
1 egg
1/4 cup light brown sugar
3 tablespoons granulated sugar

3 tablespoons mustard
1 teaspoon paprika
1/2 cup vinegar

Melt butter in pan, and cool. Beat egg, sugars, mustard, and paprika together. Then, add vinegar and beat again. Add to cooled butter and cook until thickened. Serve hot over ham slices.

Mrs. H. G. Anderson, Jr.

RAISIN SAUCE FOR HAM

1 cup raisins	2 tablespoons flour
1/4 cup margarine	1/2 cup brown sugar (packed)
2 cups water	1/4 teaspoon salt
4 tablespoons vinegar	1 teaspoon ground cinnamon
2 teaspoons prepared mustard	1/4 teaspoon ground cloves

Rinse and drain raisins. Combine margarine, water, vinegar, and mustard. Heat to boiling point. Blend together: flour, sugar, salt, and spices and stir into hot mixture. Add raisins and simmer 10 minutes. Serve hot over slices of ham. Yields 1 1/2 pints.

Mrs. Robert Waldrep

STUFFED LAMB CHOPS

4 thick loin lamb chops	3/4 cup roasted diced almonds
1 cup crumbled blue cheese	1/4 cup butter

Cut openings (pockets) in lamb chops; stuff with a mixture of blue cheese, almonds and butter. Broil on grill until cooked as you like them. Serve with additional almonds sprinkled on top. Serves 4.

Mrs. Neil Chamblee

BAKED PORK CHOPS

4 thick pork chops	4 tablespoons raw rice
4 tablespoons chopped onion	1 can tomatoes

Sprinkle chops with salt and pepper, and arrange in heavy baking dish or frying pan with cover. Cover each pork chop with one tablespoon onion and rice. Pour tomatoes over chops, and add another 1/4 teaspoon of salt. Cover and cook in 350° oven for about one hour. Serves 4.

Mrs. Harold V. Sullivan, Jr.

BAKED PORK CHOPS

4 pork chops
2 small cans tomato sauce
1/2 cup water
2 tablespoons brown sugar

Juice of 1/2 lemon
1/2 teaspoon salt
1/2 teaspoon dry mustard
1/8 teaspoon pepper

Brown chops and place in shallow greased baking dish. Then mix remaining ingredients and pour over chops and cover. Bake for 1 1/4 hours at 350 degrees. Serves 4.

Mrs. Theo L. Burriss

PORK CHOPS BAKED IN SOUR CREAM

4 pork chops
1 tablespoon oil
1 tablespoon margarine
1/2 cup water
Salt, pepper, garlic salt

1 tablespoon sugar
2 tablespoons vinegar
1 bay leaf
1/2 cup sour cream

Season 4 chops with pepper, salt and garlic salt. Dredge in flour, and brown in oil, and margarine. Put in casserole. In browning pan, add water, sugar, vinegar, bay leaf, and sour cream. Boil and pour over chops. Cover and bake for 1 1/2 hours. Uncover and let brown slightly. Bake at 350 degrees. Serves 4.

Mrs. Marshall Kowalski

PORK CHOP CASSEROLE

8 to 12 center cut chops
4 tablespoons vegetable oil
1/2 teaspoon salt
1/8 teaspoon pepper

12 thick slices onion
4 large Irish potatoes
2 cans cream of tomato soup
2 cans cream of mushroom soup

Brown chops in oil and season with salt and pepper. Place in 2 glass baking dishes, and alternate onion with potato slices. Pour mushroom soup over one casserole and tomato soup over the other. Bake at 350 degrees for 1 1/2 hours. Serves 8-12.

Mrs. James B. Pruitt, Jr.

CURRIED PORK CHOPS AND APRICOTS

6 pork chops
1 large can apricots
1 teaspoon salt
1 teaspoon curry powder
1/2 teaspoon pepper

2 cups milk
4 tablespoons butter
1/4 cup onion
4 tablespoons flour

Brown pork chops in skillet. Season with salt and pepper. Place in baking dish and top with apricots, round side up. Melt butter. Sauté onions. Blend flour and curry powder. Add to onions. Stir in 2 cups milk, and cook over low heat until thickened, stirring constantly. Pour sauce over pork chops. Leave top of apricots showing and bake one hour at 350 degrees. Serves 6.

Mrs. Richard G. Christopher III

QUICK PORK CHOP DINNER

4 pork chops (1/2-inch thick)
2 teaspoons prepared mustard
2 tablespoons flour
3/4 teaspoon salt and dash pepper

2 tablespoons fat
1 10 1/2-ounce can chicken
  rice soup
1/2 cup water

Spread mustard over chops, and sprinkle with flour, salt and pepper. Then brown thoroughly in hot fat. Place in casserole, and add chicken soup and water. Cover and place in 350 degree oven and bake for 1 hour. Uncover last 10 minutes. Serves 4.

Mrs. Allen Thomas
Iva, S. C.

FLAMBIERTES SCHWEINELENDCHEN
(PORK TENDERLOIN FLAMBÉ)

1 pork tenderloin
2 tablespoons butter
1 small can button mushrooms
3 tablespoons dry Sherry or
   Vermouth or Port
1/2 cup cream

1 teaspoon salt
1/4 teaspoon black pepper
1/2 teaspoon garlic (optional)
1 small glass brandy or
   Vodka

Trim all fat and skin from the tenderloin. Cut into finger-thick slices. Season with salt, pepper and garlic. Make ahead (standing for some hours in the refrigerator improves the flavor). At the table (a chafing dish does quite well) brown the butter, and cook the tenderloin slices slightly on both sides. Add the mushrooms (without liquid) and the Sherry. Cook until the liquid is reduced to half and pour the brandy over it. Light it quickly and let your guests watch the show. After the alcohol has burned out pour the cream over it. Stir and serve at once.

Mrs. Gerhard Wellenreuther

TOP OF STOVE BARBECUE

2 pounds pork, loin or shoulder
1/2 pound stew beef
1/2 cup vinegar
1/2 cup water

1 large onion, chopped
1 teaspoon sugar
1/3 bottle Worcestershire
1 large can tomatoes

Have butcher chop pork and beef into small cubes. Put all ingredients together and start cooking over fast heat. Remove top and simmer until meat falls apart. Serve on hamburger buns with slices of onion and dill pickles.

Mrs. May Dell Byars

HAM TETRAZZINA

3 cups cooked ham
2/3 box spaghetti
1 cup milk
1 small can Parmesan cheese
1 cup mushrooms
1 can consomme soup

3 tablespoons butter
3 tablespoons flour
1 bouillon cube
1/2 teaspoon black pepper
1/2 teaspoon celery salt
1 1/2 teaspoon salt

Cook spaghetti according to directions on box. Melt butter in sauce pan; add mushrooms and sauté. Add flour and blend carefully. Add consommé and bouillon cube. Cook until thickened. Remove from heat and stir in milk. Mix sauce with spaghetti. Add seasonings — blend in 1/2 of cheese. Add ham and blend. Place in baking dish and sprinkle remainder of cheese over top. Bake at 375 degrees until light brown (approximately 35-40 minutes). Serves 8.

Mrs. George Cole
Greenville, S. C.

BUCKAROO SHORT RIBS

2 packages meat marinade	2 garlic cloves, minced
2/3 cup tomato puree	2 tablespoons brown sugar
2/3 cup red wine	2 tablespoons prepared mustard
2 tablespoons vinegar	5 pounds lean, meaty beef short ribs

Combine ingredients thoroughly. Pierce all surfaces of meat deeply. Place in shallow broiler pan; cover with sauce. Marinate 15 minutes. Bake 2 hours, 300 degrees to 325 degrees or until done. Serves 6.

Mrs. Ellis B. Drew, Jr.

BARBECUED FRANKFURTERS

1 bottle chili sauce	2 teaspoons sugar
1/4 cup vinegar	2 teaspoons mustard
3/4 cup water	1 tablespoon Worcestershire
1 medium onion	2 tablespoons catsup
1 tablespoon butter	1 dozen franks
1/2 teaspoon pepper	

Dice onion. Mix all ingredients in casserole dish. Slit franks and add to mixture. Bake at 350 degrees for 1 hour. Serve in hotdog buns.

Mrs. Paul L. Embler

POULTRY

CHICKEN AND SCAMPI

8 single chicken breasts
1 tablespoon salt
1/2 teaspoon pepper
1/4 cup margarine
3 small onions, finely chopped
1 teaspoon garlic salt

3 tablespoons snipped parsley
1/2 cup Port wine
1 8-ounce can tomato sauce
1 pound shelled, deveined
   shrimp
1 cup rice

Debone chicken breasts. Rub chicken well with salt and pepper. Cut meat into bite size pieces. In hot margarine saute' chicken pieces until brown. Add onions, garlic salt, parsley, wine and tomato sauce. Simmer, covered, about 30 minutes or until chicken is tender. Push chicken to one side of skillet, turn up heat so tomato mixture boils, add shrimp, and cook for 3 to 4 minutes or until shrimp is done. Pile chicken pieces in serving dish, top with shrimp and garnish with a little parsley. Serve over rice. Serves 4.

Mrs. Allan P. Sloan, Jr.

CHIPPED BEEF CHICKEN

1 package chipped beef
6 chicken breasts

1 can condensed mushroom soup
1/2 can water

Place chipped beef in bottom of baking dish. Arrange boned chicken breasts on top of beef. Over above pour mushroom soup with water. Cover and cook for 2 hours at 350 degrees in preheated oven. Serves six

Mrs. W. R. Phillips, Jr.

CRUNCHY BAKED CHICKEN

1 1/2 cups crushed potato
  chips or 40 saltines
1/2 cup grated Parmesan cheese
1/4 cup chopped parsley
1 clove garlic, crushed

1/2 teaspoon salt
1/8 teaspoon pepper
2 3-pound fryers, quartered
1 cup melted butter

Mix crumbs, cheese, parsley, garlic, salt and pepper. Dip chicken in melted butter and then in crumb mix. Arrange pieces in single layer in large shallow dish. Pour remaining margarine over chicken. Bake 1 1/4 hours at 350 degrees. Serves 8.

Mrs. Sidney Harper
Westminster, South Carolina

DEVILED CHICKEN

6 or 8 chicken breasts
1/2 stick butter
2 tablespoons mustard

1/2 cup mayonnaise
Salt and pepper
1 or 2 cups Pepperidge Farm
  dressing crumbs

Melt butter. Add mustard and mayonnaise. Dip chicken that has been salted and peppered in this mixture, then roll in Pepperidge Farm crumbs. Place in baking dish and cook at 350 degrees for 1 hour. Serves 6 to 8.

Mrs. James H. Barton

LEMON-BUTTER BAKED CHICKEN

4 large chicken breasts
1 stick margarine
1/2 cup lemon juice

1/2 teaspoon salt
1/4 teaspoon pepper
1/4 teaspoon paprika

Combine ingredients except chicken. Chill chicken in the sauce for 4 to 5 hours. Bake at 350 degrees about 1 to 1 1/4 hours or until tender. Serves 4.

Mrs. Stuart M. Brown

"Oh the pleasure it is. . .
to know that a perfect meal awaits us!"
— Brillat-Savarin

ROLLED CHICKEN BREASTS

3 large chicken breasts
  boned, skinned and halved
6 thin slices boiled ham
2 tablespoons butter

6 ounces natural Swiss cheese,
  cut in 6 sticks.
1/4 cup all-purpose flour

Place chicken pieces, boned side up, on cutting board. Working from center out, pound chicken lightly with wooden mallet to make cutlets about 1/4 inch thick. Sprinkle with salt. Place a ham slice and a cheese stick on each cutlet. Tuck in sides of each, and roll up as for jelly roll, pressing to seal well. Skewer or tie securely. Coat rolls with the 1/4 cup flour; brown in the butter or margarine. Remove chicken to 11 x 7 x 1 1/2 inch baking pan.

SAUCE

1/2 cup water
1 teaspoon chicken flavor
  gravy base
1 3-ounce can sliced drained
  mushrooms

1/3 cup sauterne
2 tablespoons flour
1/2 cup cold water
Toasted sliced almonds

In same skillet, combine first water, the gravy base, mushrooms, and wine. Heat, stirring to incorporate any crusty bits from skillet. Pour mixture over chicken in baking pan. Cover and bake at 350 degrees 1 to 1 1/4 hours. Transfer chicken to warm serving platter. Blend the 2 tablespoons flour with the 1/2 cup cold water. Add to gravy in baking pan. Cook and stir until thickened. Pour a little gravy over chicken. Garnish with toasted sliced almonds. Serves 6.

Mrs. Sidney Paine

CHICKEN CACCIATORE

1/4 cup olive oil
1 fryer, cut up
2 medium onions, sliced
2 cloves garlic, minced
1 8-ounce can seasoned
   tomato sauce

1 teaspoon salt
1/4 teaspoon pepper
1/2 teaspoon celery seed
1 teaspoon oregano
1 or 2 bay leaves
1/4 cup cooking sauterne

Brown chicken in oil. Remove from oil. Cook onions and garlic until tender. Combine remaining ingredients, except wine. Return chicken to skillet. Pour over sauce mixture. Cover and simmer 45 minutes. Add wine and cook 20 minutes more, turning occasionally (or until fork tender). Arrange on large platter of spaghetti. Serves 4 to 6.

Mrs. Ellis B. Drew, Jr.

What is sauce for the goose may be sauce
for the gander but is not necessarily
sauce for the chicken, the duck, the turkey
or the guinea hen. — Alice B. Toklas

CHICKEN CASSEROLE

4 chicken breasts, halved and boned
8 strips bacon
1/2 pint sour cream

1 can mushroom soup
1 large jar Libby's chopped beef

Line casserole with beef. Roll breasts up and wrap with bacon. Place chicken on the beef. Mix sour cream and soup. Pour over chicken. Bake 1 1/2 hours at 300 degrees. Serves 8.

Mrs. David Hunter

BUTTERED CHICKEN BREASTS

8 split chicken breasts
1 stick margarine or butter
1 teaspoon salt
1/4 teaspoon pepper

3 cups of water
2 teaspoons of fresh
    chopped or canned parsley

Place the chicken breasts in a shallow pyrex baking dish or aluminum pan. Sprinkle with salt, pepper, and chopped parsley. Cut butter in small chunks and put on top of the chicken. Pour the 3 cups of water in the baking dish (more may be added if needed as it cooks). Cover the container with foil and cook at 350 degrees for 1 1/2 hours. Serves 6 to 8.

Mrs. Walter C. Duffie

He that banquets every day never makes a good meal.
—Thomas Fuller

CHICKEN BROCCOLI CASSEROLE

1 small onion
1 stalk celery
4 chicken breasts
2 packages frozen broccoli
    spears
2 cans cream of chicken soup

1 cup mayonnaise
3 teaspoons fresh lemon juice
3/4 teaspoon curry powder
Ritz crackers
1 1/4 cup grated sharp cheese

Boil chicken with onion, celery and salt until tender. Cook broccoli and drain. Place broccoli in 9 x 13 baking dish. Cut chicken in small pieces and place over broccoli. Mix soup, mayonnaise, lemon juice and curry powder and pour over chicken. Sprinkle grated cheese over soup mixture. Make thin crust of Ritz crackers and sprinkle over top of cheese. Cook at 350 degrees for 45 minutes. This is good warmed over. Serves 8.

Mrs. James Smith

CHICKEN GREEN PEA CASSEROLE

3 cups chopped chicken
1 8-ounce box noodles
2 cups milk (or broth, or 1 each)
2 tablespoons flour
2 tablespoons butter
1/2 teaspoon onion

1 can mushroom soup
2 hard-cooked eggs
1 cup Le Seur English peas
1 small jar chopped pimientos
1 can chow mein noodles

Cook noodles in broth; add chicken, eggs, pimientos and peas. Make gravy of milk, flour and butter. Add onion and soup. Cook until thick; pour over noodles and chicken mixture. Bake at 350 degrees for 25 to 35 minutes. For last 10 minutes top with chow mein noodles. Serves 8. For freezing, omit the boiled eggs.

Mrs. W. Glenn Garrison

CHICKEN-WILD RICE CASSEROLE

2 whole broiler-fryer chickens
    (3 pounds each)
1 cup water
1 1/2 teaspoons salt
1 cup dry sherry
1/2 teaspoon curry powder
1 medium onion

1/2 cup sliced celery
1 pound fresh mushrooms
1/4 cup margarine
2 6-ounce packages long grain
    wild rice (with seasonings)
1 cup sour cream
1 can cream of mushroom soup

Place chicken in deep kettle. Add water, sherry, salt, curry powder, onion and celery. Bring to boil; cover tightly. Reduce heat and simmer one hour. Remove from heat, strain broth. Refrigerate chicken and broth. When chicken is cool, remove meat from bone. Cut into bite size pieces. Sauté mushrooms in butter until golden brown. (Reserve enough to circle top of casserole) Measure chicken broth, use as part of liquid for cooking rice. Follow package directions for firm rice. Combine chicken, rice, and mushrooms. Blend sour cream and undiluted mushroom soup. Toss together with chicken mixture. Put in 3 1/2 or 4 quart casserole. Arrange reserved mushrooms on top of casserole. Cover. Bake in 350 degree oven for 1 hour. Serves 10 to 12.

Mrs. Reese Fant

CHICKEN CHOW MEIN

1 1/2 cups sliced celery
1 large bell pepper
3 tablespoons margarine
2 cups chicken broth
2 tablespoons cornstarch
1/2 cup cold water
3 tablespoons soy sauce

1/2 envelope onion soup mix
3 cups cooked chicken
2 3-ounce cans mushrooms
1 5-ounce can water chestnuts
1 1-pound can bean sprouts
1 can Chow-mein noodles

Slice celery and pepper in strips. Cook in margarine for 5 minutes. Dice chicken and add to broth. Blend cornstarch with water and soy sauce. Add to chicken. Add onion soup mix. Cook and stir until mixture thickens. Drain mushrooms, water chestnuts, and bean sprouts. Add to chicken mixture and cook for 15 minutes on medium heat. Serve with Chow-mein noodles. Serves 6.

Miss Julia Timmerman

QUICK-CHICKEN CHOW MEIN

1/2 cup milk
1 can condensed cream of
  chicken soup

1 small can boned chicken
1 can mixed Chinese vegetables
2 teaspoons soy sauce

Mix above ingredients and serve hot over chow mein noodles. Serves four.

Mrs. A. Owen Meredith

CHICKEN PIE

6 tablespoons butter
6 tablespoons flour
1/2 teaspoon salt
1/4 teaspoon pepper

1 3/4 cups chicken broth
2/3 cup milk
2 cups cut-up cooked chicken
Pastry for 9-inch 2 crust pie.

Divide pastry, using about 2/3 of it to line baking dish. Melt butter, add flour, seasoning; let bubble. Add liquid and cook until thickened. Add chicken. Use remaining 1/3 pastry for strips across top of dish. Bake at 425 degrees for 25 minutes. Serves 6.

Mrs. Joe Prevost, Jr.

CHICKEN SALAD

1 cup sour cream
1/2 cup mayonnaise
2 tablespoons lemon juice
1 tablespoon Worcestershire
1 teaspoon salt

Pepper to taste
7 cups diced chicken
1 cup chopped pecans
1/2 cup finely chopped celery

Mix sour cream, mayonnaise, lemon juice, Worcestershire sauce, salt and pepper. Pour over the chicken, pecans, and celery. Toss lightly. Serve on lettuce or tomato. Serves 8.

Mrs. Charles J. Riddle, Jr.

HOT CHICKEN SOUFFLE

13 slices of white bread
7 cups chicken, hen
1 cup green pepper
1/2 cup chopped onion
1/2 cup pimento
1 cup celery
2 cups grated sharp cheese

1 cup mayonnaise
1 1/2 tablespoons plain flour
Dash pepper
5 eggs, beaten
4 cups milk
2 cans mushroom soup

Cube 4 slices of bread. Place on bottom of baking dish. Combine chicken, vegetables, mayonnaise, salt and pepper. Spoon over cubed bread. Trim remaining slices of bread and crumble over chicken mixture. Combine eggs and milk. Pour over all. Cover and chill 1 hour or overnight. When ready to bake, spoon soup on top. Cook in slow oven, 325 degrees, for 1 hour or until set. Sprinkle cheese over top, the last few minutes of baking. Serves 14.

Mrs. J. Donald Brown, Jr.

CHICKEN TETRAZZINI

1 large hen
2 green peppers, chopped
2 onions, chopped
1 small bunch celery, chopped
1 cup mushroom soup

2 cans tomatoes (medium size)
1 can English peas, drained
1 pound package vermicelli
Salt and pepper to taste
Grated American cheese

Cook hen and cut up in pieces. Sauté onions, celery and green peppers until tender. Cook vermicelli, drain. Add all ingredients. Use enough broth to make it moist. Pour in two long casseroles. Cover with grated cheese and bake at 400 degrees until cheese is slightly brown.

Mrs. Jerry C. Sloan
Pendleton, S. C.

BARBECUE CHICKEN WITH MUSHROOMS

Fry 8 chicken breasts

SAUCE

Juice of 1 lemon
1 can mushrooms
1 tablespoon Kitchen
Bouquet sauce

1 teaspoon Worcestershire
1 teaspoon A-1 sauce
1 teaspoon Tabasco

Mix liquid ingredients. Put chicken in roaster and pour sauces over it. Pour sliced mushrooms and 1 cup boiling water over chicken (use mushroom juice as part). Bake covered 1 hour in 350 degree oven, basting frequently.

Mrs. Beaty Jackson

BARBECUE SAUCE FOR CHICKEN

1 cup water
1/2 cup vinegar
4 tablespoons sugar
1 teaspoon salt
1 teaspoon garlic salt

1/2 teaspoon black pepper
1 teaspoon dry mustard
1 teaspoon paprika
1/4 cup margarine

Combine above ingredients and heat until margarine is melted. Half or quarter chicken. Salt and grease with vegetable oil each piece of chicken. Cook over hot coals, basting often, until done – about 1 hour. This is enough sauce for 1 chicken.

Mrs. C. Marshall Kowalski

CHINESE BARBEQUED CHICKEN

1 tablespoon vegetable oil
1/4 cup soy sauce
3/4 teaspoon dry mustard
1/4 teaspoon ground ginger

1 small clove garlic, minced
1 fryer, 3 pounds quartered
Cooked French Green Beans,
   optional

Mix all ingredients except chicken and beans. Put chicken in shallow baking pan and brush on all sides with the mixture. Let stand 30 minutes. Bake in oven at 350 degrees for 50 minutes, turning once or twice and brushing with the sauce. Serve with green beans if desired. Serves 4.

Mrs. Fritz Waidner

LOW CALORIE BARBEQUE CHICKEN

2 3-pound fryers in pieces or
   quartered
3 cups tomato juice
1/2 cup vinegar
1 tablespoon sugar
4 medium onions (sliced)

3 tablespoons Worcestershire
1/2 cup catsup
4 teaspoons prepared mustard
1 teaspoon pepper
2 teaspoons salt

Place chicken in broiler pan and pour above mixture over it. Cook for 1 hour or until tender at 350 degrees, basting often with sauce.

Mrs. James C. Marchbanks
Mrs. H. G. Anderson, Jr.

CHICKEN AND ARTICHOKES IN SHERRY

1 stick margarine
1/2 pound sliced mushrooms
4 pounds chicken pieces
1 teaspoon salt
1/8 teaspoon pepper

2 packages frozen artichoke
  hearts
1 1/2 cups dry sherry
1/2 cup water
2 tablespoons cornstarch

Melt margarine. Saute'mushrooms and set aside. Salt and pepper the chicken and brown in remaining margarine. Add artichokes, sherry, 1/2 cup water, and mushrooms. Cover. Simmer 30 minutes. Combine cornstarch and 3 tablespoons water. Stir into liquid and cook until thickened. Serves 8.

Mrs. Robert E. Jones

CHICKEN BREAST IN SHERRY

10 chicken breasts
1 stick butter
2 cans cream of chicken soup
1/2 soup can of water

3/4 cup sherry
1 pound mushrooms
Salt and pepper

Salt and pepper chicken; brown in butter. Remove chicken from skillet and place in baking dish. To the butter add soup, water, sherry and mushrooms. Cook this for 5 minutes, then pour it over the chicken. Bake at 325 degrees for one hour. Serves 10.

Mrs. Kathryne Moore
Memphis, Tennessee

CHARCOAL-MEAT SAUCE

1 cup Worcestershire
1/4 cup wine vinegar
1/4 cup plus 1 tablespoon
  light brown sugar

1 teaspoon garlic powder
1/2 teaspoon garlic salt

This sauce used for basting meat cooked on a covered grill with 4 air vents. Place charcoal at one end and open vent under coals. Place meat at other end of grill and open vent over meat. Place hickory wood on top of coals when you place meat on grill. Baste every 15-20 minutes until ready.

Use turkey breast, chicken halves or quarters, or roast. Salt meat with garlic salt the night before. Turkey should be salted 24 hours ahead. Have meat at room temperature (5 pound turkey breast takes around 4 to 4 1/2 hours; a 3 pound roast takes around 1 to 1 1/2 hours. Chicken takes 1 to 1 1/2 hours). Add hickory (soaked in water for several hours) when needed. Hickory will make meat turn slightly pink.

Mrs. Forest Suggs, Jr.

STEAMED DOVES

1 dozen doves
Salt
Pepper
1 cup bacon drippings

1 cup cooking oil
Flour
1 tablespoon Kitchen Bouquet

Salt and pepper doves as you would chicken to fry. Let doves stand 12 hours before cooking or at least six hours with salt and pepper on them. Roll doves in flour as you would flour chicken to fry. Put 1 cup of bacon drippings and 1 cup of any kind of cooking oil in 12 inch frying pan for one dozen doves, (a black iron frying pan is best). Brown doves real well on both sides until they are crisp. Pour all but a very small amount of grease off your doves, cover doves with cold water and add 1 tablespoon of Kitchen Bouquet. As soon as the water begins to bubble, cover and turn the heat to low and cook for two hours, turning birds several times. When the breasts of the doves are tender and stick easily they are ready to eat. Quail may be cooked by this recipe also. Two to three doves per person. Serves 4.

Mrs. Hugh E. Vincent, Jr.

ROAST WILD DUCK

3 wild ducks
Celery leaves
1 cup butter melted
1/2 cup dry red wine

1 teaspoon salt
Freshly ground black pepper
Apricot sauce

Rub cavities with salt and pepper. Fill the cavities with celery leaves. Brush skin with 1/2 cup butter. Roast ducks breasts side up in a hot oven 450 degrees for 30 minutes, basting every 5 minutes with wine and remaining 1/2 cup butter. Carve ducks and keep hot over boiling water. Save the juices to add to apricot sauce.

APRICOT SAUCE

2 1/2 cups canned
  apricots, drained
1 teaspoon grated orange rind
2 cups dry red wine

6 tablespoons butter
3 duck livers, (cut up)
Duck juices
Freshly ground black pepper

Press apricots through a coarse sieve. Combine apricots, orange rind, wine, butter and pepper in the top of a double boiler. Cook over direct heat for 5 minutes. Press duck livers through a coarse sieve and add apricot mixture with duck juices. Place over hot water and simmer 5 minutes, stirring constantly, until smooth and lightly thickened. Pour over duck and serve immediately.

Mrs. Fritz Waidner

WILD DUCK

1 pound link sausage
2 large onions
1 cup rice
1 can consomme

4 slices bacon
1 pinch sage
2 or 3 ducks
Salt and pepper

Fry 1 pound link sausage, cut in half. Remove sausage from pan and saute' sliced onions until tender. Drain onions and put rice in sausage grease stirring until each grain is coated. Put rice, sausage, onion in Dutch oven or roaster, season with salt, pepper, and sage. Add 1 can consomme. Place ducks on top of this. Cover each duck with 2 slices of bacon. Cover tightly, bake in oven 5 hours at 250 degrees. Serves 2 people per duck.

Mrs. J. Donald King

JELLIED GOOSE WITH WINE

1 twelve pound goose quartered	3 carrots
2 large onions, sliced	1 lemon, sliced
8 tablespoons chopped parsley	1 cup dry white wine
2 bay leaves	3 envelopes unflavored gelatin
1 teaspoon thyme	1 teaspoon chives
1 whole clove	1 tablespoon salt
2 garlic cloves	10 peppercorns, crushed

Place goose, onions, 6 tablespoons parsley, bay leaves, thyme, clove, garlic, carrots, lemon, salt and peppercorns in large pot with water to cover. Bring to a boil, cover, reduce heat and simmer for one hour. After first 30 minutes remove carrots, slice and save them. When goose is done, remove it. Let it cool, remove the skin and slice it thin. Strain hot broth through sieve or cheesecloth. Skim off fat. Add 3 cups broth to wine in which gelatin has been softened. Stir until gelatin is dissolved, chill until syrupy. Pour a thin layer of gelatin mixture into bottom of 2 quart mold. Decorate with 3 scored lemon slices, 3 carrot slices and chives to form flower spray. Chill gelatin layer until firm, then fill mold with alternate layers of goose and carrots. Combine the two tablespoons parsley with remaining gelatin mixture and pour into mold. Chill 4 hours. Serves 6.

Mrs. Fritz Waidner

BAKED ROCK CORNISH HEN WITH WILD RICE

8 Rock Cornish hens
(one pound each)
1 can consommé
2 cups Karo syrup
1 cup dry white wine

1 stick butter
3 teaspoons salt
1 teaspoon pepper
1 teaspoon accent

Hens may be split in half or served whole. Season with salt, pepper, and accent. Place on rack in shallow roasting pan. Combine consommé, Karo syrup, butter and wine in double boiler. Roast hens, uncovered, about 1 hour in pre-heated 350 degree oven, basting frequently with sauce. To brown turn up oven to 400 degrees during last 10 minutes of roasting time. Directions for wild rice below.

WILD RICE WITH MUSHROOMS

1 package of wild rice
1 can consommé

1 1/2 cups finely chopped
mushrooms

Follow directions on package for cooking wild rice, but substitute half the water with consommé. Add mushrooms to rice before cooking. Serve roasted hens on bed of rice. Serves 8.

Mrs. Ted Owen

GOOD-BYE TURKEY

1 can cheddar cheese soup
1 1/2 cups turkey broth or
1 1/2 cups water and 2 chicken
bouillon cubes, dissolved

1 1/3 cups minute rice
14 to 18 asparagus spears
2 cups turkey, chopped
1 tablespoon turkey broth

Set aside 1/2 cup cheese soup. Combine remaining soup with 1 1/2 cups broth in skillet. Bring to boil. Remove from heat. Stir in minute rice. Top with asparagus and turkey. Pour remaining soup and broth over turkey. Simmer 5 minutes. Sprinkle with toasted almonds or paprika. Serves 4 to 6.

Mrs. Wes Williams
St. Petersburg, Florida

CHEESE and EGG

CHEESE PUDDING

10 slices bread
1/2 stick butter
1/2 pound grated cheese

3 eggs, beaten
2 cups of milk
1/2 teaspoon salt

Remove crust, butter well, cut in cubes. Mix together. Let stand several hours before baking. Bake for 1 1/2 hours at 300 degrees.

Mrs. Paul L. Embler
Mrs. James B. Pruitt, Jr.
Mrs. W. C. Johnston
Mrs. Harold V. Sullivan

CHEESE SOUFFLÉ

3 tablespoons margarine
3 tablespoons flour
1 cup milk
1/2 teaspoon salt

Dash of pepper
1 cup grated cheese
3 eggs, separated

Make a cream sauce by melting butter and mixing in flour, then gradually adding milk, stirring constantly until it boils to avoid lumping. Add salt and pepper. Boil gently a few moments, then remove from heat, add cheese and stir. Beat egg yolks and whites separately. Add yolks and mix well. Fold in stiffly beaten whites. Pour into greased dish and bake at 350 degrees for 20 minutes or until set. Serve **immediately,** as it begins to fall as soon as removed from oven. Serves 4 to 5.

Mrs. C. Edwin Roberts
Charleston, S. C.

APPLE YARD SCRAMBLED EGGS

1 1/3-cup light cream
1 teaspoon grated lemon rind
16 eggs
2 teaspoons salt
1/2 teaspoon white pepper
1/4 teaspoon oregano

1/4 teaspoon basil
1/4 teaspoon powdered rosemary
1/2 cup grated cheddar cheese
1/2 cup grated parmesan cheese
1 stick butter

Pour cream into bowl with grated lemon rind. Let stand 15 minutes. Beat eggs slightly and add salt, pepper, and herbs. Mix well. Add cheeses. Strain cream and add to egg mixture. Melt butter in large, heavy skillet. Pour in egg mixture. Cook over very low heat, stirring from time to time until mixture just sets. Be careful not to overcook. Serves 8.

Mrs. Samuel R. Moorhead, Jr.

Cooks are not to be taught in their own kitchen. — Thomas Fuller

EGGS A LA KING

1 10 1/2-ounce can condensed
  cream of mushroom soup
1/2 cup milk

4 hard cooked eggs
4 corn muffins
Chopped parsley

In medium saucepan, combine soup and milk, mixing well. Bring to boiling point, stirring constantly. Carefully stir in eggs; re-heat gently. Serve hot, over toasted corn muffins. Sprinkle with parsley. Serves 4.

Mrs. J. Philip Noury

POACHED EGGS A LA BEARNAISE

1 pound fresh minced mushrooms
3 tablespoons minced spring
  onions
3 tablespoons butter
1 1/2 tablespoon flour
2 tablespoons white wine
1/2 cup heavy cream

1/2 teaspoon salt
Dash pepper
8 pastry shells
8 poached eggs
2 cups Bearnaise Sauce
Sprigs of parsley

Wipe mushrooms with damp towel. Mince mushrooms and onions. Saute' mushrooms and onions in butter for 8 minutes. Add flour and stir over moderate heat for 3 minutes. Stir in wine and simmer for 3 minutes. Stir in 2/3 of cream and seasonings. Simmer 3 minutes, adding more cream, a little at a time if mixture becomes too thick. Heat pastry shells and poach eggs. Place eggs in shells and spoon mushroom mixture over eggs. Top with Bearnaise Sauce. Garnish with parsley.

BEARNAISE SAUCE

1 teaspoon chopped shallots
1 teaspoon chopped tarragon
1 teaspoon chopped chervil
2 pepper corns
Pinch salt

1/4 cup tarragon vinegar
5 egg yolks
3/4 cup melted butter
Pinch of cayenne pepper

Simmer first five ingredients in vinegar over low heat until vinegar is reduced by 2/3. Cool to lukewarm. Add egg yolks, and beat briskly with a wire whisk. Place over low heat and gradually add butter. Whisk until sauce thickens. Strain sauce. Season with cayenne pepper. Serves 6.

Mrs. J. Gary Early

Cheese — milk's leap toward immortality.
— Clifton Fadiman

"KING'S INN SPECIAL"

MACARONI MOUSSE

1 cup macaroni broken in
  two-inch pieces
1 1/2 cups scalding milk
1 cup soft bread crumbs
1/4 cup melted butter
1 pimento, chopped
1 tablespoon chopped parsley

1 tablespoon chopped onion
1 1/2 cups Kraft American
  Cheese grated or Nukraft
3/8 teaspoon salt
1/8 teaspoon pepper
Dash of paprika
3 eggs

Cook the macaroni in boiling salted water, blanch in cold water and drain. Pour the scalding milk over the bread crumbs, add the butter, pimento, parsley, onion, grated cheese and seasonings. Then add the well-beaten eggs. Put the macaroni in a thickly buttered loaf pan and pour the milk and cheese mixture over it. Bake about 50 minutes in a slow oven, or until the loaf is firm and will hold its shape when turned out on a platter. Serve with mushroom sauce.

SAUCE

1 1/2 cups milk
1/2 cup liquor drained from
  mushrooms
1 tablespoon butter
4 tablespoons flour

1 small can mushrooms
1/4 teaspoon salt
1/8 teaspoon pepper
Dash of paprika

Make a sauce of the milk, mushroom liquor, butter, flour and seasonings, and when thick add mushrooms.

Mrs. Bob King

"Who doth ambition shun,
And loves to live i' the sun,
Seeking the food he eats,
And pleased with what he gets."
—Shakespeare

VEGETABLES

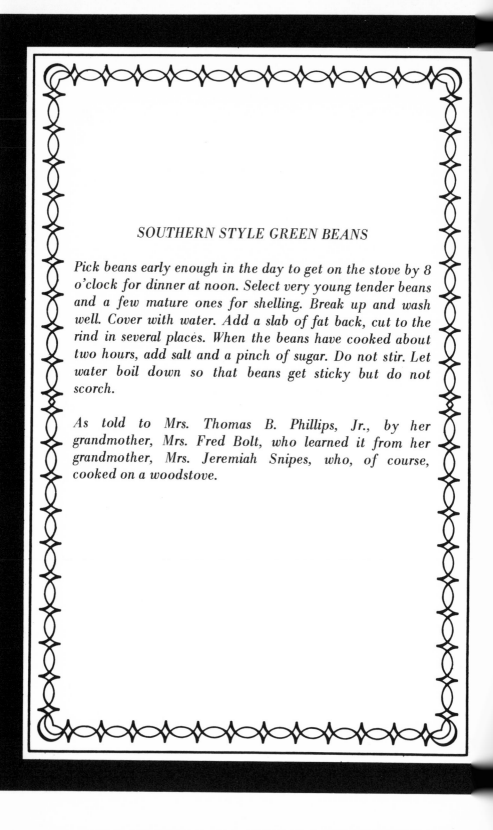

SOUTHERN STYLE GREEN BEANS

Pick beans early enough in the day to get on the stove by 8 o'clock for dinner at noon. Select very young tender beans and a few mature ones for shelling. Break up and wash well. Cover with water. Add a slab of fat back, cut to the rind in several places. When the beans have cooked about two hours, add salt and a pinch of sugar. Do not stir. Let water boil down so that beans get sticky but do not scorch.

As told to Mrs. Thomas B. Phillips, Jr., by her grandmother, Mrs. Fred Bolt, who learned it from her grandmother, Mrs. Jeremiah Snipes, who, of course, cooked on a woodstove.

ASPARAGUS CASSEROLE

1 can or jar of asparagus
1/2 can cheddar cheese soup

1/2 cup herb seasoned dressing

Place asparagus in casserole. Top with cheddar cheese soup. Top this with dressing. Heat at 325 degrees for 30 minutes or until topping is browned. Serves 4-6.

Mrs. Norman Avinger

ASPARAGUS CASSEROLE

1 15-ounce can asparagus
1 10 1/2-ounce can mushroom soup
1/2 cup shredded cheese
1/2 teaspoon salt

1/4 teaspoon pepper
1/2 cup cracker crumbs
1/2 stick margarine

Drain asparagus; place in shallow casserole; add mushroom soup undiluted, salt, pepper and cheese. Place pats of butter on top. Sprinkle cracker crumbs over entire casserole. Bake at 350 degrees for 30 minutes. Serves 4.

Mrs. Stuart M. Brown

CRUNCHY ASPARAGUS CASSEROLE

2 number 303 cans green
  asparagus spears
4 hard-cooked eggs, sliced
1 teaspoon salt
1/2 teaspoon pepper

3/4 teaspoon paprika
1 10 1/2-ounce can cream
  of mushroom soup
1 cup cornflake crumbs
1/4 pound cheese, grated

Drain asparagus, saving liquid; arrange in buttered casserole. Cover with egg slices, adding salt and pepper. Dilute soup with liquid from 1 can asparagus. Pour over asparagus and eggs. Cover with crumbs, top with cheese. Sprinkle with paprika. Bake at 400 degrees for 20-25 minutes. Serves 6.

Mrs. F. Spencer Shirley

ASPARAGUS PARMESAN

3 pounds asparagus
1 tablespoon grated
   Parmesan cheese
1/2 cup flour
1 egg
2 tablespoons dry white wine

1 cup dry bread crumbs
1/4 teaspoon garlic powder
1/2 cup olive oil
· 1 teaspoon salt
1/2 teaspoon freshly ground
   pepper

Break off tough ends of asparagus stalks. Dip stalks first in flour, then in egg beaten with wine, then into crumbs combined with cheese, garlic powder, salt and pepper. Sauté in olive oil for ten minutes or until tender. Serves 6.

Mrs. Fritz Waidner

Vegetarianism is harmless enough, although it is apt to fill a man with wind and self-righteousness. — *Robert Hutchinson*

ASPARAGUS SOUFFLÉ

1/4 pound of butter
3 heaping tablespoons of flour
3 cups of milk
2 number 303 cans of
   asparagus spears
Salt

Pepper
Paprika
2 cups grated sharp
   Cracker Barrel Cheese
1/2 cup whole pecans or
   almonds

Melt butter, stir in flour until well blended, add milk a little at a time and cook until creamy and thick. Season with salt and pepper. Put a layer of asparagus in greased casserole, then a layer of cheese and cover with cream sauce. Continue with layers until casserole is filled. Top with cheese and nuts and sprinkle with paprika. Bake at 350 degrees for about 30 minutes until cheese is light brown. Serves 8-10.

Mrs. Walter C. Duffie

BAKED BEANS

1 16-ounce can pork and beans
1/4 green pepper, diced
1 small onion, diced
3/4 cup light brown sugar
1 teaspoon dry mustard

1 tablespoon Worcestershire
2 tablespoons barbecue sauce
1 small can tomato sauce
4 strips bacon
1 cup grated sharp cheese

Sauté green pepper and onion and combine with remaining ingredients. Bake at 375 degrees for 1 1/2 hours. Fry 4 strips bacon. Break and mix with above when bean mixture is done. Cover top of mixture with grated sharp cheddar cheese. Return to oven and bake until cheese melts and is slightly browned. Serves 4 to 6.

Mrs. Alan Blanchard

BAKED BEANS

1 medium onion
1 medium bell pepper
3 slices bacon

2 1-pound cans pork and beans
1/2 cup molasses
1 tablespoon mustard

Fry bacon. Drain. Sauté onion and bell pepper in drippings. Add remaining ingredients including crumbled bacon. Bake at 350 degrees for 1 hour in a covered casserole. Serves 4 to 6.

Mrs. Chris Suber

EASY BEAN CASSEROLE

1 can French green beans
1 can mushroom soup

3 slices cheese
1 can French fried onions

Drain beans and put beans in a thin pyrex pie dish. Pour soup over beans. Cover with cheese slices. Cook at 300 degrees until cheese is completely melted. Remove from oven and cover with onions. Serves six.

Mrs. W. L. Hendrix
Greenwood, S. C.

FRENCH BEAN CASSEROLE

2 4-ounce cans sliced mushrooms	2 teaspoons soy sauce
1 medium size onion (chopped)	1 teaspoon salt
1 stick margarine	1/2 teaspoon pepper
1/4 cup flour	1 teaspoon Accent
2 cups warm milk	3 packages frozen French beans
3/4 cup sharp cheese	1 5-ounce can water chestnuts
1/8 teaspoon Tabasco sauce	3-ounce package sliced almonds

Saute' mushrooms and onions in margarine. Add flour, stir and cook until smooth. Add milk and stir, making a smooth cream sauce. Add next six ingredients and simmer until cheese melts. Cook beans by directions on package. Drain and combine with above sauce. Add water chestnuts (sliced thin). Pour into 2 quart buttered casserole. Cover with almonds. Bake at 375 degrees until bubbly, approximately 35 minutes. Serves 8.

Mrs. Robert Hunt

One morning in the garden bed,
The onion and the carrot said
Unto the parsley group:
"Oh, when shall we three meet again?
In thunder, lightning, hail or rain?"
"Alas," replied in tones of pain,
The parsley, "In the soup."

GREEN BEAN CASSEROLE

4 cups cooked green beans	1/2 cup sugar
8 slices crisp bacon	1/2 cup vinegar
1 medium onion (chopped)	

Alternate (two layers) beans, bacon, onion; repeat with onion on top. Put sugar and vinegar in a little bacon grease and boil for one minute. Pour over beans. Bake at 325 degrees for 1 1/2-2 hours. Serves 8 to 10.

Mrs. Michael Little

PENNSYLVANIA DUTCH STYLE GREEN BEANS

6 strips bacon
1 small onion, chopped
1 tablespoon cornstarch
1/2 teaspoon dry mustard
1/4 teaspoon salt
1/2 cup cooking liquid
  from beans

3 cups cooked green beans, drained
  (cook in salt water only)
2 tablespoons brown sugar
1 1/2 tablespoons vinegar
3 tablespoons blanched almonds

Fry bacon in skillet until crisp. Remove and crumble. Drain off all but 2 tablespoons drippings, add onion and brown lightly. Stir in cornstarch, mustard and salt. Stir reserved liquid from beans into skillet. Cook, stirring until mixture boils. Blend in beans, brown sugar, and vinegar. Put into small casserole and sprinkle with crumbled bacon and almonds. Bake 20-30 minutes at 350 degrees. Serves 8.

Mrs. Cliff Bryant

*Eat enough and it will make
you wise. — John Lyly*

MUSHROOM-LIMA BEAN CASSEROLE

2 cups cooked lima beans
1 large can mushrooms
1/2 pound Swiss cheese
1 tablespoon onion

4 tablespoons butter
3 tablespoons flour
1/2 cup milk
1 tablespoon butter

Melt butter in sauce pan, blend in flour. Add juice from mushrooms and milk to make white sauce. Add grated cheese to sauce. Sauté mushrooms and onion in 1 tablespoon butter. Put beans in a casserole dish. Blend in mushrooms (reserving enough for top), onions and sauce. Top with mushrooms. Bake at 350 degrees for 20 minutes (until bubbly). Serves 6.

Mrs. Sam T. Haddock

HARVARD BEETS

2 cups beets
1/2 cup sugar
2 tablespoons butter
1 tablespoon flour

1/2 teaspoon salt
1/4 cup vinegar, mixed with
1/4 cup beet juice, or water

Melt butter in saucepan or double boiler. Add flour. Stir. Add sugar, salt, and the liquid gradually. Cook until clear, stirring constantly. Add beets and heat thoroughly. Serves 4.

Mrs. Ike Schwartz
Raleigh, N. C.

BEETS IN ORANGE SAUCE

3 tablespoons sugar
2 tablespoons flour
1 teaspoon salt

1 tablespoon butter
1/2 cup orange juice
8 or 10 hot cooked beets

Combine sugar, flour, salt. Add butter. Blend to a smooth paste over low heat. Stir orange juice in slowly. Cook until mixture thickens slightly, stirring constantly. Pour the orange sauce over 8 or 10 hot, cooked beets. Serves 4.

Mrs. Ernest W. Garrison, Jr.

BROCCOLI CASSEROLE

1 package of cut broccoli
1 cup grated sharp cheese
1 can mushroom soup
1/4 cup mayonnaise
1/4 cup milk

1 beaten egg
Grated onion — optional
Butter
1 cup dry bread crumbs

Cook broccoli according to directions, leaving out salt. Drain and put in casserole. Dot with butter. Mix the remaining ingredients thoroughly and pour the mixture over broccoli. Sprinkle buttered dry bread on top. Bake at 325 degrees for 45 minutes. Serves 4.

Mrs. C. Tom Tolly, Sr.
Honea Path, S. C.

HOLLANDAISE SAUCE FOR BROCCOLI

3 egg yolks
2 tablespoons lemon juice
1/2 cup cold butter

1/4 teaspoon each salt,
sugar, dry mustard and
hot pepper sauce

Beat together egg yolks, lemon juice and seasonings in top double boiler. Divide butter in thirds. Add 1/3 of butter to the egg mixture. Cook over hot water, stirring constantly, until butter is melted. Add second 1/3 of butter when this is melted. Repeat with third portion. Stir constantly. As butter melts sauce thickens. Remove from heat. Serve hot or room temperature. Serves 5.

Mrs. James Halford, Jr.

SAUCE FOR BROCCOLI

2 tablespoons butter
2 tablespoons oil
1 1/2 teaspoons Worcestershire
1 teaspoon mustard

1 tablespoon vinegar
1/4 teaspoon salt
1/8 teaspoon pepper
1/8 teaspoon red pepper

Mix all ingredients and heat until butter melts. Pour over cooked broccoli before serving.

Mrs. Larry Kowalski

We may live without poetry, music, and art;
We may live without conscience, and live
without heart;
We may live without friends; we may live
without books;
But civilized man cannot live without cooks.
— E. R. Bulwer-Lytton

STUFFED CABBAGE

1 3-pound cabbage
1 pound ground beef
1 egg
1/2 teaspoon salt

1/2 teaspoon pepper
1/2 teaspoon garlic salt
1/4 cup water

PREPARE CABBAGE LEAVES: Use a firm head of cabbage. With sharp knife, cut core out of cabbage to depth of 3 inches. Rinse well under running cold water. Put cabbage in pan of slightly salted, boiling water over high heat. Put core side down in pan. Remove from heat when leaves are wilted. You may have to remove outer leaves first and let inside leaves cook a little longer. Drain leaves on paper towels until cool enough to handle.

STUFFING
Mix beef, egg, salt, pepper, garlic salt and water. Take a heaping teaspoon of beef mixture and place on cabbage leaf. Make roll by folding in sides of cabbage leaf and rolling. Place seam side down in 3 quart casserole.

SAUCE

1 8-ounce can tomato sauce
1 medium onion, chopped
3 tablespoons sugar
1/2 cup fresh lemon juice

1/2 teaspoon citric acid pieces
1 1/2 sauce cans water
1/2 teaspoon salt
1/2 teaspoon pepper

Combine and cover cabbage rolls with the above ingredients. Cover casserole and heat in 400 degree oven until it boils (about 20 minutes), then cut heat down to 300 degrees for 1 1/2 hours. Serves six.

Mrs. Larry Forgang

"Men usually like food." — Emily Post

GLAZED CARROTS

8 large carrots
1 cup water
1/2 cup sugar

1/2 stick margarine
1/2 teaspoon salt
3 tablespoons orange marmalade

Peel and cut carrots in desired shape. Cook slowly in water in covered sauce pan about 20 minutes until tender. Add more water if necessary. Add sugar, margarine, salt and marmalade. Cook 3 to 5 minutes longer. Serves 6.

Mrs. William J. Bolt

CORN AND CHEESE PUDDING

1/2 cup milk
1 teaspoon sugar
1 teaspoon salt
1/2 teaspoon pepper

1 1-pound can cream-style corn
2 eggs
1 cup grated cheese

Add milk, sugar, salt and pepper to corn. Beat eggs; add with cheese. Pour into 1 quart buttered casserole. Set in pan of warm water. Bake at 325 degrees for 1 hour and 15 minutes. Serve at once. Serves four.

Mrs. Robert C. Herndon

CORN CREOLE CASSEROLE

1 medium onion (chopped)
1 green pepper (chopped)
1 stick margarine
4 tablespoons flour
2 cups cooked rice
2 cups whole kernel corn

2 cups canned tomatoes (mashed)
2 hard-cooked eggs (chopped)
1 teaspoon Worcestershire
1/2 teaspoon Tabasco sauce
1 teaspoon salt
1 cup grated cheese

Slightly brown onion and green pepper in margarine. Add flour and brown. Add remaining ingredients except cheese; mix well. Pour into greased casserole. Cover with cheese. Bake at 350 degrees until cheese melts. Serves 6 to 8.

Mrs. Robert L. Waldrep

115

GRILLED CORN ON COB

4 ears of corn

Use medium size ears of corn for best results on the grill. Open outer husks of corn and remove silk. Replace husks. Wrap closely in aluminum foil. Place in hot coals or on grill and cook 15 to 20 minutes (until tender). Remove from husks, add butter, seasonings and serve immediately. Serves 4.

Mrs. Neil Chamblee

EGGPLANT
SWEET AND SOUR SHIBUI

1 large eggplant
1 10 1/2-ounce can
  mushroom soup
1/2 pint whipping cream
1/2 teaspoon nutmeg
1 teaspoon curry power
2 cans whole anchovies
  (drained)

1 can smoked oysters
1 can maraschino cherries
  (drained)
1 can mandarin orange sections
  (drained)
1 cup Bugles
2 teaspoons brown sugar
1 envelope onion soup mix

Parboil eggplant. Remove from water and puree. Add mushroom soup, whipping cream, nutmeg and curry powder. Mix well. Then add anchovies, oysters, maraschino cherries and mandarin orange sections. Place in a casserole. Sprinkle top liberally with Bugles, brown sugar, and onion soup mix. Bake in 350 degree oven until it bubbles, about 30 minutes. May be served over Chung-King noodles. Serves 4.

Mrs. Leon Daniel
Tokyo, Japan

KRAUT SALAD

1/3 cup sugar
1/4 cup vinegar
1 medium can kraut
  with caraway seeds

1/2 cup chopped celery
1/2 medium chopped green pepper
1 medium onion,minced fine

Mix sugar and vinegar over low heat until sugar is dissolved. Cool. Mix with other ingredients and chill. Will keep indefinately. Serve with beef roasts. Serves 8-10.

Mrs. George Campbell
Greenville, S. C.

MUSHROOMS IN SOUR CREAM

1 pound fresh mushrooms
3 tablespoons butter
1 1/2 tablespoons flour
1 cup sour cream

1/2 teaspoon lemon juice
1/2 teaspoon salt
1/4 teaspoon pepper

Wash mushrooms and slice not too thinly. Saute them 10 minutes in butter. Sprinkle with flour and continue cooking another 5 minutes, stirring carefully. Add the sour cream, lemon juice, salt and pepper. Keep heat low and cook for 15 minutes longer. These are simple to keep hot and serve in a chafing dish. Serves 4.

Mrs. Richard Shawn

OKRA CASSEROLE

6 slices bacon
2 medium size onions
2 green bell peppers

4 medium size tomatoes or 1 can
4 to 6 cups okra, sliced

Fry bacon. Remove from pan. Chop onions and peppers. Add to bacon drippings and cook until onions are golden. Chop tomatoes and add to onion. Cook covered 20 minutes over medium low heat (until tender). Add okra and cook until tender. Place in casserole dish. Top with crumbled bacon and parsley if desired. Serves 8.

Mrs. Thomas B. Phillips, Jr.

ONION CASSEROLE

1 can mushroom soup   6 medium onions
1/2 teaspoon salt   1/4 teaspoon pepper
1 tablespoon butter

Fill buttered casserole with fresh sliced onion rings. Add seasonings
and mushroom soup. Top with pats of butter. Bake in 350 degree
oven for one hour. Serves 6.

Mrs. Robert E. Jones

SAVORY BAKED ONIONS

5 or 6 large white onions   1/4 cup margarine
1 teaspoon salt   1/4 cup hot water
1/4 teaspoon pepper   1/4 cup vinegar
1/4 cup sugar

Peel onions and cut in thick slices. Place onions in baking dish.
Combine remaining ingredients and pour over onions. Cover and
bake at 350 degrees for 1 hour. Serves 6 to 8.

Mrs. Martha Bleckley Barnes
Clemson, S. C.

SWISS ONION PIE

3 strips bacon   Few grains pepper
6 medium-size onions   Dash ground nutmeg
2 eggs   Dash ground cloves
1 tablespoon flour   1/2 cup milk
2 teaspoons sugar   1 unbaked 9-inch pie shell
1/2 teaspoon salt

Set the oven for hot, 400 degrees. Cut the bacon in small pieces. Wash and peel the onions and cut in very thin slices. Put the bacon in a skillet over low heat. Add the onions and cook, stirring frequently, until the onions are transparent but not brown. Remove them from heat and let stand until slightly cooled. Put the eggs in a bowl and beat them slightly with a fork. Add the flour, sugar, salt, pepper and spices and continue to beat until smooth and well blended. Stir in milk. Spread the onion mixture in the pie shell. Pour the egg mixture over the top. Bake 30 minutes or until the crust is brown and the filling is set. Serves 6.

Mrs. W. L. Thompson

CREOLE PEAS

1 small onion	1 Number 3 can green peas
1/2 green pepper	1 2-ounce can tomato soup
2 tablespoons bacon drippings	Salt and pepper to taste

Brown onions and green pepper in drippings. Drain juice from peas. Add peas and tomato soup. Cook slowly for 30 or 40 minutes. Serves eight.

Mrs. William F. Bolt

Give no more to every guest
Than he is able to digest;
Give him always of the prime,
And but little at a time. — Swift

ENGLISH PEA CASSEROLE

1 large can tiny peas
2 hard boiled eggs
1/2 small onion
1 small can pimento
1/2 teaspoon salt

1/4 teaspoon pepper
1 10 1/2-ounce can mushroom soup
Cracker crumbs
Butter

Drain peas and mix with grated hard boiled eggs, onion, diced pimento, and seasonings. Fold in mushroom soup and pour into a small casserole. Sprinkle with cracker crumbs and dot with butter. Bake at 375 degrees for 30 minutes. Serves 6.

Mrs. Michael Glenn

SWEET POTATO CASSEROLE

1 1/2 to 2 pounds canned yams
3 tablespoons butter
6 tablespoons brown sugar
1/2 teaspoon salt
3 eggs, separated
1/2 cup orange juice
1/2 cup milk

1/2 teaspoon nutmeg
1 teaspoon cinnamon
1/4 teaspoon ginger
1 tablespoon honey or syrup
1/2 cup chopped pecans
Marshmallows

Beat yams with electric mixer until smooth. Add all other ingredients except egg whites, pecans, and marshmallows. Beat well. Fold in pecans. Beat egg whites until stiff peaks form, fold into mixture. Turn into well buttered casserole. Bake at 400 degrees for 50 minutes. Cover top with marshmallows last 5 or 10 minutes. Serve at once. Serves 6-8.

Mrs. Fred E. Green

SWEET POTATO CASSEROLE

3 cups mashed sweet potatoes
1 cup sugar
2 eggs
1 stick oleo
1 teaspoon vanilla

1/2 cup milk
1 cup brown sugar
1/3 cup flour
1/2 stick oleo
1 cup chopped nuts

Combine first 6 ingredients and pour into greased casserole. Mix brown sugar, flour, 1/2 stick oleo and nuts. Pour over potatoes. Bake at 350 degrees for 35 minutes. Serves 8.

Mrs. R. J. Willis, Jr.

"Be painstaking with your sauce."
— Escoffier

ORANGE HALVES STUFFED WITH SWEET POTATOES

8 medium sweet potatoes
4 large oranges
1/2 stick butter
1/4 teaspoon powdered nutmeg
1/8 teaspoon powdered cloves

2 tablespoons brown sugar
1/2 cup white raisins
1 cup pecans
1/2 cup sherry
48 small marshmallows

Scrub potatoes and grease them. Bake at 400 degrees for 45 minutes. Remove hot potatoes from shell and add butter, nutmeg, cloves, brown sugar, raisins, pecans and sherry. Cut oranges in half and scoop out fruit. Remove seeds and add orange juice and fruit to mixture. Whip until fluffy. Spoon potato mixture into orange halves. Place six marshmallows on top of each. Place orange halves in muffin pan and bake at 350 degrees for twenty minutes. Serves 8.

Mrs. Ted Owen

CHEESE PUFFED POTATO CASSEROLE

4 eggs – separated
1 cup shredded cheese
1/2 teaspoon celery salt
1/4 cup chopped parsley
1/2 teaspoon salt

4 cups seasoned mashed potatoes
2 teaspoons chopped onion
2 teaspoons green pepper
1/4 teaspoon paprika

Beat egg yolks with potatoes. Stir in cheese, onion, pepper, parsley and salt. Just before baking, beat egg whites and fold in potatoes. Spoon into buttered casserole (7 x 13). Sprinkle with paprika. Bake at 375 degrees for 25 minutes. Serves 6.

Mrs. Marquis Peek
Encinitas, California

KARTOFFELKNOEDEL (POTATO DUMPLINGS)

2 pounds baked white potatoes
1 teaspoon salt
1 tablespoon majoram
1 egg

2 tablespoons flour
2 tablespoons crumbs
2 tablespoons chopped parsley
1/4 teaspoon pepper

Prepare 2 pounds baked potatoes. Peel them while still hot and keep them cool for a day (not refrigerated). Chop potato in a meat grinder. Add 1 teaspoon salt, 1 tablespoon majoram, 1 egg, 1/4 teaspoon pepper, 2 tablespoons flour, 2 tablespoons crumbs and 2 tablespoons chopped parsley. Mix all ingredients well together and form little balls of 1.5" diameter. Drop the balls into a mixture of 2 quarts boiling water and 1 tablespoon of salt. Boil the dumplings until they float for 5 minutes atop the water. Serves 4. *Serve together with "Sauerbraten".*

Mrs. Hermann Buchert

122

MASHED POTATO CASSEROLE

6 medium potatoes (boiled)
1 1/2 cups cottage cheese
1/3 cup sour cream
Chopped onion to taste

1/6 teaspoon white pepper
1/4 cup melted butter
1/4 cup slivered almonds

Mash cooked potatoes (no milk). Mix in cottage cheese, sour cream, onion, white pepper (an electric hand mixer works well). Turn into 1 1/2 quart casserole dish. Drizzle melted butter over top and then sprinkle on slivered almonds. Bake at 350 degrees for 30 minutes. Serves 6.

Mrs. Clyde A. Perkins, Jr.

QUICK SCALLOPED POTATOES

2 tablespoons butter
2 tablespoons flour
3/4 teaspoon salt

1 3/4 cups milk
5 cups potatoes, sliced
Grated cheese

Melt butter in saucepan; stir in flour and salt. Add milk slowly, stirring constantly until sauce boils and thickens. Add potatoes and heat with occasional stirring until the sauce boils again. Pour potatoes and sauce into a greased casserole; cover with cheese, cover and bake at 350 degrees for 30 minutes or until potatoes are tender. Serve hot. Serves 5.

Mrs. Everett Newman

SCALLOPED POTATOES

6 large potatoes
6 large onions
1 10 1/2-ounce can mushroom soup

1/2 cup milk
6 teaspoons salt
2 teaspoons pepper

Grease a baking dish. Place a layer of sliced potatoes on bottom and salt and pepper. Now place a layer of sliced onions, alternating onions and potatoes until all are used up. Pour over all a can of mushroom soup mixed with 1/2 cup of milk. Bake in a 325 degree oven for 2 hours, uncovering for last 1/2 hour of cooking. Serves 4.

Mrs. Raymond B. Fretwell

SWEET POTATO AMBROSIA

6 to 7 cups sliced sweet potatoes
1 9-ounce can crushed pineapple
1 lemon
1 orange

1/2 cup light brown sugar
1/2 cup butter
1/2 teaspoon salt
Flaked coconut (optional)

Thinly slice lemon, orange and sweet potatoes. Alternate layers of potatoes, orange and lemon. Combine pineapple, sugar, butter and salt. Pour over potatoes. Sprinkle coconut on top if desired. Bake 30-40 minutes (until tender) in 350 degree oven. Serves 8.

Mrs. Richard G. Christopher
Hodges, S. C.

DRESSING FOR BAKED POTATOES

4 sticks margarine
1 pint Kraft mayonnaise
1 8-ounce container of cream
    cheese and chives

2 tablespoons Worcestershire
1/2 teaspoon garlic salt

Combine margarine and mayonnaise in mixer. Beat 2 minutes. Add Worcestershire sauce and garlic salt. Add cream cheese and chives with spoon last. (This is a delicious topping to use in place of butter.) Yields about 1 quart.

Miss Ann Holden

SOUR CREAM AND CHEESE SAUCE

1 cup sour cream
1 stick soft butter
1 cup shredded cheddar cheese

1/4 cup chopped green onions
1/8 teaspoon salt

Combine all ingredients and serve at room temperature on baked potatoes. Serves 6.

Mrs. Robert C. Brown

BROWN RICE

1 stick butter
1 large onion
1 can beef broth

1 can beef consommé
1 cup rice (not minute rice)

Chop onion and sauté in butter. In casserole put onion and butter mixture, both cans of soup and rice (uncooked). Bake at 350 degrees for 1 hour. Rice should be firm but not dry when done. Serves 5-6.

Miss Gladys Johnston
Columbia, S. C.

GREEN RICE

3 cups cooked rice
1/4 cup grated Parmesan cheese
1/4 cup chopped parsley
2 eggs, well beaten
1 cup milk

1/4 cup melted butter
1 1/2 teaspoons salt
1 tablespoon Worcestershire
2 tablespoons grated onion

Mix all ingredients well and place in a 2-quart casserole. Bake in 325 degree oven for 45 minutes. Serves 6.

Mrs. C. L. Mayo

SOUTH CAROLINA RICE

1 cup white long grain rice
1 can beef broth
1 can beef consommé
1 can chopped mushrooms

1/2 cup chopped onion
1/4 cup chopped green pepper
1/2 stick margarine

Sauté mushrooms and onion in butter. Add green pepper. Put all ingredients in casserole. Bake uncovered one hour at 350 degrees. Cover every 15 minutes for 5 minutes to steam. Serves 8.

Mrs. Sam Taylor

SOUR CREAM PILAFF

3 cups chicken stock or
   3 tablespoons chicken stock base
   dissolved in 3 cups hot water
1 tablespoon lemon juice
1 1/2 teaspoons salt
1/4 teaspoon pepper
1/2 bay leaf

1 stick butter
1 1/2 cups uncooked rice
1 can (3 to 4 ounce) mushroom
   slices (drained)
1 cup commercial sour cream
Chopped chives or parsley

Place chicken stock, lemon juice, salt, pepper, bay leaf, and 1/4 cup of the butter in top of a double boiler. Heat over direct heat until stock starts to simmer. Add rice, cover and cook over boiling water for 35 minutes or until rice is tender and all liquid is absorbed. Remove bay leaf; stir in remaining 1/4 cup butter, drained mushrooms and sour cream. Heat through. Sprinkle with chopped chives or parsley. Serves 6.

Mrs. Donald C. Roberts

BAKED SQUASH RING

3 cups cooked squash
1/4 cup melted butter
1/4 cup milk
3 eggs, well beaten

1 teaspoon salt
1/8 teaspoon pepper
1/4 cup buttered bread crumbs
1 tablespoon minced onion

Cut up washed squash and cook covered in a small amount of water until tender. Force through coarse sieve. Add other ingredients, blend well, and turn into a well greased ring mold. Set ring in a pan of hot water and bake at 350 degrees for 45 minutes or until inserted knife comes out clean. To remove squash ring, place serving dish over ring, then turn dishes quickly. Fill center with buttered peas or other vegetables. Serves 6 to 8.

Mrs. John A. Holman

SQUASH SUPREME

White sauce
2 pounds yellow squash
1/2 pound sharp cheese
1 teaspoon salt

1 teaspoon pepper
Bread crumbs
Butter

Prepare a thick white sauce. Grate cheese and add to white sauce. Stir until cheese melts. Wash squash and cut in small pieces. In a large casserole, place a layer of squash, salt, pepper and sauce. Repeat until all the squash and sauce are used. Place bread crumbs on top and dot with butter. Bake, uncovered, at 350 degrees for 25 to 30 minutes.

Mrs. R. Allen Jones
Atlanta, Georgia

I like to shell peas that are fresh from a shop.
I start at the tail-end instead of the top
So they will explode with a wonderful POP!
— Aileen Fisher

SQUASH CASSEROLE

1 1/2 pounds squash
    cooked and mashed
1 can cream of chicken soup
1/4 cup milk

1 small onion chopped or grated
1/2 teaspoon salt or to taste
1/4 teaspoon pepper
Butter
Cheese Ritz crackers

Mix ingredients with small amount of cheese Ritz cracker crumbs and top with more crumbs and butter pats. Cook at 325 degrees for 30 minutes. Serves 4 to 6.

Mrs. W. Glenn Garrison

SQUASH CASSEROLE

1 pound squash
1 tablespoon bacon grease
1 tablespoon brown sugar
1/4 teaspoon salt
1/8 teaspoon pepper

1 large egg
1/2 stick margarine
1 small onion (chopped)
1/2 can cream mushroom soup
2 cups bread crumbs

Cook squash, bacon grease, brown sugar, salt and pepper over low heat for 20 minutes. Add one large egg, margarine, chopped onion, mushroom soup and bread crumbs. Bake in casserole dish for 30 minutes at 350 degrees. Serves 6.

Mrs. Virgil McCormick

SQUASH CASSEROLE

1 1/2 pound summer squash or
   2 10-ounce frozen packages
1 carrot grated
1 medium onion, chopped
3/4 cup sour cream

1/2 stick butter
1 can cream of chicken soup
1/2 package of seasoned
   bread crumbs
Salt and pepper to taste

Cook squash until soft enough to mash. Add onion and all other ingredients except crumbs. Dot with butter. Bake 30-40 minutes at 350 degrees. Serves 6.

Mrs. Fritz Waidner

SQUASH CORN PUDDING

1 1/2 cups squash, canned,
   frozen or fresh, drained
1 can cream style corn
2 eggs
1 cup bread crumbs

2 tablespoons oil
Potato chips
Paprika
Salt, sugar, pepper to taste

Combine all ingredients and put into buttered casserole. Bake at 350 degrees for 30-40 minutes. Sprinkle crushed potato chips and a dash of paprika over top. Serves 6.

Mrs. G. Carey Hayes

SQUASH SOUFFLÉ

6 medium summer squash
2 slices white bread
1/2 cup milk
1 egg

1 small white onion
1/2 teaspoon salt
1/4 teaspoon pepper
Bread crumbs

Cut squash in medium size pieces. Boil in unsalted water until tender. Drain and mash well. Soak 2 pieces of bread in milk. When well soaked, blend into squash. Add one egg and beat well into mixture. Add onion, salt and pepper. Bake in greased casserole for 35 minutes at 350 degrees. Sprinkle with bread crumbs and dots of butter before baking if desired. Serves 6.

Mrs. Larry Kowalski

TOMATO — ASPARAGUS BAKE

4 large tomatoes
2 cans asparagus spears
1 small can Parmesan cheese

1 onion diced (if desired)
1 teaspoon salt

Wash tomatoes. Cut stem from one end and a small slice from other end. Cut tomato in half and place in baking dish. Sprinkle 1/8 teaspoon salt on each half. Lay 3-4 asparagus spears on top of each half. Top with onion cubes. Bake in oven 350 degrees for 25 minutes. Remove and sprinkle cheese generously on top each tomato. Return to oven. Broil for 1-2 minutes. Serves 8.

Mrs. Richard G. Christopher III

*A man once asked Diogenes what was the
proper time for supper, and he made answer,
"If you are a rich man, whenever you please;
and if you are a poor man, whenever you can."
— Diogenes Laertius*

HERB BROILED TOMATOES

4 large tomatoes, halved
1 teaspoon basil (chopped)
  (fresh if possible)
1/2 teaspoon grated lemon rind
4 tablespoons bread crumbs
Salt and pepper

2 tablespoons parsley
  (chopped fresh)
2 tablespoons olive oil
  (or melted butter)
1 clove garlic (crushed)

Arrange tomatoes cut side up on baking sheet. Sprinkle with salt and pepper. Combine remaining ingredients (a blender makes it easy) and spread over tops of tomatoes. Cook at 400 degrees for 15 minutes. Serves 8. Topping may be prepared ahead.

Mrs. Samuel R. Moorhead, Jr.

SCALLOPED TOMATOES AND CHEESE

1 Number 3 can tomatoes
Salt and pepper
2 teaspoons sugar

1 1/2 cups soft bread crumbs
1/4 cup melted butter
1 cup grated American cheese

Season tomatoes to taste with salt and pepper. Add sugar. Combine crumbs and melted butter. Arrange alternate layers of tomatoes, cheese, and crumbs in casserole, ending with crumbs. Bake at 350 degrees for 15 to 20 minutes. Serves 6.

Mrs. E. Cecil Campbell

STEWED TOMATOES

1 3/4 cups canned tomatoes or
  cooked fresh tomatoes
1 teaspoon minced onion
3/4 teaspoon sugar

1 tablespoon butter
1/4 cup bread crumbs
1 teaspoon black pepper

Simmer together all ingredients over medium heat for 10 minutes. Serves 2.

Mrs. Robert C. Herndon

VEGETABLE CASSEROLE

1 Number 2 can English peas	1 1/2 cups grated cheese
1 small can mushrooms	2 tablespoons butter
1 small (4 ounce) can pimentos	2 tablespoons flour
2 large green bell peppers	1 teaspoon salt
1 quart small potatoes	Dash cayenne pepper

Remove inside pulp of green peppers and chop very small. Combine peppers and mushrooms and cook until peppers are tender. Cook Irish potatoes until tender. Cut pimentos into small pieces. Make white sauce of butter, flour, salt and cayenne, liquid from peas, mushrooms and pimentos. Dissolve one cup of cheese in it. Mix all ingredients into the cream sauce with a fork. Put into a greased baking dish. Cover the top with the remaining cheese and bake at 350 degrees for 30 to 45 minutes. Serve at once in baking dish. (Small potatoes may be made by being scooped out of large ones.) Serves 8 to 10.

Mrs. James Halford, Sr.
Johnston, S. C.

MARINATED VEGETABLES

1 1-pound can French beans	4 celery sticks, diced
1 1-pound can peas	1 medium onion, sliced
1 1-pound can bean sprouts	1/2 medium green pepper
1 can pimento, diced	

Mix together above ingredients in large bowl. Pour over marinade. Cover and let sit at least overnight before serving.

MARINADE

3/4 cup vinegar	1/2 cup oil
1/2 cup sugar	1 teaspoon salt

Mix all together. Serves 4 to 6.

Mrs. James F. White
Columbia, S. C.

CHILLED CUCUMBER GAZPACHO

1/4 cup almonds, ground
2 shallots, peeled and chopped
1 teaspoon salt
1 teaspoon white pepper
2 eggs
1 cup salad oil
1 cup cider vinegar
1 can (16 ounces)
   Italian tomatoes

2 medium cucumbers,
   peeled and chopped
1 teaspoon ground cloves
1 teaspoon ground cumin
Pinch cayenne pepper
3 slices stale white bread
4 cups chicken stock
1 cup heavy cream
Seedless grapes, peeled

Put almonds, shallots, salt, white pepper, eggs, salad oil and cider vinegar in blender. Blend until smooth and set aside in a bowl. Put remaining ingredients, except grapes, in blender, and when smooth, combine them with those in bowl. Chill. Put 5 or 6 seedless, peeled grapes in bottom of each individual serving bowl, and fill with Gazpacho. When desired, freeze Gazpacho, and add grapes at time of serving. Serves 8-10.

Mrs. David Kelley

CREAM OF TOMATO

1 small can tomatoes
5 tablespoons butter
5 tablespoons flour
1 teaspoon salt

1/4 teaspoon minced onion
1 cup whole milk
1/2 cup water
1/4 teaspoon soda

Place tomatoes, onions and salt in pan. Boil a few minutes. In another pan, melt butter, add flour, then milk and water. Bring to the boiling point. Add soda to tomato mixture and combine the mixtures. Serve hot with saltine crackers or corn bread. Serves 4.

Mrs. J. Prue Garrison

HEARTY SOUP

2 tablespoons bacon fat
  optional
1 pound ground beef
1/4 cup minced onion
3 cups canned tomato juice
1 cup water

2 cans of condensed celery soup
Bay leaf
1/4 teaspoon garlic salt
1 teaspoon sugar
2 cups grated raw carrots

Brown meat in hot fat or alone. Combine meat and all other ingredients in kettle and simmer about an hour. Serves 8.

Mrs. J. S. Ezelle

ONION SOUP

1 1/2 cups thinly sliced onions
3 tablespoons butter
6 cups beef or chicken broth
1/2 teaspoon ground black pepper

6 slices French bread
1 cup grated Parmesan cheese
Cognac or dry sherry

Saute onions in butter until well browned but not burned. Add broth and pepper. Cover and cook over low heat or in 275 degree oven for 30 minutes. Put the soup into a casserole and cover with toasted French bread. Sprinkle the Parmesan cheese over the toast and heat in the oven for about 10 minutes or until cheese is melted. Add a dash of cognac or dry sherry. Serves 6.

Mrs. Fritz Waidner

Taking food and drink is a great enjoyment
for healthy people, and those who do not
enjoy eating seldom have much capacity for
enjoyment or usefulness of any sort.
— Charles W. Eliot

NOTES

BREADS

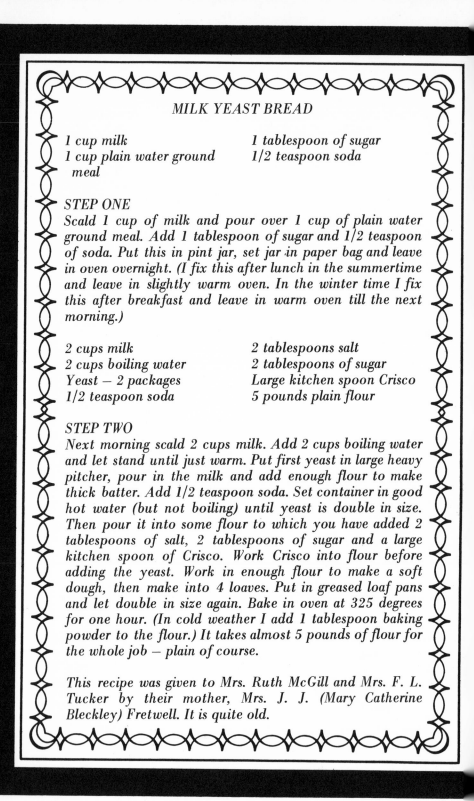

MILK YEAST BREAD

1 cup milk	1 tablespoon of sugar
1 cup plain water ground meal	1/2 teaspoon soda

STEP ONE

Scald 1 cup of milk and pour over 1 cup of plain water ground meal. Add 1 tablespoon of sugar and 1/2 teaspoon of soda. Put this in pint jar, set jar in paper bag and leave in oven overnight. (I fix this after lunch in the summertime and leave in slightly warm oven. In the winter time I fix this after breakfast and leave in warm oven till the next morning.)

2 cups milk	2 tablespoons salt
2 cups boiling water	2 tablespoons of sugar
Yeast — 2 packages	Large kitchen spoon Crisco
1/2 teaspoon soda	5 pounds plain flour

STEP TWO

Next morning scald 2 cups milk. Add 2 cups boiling water and let stand until just warm. Put first yeast in large heavy pitcher, pour in the milk and add enough flour to make thick batter. Add 1/2 teaspoon soda. Set container in good hot water (but not boiling) until yeast is double in size. Then pour it into some flour to which you have added 2 tablespoons of salt, 2 tablespoons of sugar and a large kitchen spoon of Crisco. Work Crisco into flour before adding the yeast. Work in enough flour to make a soft dough, then make into 4 loaves. Put in greased loaf pans and let double in size again. Bake in oven at 325 degrees for one hour. (In cold weather I add 1 tablespoon baking powder to the flour.) It takes almost 5 pounds of flour for the whole job — plain of course.

This recipe was given to Mrs. Ruth McGill and Mrs. F. L. Tucker by their mother, Mrs. J. J. (Mary Catherine Bleckley) Fretwell. It is quite old.

EASY BISCUITS

2 cups self-rising flour   1 cup milk
3 tablespoons mayonnaise   Dash of salt

Combine all ingredients and blend well. Pour into greased muffin tins and bake in a preheated 400 degree oven 10 to   12 minutes. Yields to 12.

Mrs. Alan Blanchard

SOUTHERN BISCUITS

2 cups sifted plain flour   2/3 cup shortening
3 teaspoons baking powder   Milk to work well
1 teaspoon salt

Combine all of the ingredients and roll out to 1/2 to 3/4 inch thickness. Cut with a biscuit cutter and place on a cookie sheet. Bake at 500 degrees for 10 minutes. Yields 10 to 12.

Mrs. Jack Ellenberg
Greenwood, S. C.

WHOLE WHEAT BISCUITS

2 cups whole wheat flour   1/2 teaspoon baking soda
1/2 cup plain flour   2 tablespoons shortening
2 teaspoons baking powder   1 cup buttermilk
1 teaspoon salt

Mix sifted flour with baking powder, salt, soda, and shortening. Add buttermilk, mixing lightly until dough holds together. Transfer dough to floured board. Knead lightly, and roll dough 1/2 inch thick. Cut into desired shape with floured cutter. Bake on lightly greased cookie sheet for 15 minutes at 425 degrees. Serves 8.

Mrs. Ted Owen

WILLIE MAE'S ANGEL BISCUITS

4 cups self-rising flour
1/2 cup shortening
1 teaspoon soda

1/3 cup sugar
1 1/2 cups buttermilk
1 package yeast dissolved in
1/4 cup warm water

Blend shortening and sifted flour until crumbly. Add remaining ingredients and mix well. Roll out on floured board and cut or pat to desired size by hand. Remaining dough may be covered in a bowl and kept in the refrigerator for several days and used as needed. Bake biscuits at 400 degrees for 15 minutes. Yields 36.

Mrs. C. Patrick Killen

YEAST BISCUITS

5 cups plain flour
1/4 cup sugar
3 teaspoons baking powder
1 teaspoon salt
1 teaspoon soda

1 cup shortening
1 package yeast (dry)
2 tablespoons warm water
2 cups buttermilk

Mix the dry ingredients with the shortening. Mix the package of yeast with the warm water; add this to the buttermilk and mix with flour to form dough. Place dough in greased bowl and allow to rise (about 2 hours) in a warm place, or place in refrigerator overnight. After dough rises, roll out and make biscuits. Bake at 350 degrees for 20 minutes or until bread is light brown. Yields 50.

Mrs. Mae Woodward

CORN BREAD

1 egg
1 1/2 cups self-rising corn meal
1 to 1 1/2 cups buttermilk

2 1/2 tablespoons Crisco
2 tablespoons flour

Blend ingredients in bowl. Pour into round or square greased 8-9 inch pan. Bake in a preheated 400 degree oven for 30 minutes. Serves 4.

Mrs. F. Smith Pruitt

SOUTHERN CORN BREAD

1 1/2 cups corn meal
1 cup flour
3/4 teaspoon baking soda
2 teaspoons baking powder
1 teaspoon salt

1 tablespoon sugar
1 egg, beaten
2 cups buttermilk
2 tablespoons oil

Sift together all the dry ingredients, set aside. In a large mixing bowl, beat the egg, add buttermilk and oil. To this mixture, add the dry ingredients. Stir well, and pour into a greased pan or skillet. Bake at 425 degrees for 25 minutes. Serves 6.

Mrs. Fred A. Shirley

HOMEMADE BREAD

5 cups lukewarm water
3 packages yeast
2 tablespoons sugar
5 pounds flour

2 heaping tablespoons salt
1 3/4 cups sugar
1 cup shortening

Sprinkle yeast and 2 tablespoons sugar over lukewarm water. Set aside until yeast has puffed to top and covered the water surface. Sift flour into very large bowl, adding the sugar and salt to the flour as it is sifted. Place shortening in center. Pour yeast water over shortening. Stir together until dry ingredients are moistened. Turn out and knead (at least 10 minutes) on floured surface until dough is smooth and slightly shiny. Put in large bowl, grease top of dough, cover, and let rise until double in bulk. Work down slightly. Divide into 5 portions and place in loaf pans. Cover and let rise to just above top of pan. Cook until tops are well browned. Bake at 350 degrees for 15 minutes, then 325 degrees for 40 minutes. As soon as bread is taken from oven, brush tops with melted butter. Yields 5 large loaves. Note: This bread freezes well.

Mrs. David Shores

MUSTARD BREAD

1 loaf French Bread
1/2 cup chopped onions
2 tablespoons parsley
1/4 cup butter

2 tablespoons prepared mustard
2 tablespoons sesame or
  poppy seeds

Cream butter; blend in onions and parsley. Split loaf long ways, spread with butter mixture, then with mustard. Top with seeds. Bake for 12 minutes at 350 degrees. Serves 4 to 6.

Mrs. Marshall Kowalski

NUT BREAD

2 1/2 cups sifted flour
2/3 cup sugar
3 teaspoons baking powder
1/4 teaspoon salt

1 cup chopped nuts
1 egg, well beaten
1 cup milk

Sift together flour, sugar, baking powder, and salt into mixing bowl. Add nuts, egg and milk. Mix well. Pour into greased,large loaf pan. Bake at 350 degrees for 45 minutes. Yields 1 loaf.

Mrs. Richard Shawn

BANANA-DATE NUT BREAD

1 1/2 cups sugar
1 stick margarine
1 1/2 cups buttermilk
1 1/2 teaspoons soda
2 eggs

3 cups flour, unsifted
1 cup mashed bananas
1 cup chopped nuts
1 cup chopped dates

Cream sugar and margarine. Add eggs and beat. Add flour, soda, and buttermilk. Then add bananas, nuts, and dates. Mix well. Line pans with foil. Make foil larger than pan. Cook at 350 degrees for 1 hour or until toothpick inserted in center comes out clean. Cool in pan. Makes 2 loaves.

Mrs. Dennis Stoudenmire
Honea Path, S. C.

BANANA NUT BREAD

1 1/2 cups sugar
2/3 cup shortening
2 eggs, separated
1 cup mashed ripe bananas
4 tablespoons sour milk
  or buttermilk
1 teaspoon vinegar

1 teaspoon baking soda
1 tablespoon warm water
1/2 cup chopped pecans or
  walnuts
1 1/2 cups presifted flour
1 teaspoon vanilla
1/4 teaspoon salt

Preheat oven to 325 degrees. Grease a 9 1/2-inch loaf pan. In mixing bowl beat sugar and shortening until blended. Beat in egg yolks and bananas. Combine sour milk and vinegar. Stir in banana mixture. Dissolve baking soda in water. Stir into batter. Stir in nuts, flour, vanilla, and salt. Beat egg whites until stiff but not dry. Fold into batter. Turn batter into pan. Bake for 1 hour.

Mrs. William D. McClellan
Manchester, Georgia

No clock is more regular than the belly.
— Rabelais

CRANBERRY NUT BREAD

3/4 cup sugar
1 egg
1 1/4 cups orange juice
1 tablespoon grated orange rind

3 cups Bisquick Mix
3/4 cup chopped nuts
1 cup chopped cranberries
  (fresh or frozen)

Mix sugar, egg, orange juice, rind, and Bisquick. Beat vigorously for 30 seconds. Batter may still be lumpy. Stir in nuts and cranberries. Pour into well-greased loaf pan. Bake at 350 degrees for 55-60 minutes.

To bake in cans for round slices: Divide batter among 3 well-greased Number 2 cans or 5 greased soup cans. Fill slightly more than half full. Bake Number 2 cans 45 to 50 minutes, and soup cans for 40 minutes.

Mrs. Michael Glenn

CASSEROLE ONION BREAD

1 cup milk
3 tablespoons sugar
2 teaspoons salt
1 1/2 tablespoons shortening
1 cup warm water
2 packages yeast
4 1/2 cups flour

1 teaspoon onion salt
1/2 teaspoon celery salt
3 tablespoons butter
1 cup coarsely chopped onion
1 egg yolk
1 teaspoon water

Scald milk over medium heat; remove; add sugar, salt, and shortening. Stir and cool to lukewarm. Put warm water in large bowl. Add yeast. Dissolve, and add milk mixture. Sift flour and salts, and add at one time to yeast mixture. Stir until well blended; cover with towel and let rise in warm place until tripled in bulk. Then stir down; beat vigorously and turn into a 2-quart casserole and place in 375 degree oven for 1 hour.
While bread is baking, melt butter, add onion and cook 5 minutes. Cool. Beat egg yolk and add water and mix with onion. After bread has baked 40 minutes, spoon onion over top. Bake 20 minutes more. Can be made the day before. When cold, slice. Brush slices with melted butter, and return to casserole. Cover with foil and warm in oven. Serve hot!

Mrs. Forest Suggs

PINEAPPLE-WALNUT BREAD

1 large can crushed pineapple
2 cups flour
1/2 cup sugar
3 teaspoons baking powder
1 teaspoon salt

1/2 teaspoon baking soda
3/4 cup chopped walnuts
1/4 cup butter (melted)
1 1/2 teaspoons vanilla
1 egg

Preheat oven to 350 degrees. Grease a 9x5x3 inch loaf pan. Drain pineapple well. Into large bowl sift flour with sugar, baking powder, salt, and soda. Add walnuts, mix well. Add egg, pineapple, butter and vanilla with wooden spoon, stir just until blended. Turn into pan. Bake 1 hour or until cake tester comes out clean. Cool in pan on wire rack. Slice thinly. Then slice into 1/2 inch strips. Place on serving plate.

Mrs. M. L. Propp

PUMPKIN BREAD

3 cups of sugar
1 cup salad oil
4 eggs
3 1/2 cups sifted flour
2 teaspoons ground cinnamon
2 cups nuts

1 teaspoon ground nutmeg
2/3 cup of water
2 cups canned pumpkin
(or 1 can pumpkin pie
filling or 2 cups mashed
sweet potatoes)

Combine sugar and salad oil; beat well. Add eggs and beat. Combine dry ingredients and add to egg mixture alternately with water. Stir in pumpkin and nuts. Pour batter in 3 greased loaf pans; bake at 350 degrees for 1 hour. Slice and spread with butter or cream cheese. Makes 3 loaves.

Mrs. Dan Chamblee

The bagel, an unsweetened doughnut with rigor mortis. — Beatrice and Ira Freeman

SCOTCH SHORT BREAD

1 pound butter
2 tablespoons Crisco
1 1/2 cups light brown sugar
1 egg

1/4 teaspoon salt
1/2 teaspoon baking powder
4 or 5 cups flour

Mix all ingredients together except flour. Gradually add flour until mixture will roll out easily. Will be soft. Cut in squares and crimp edges with fork. Bake at 325 degrees for 20-25 minutes or until lightly browned.

Mrs. Joe Crudup, Jr.

SPOON BREAD

1/2 cup yellow corn meal
2 cups milk, scalded
2 tablespoons melted butter
3 eggs, separated

1 teaspoon salt
1/2 teaspoon baking powder
1/4 teaspoon cream of tartar

Stir corn meal gradually into hot milk; cook until thick (2-4 minutes) stirring constantly. Remove from heat, add butter and let cool a few minutes. Beat egg yolks with salt and baking powder until thick and lemon-colored. Beat egg whites with cream of tartar until very stiff. Stir egg yolks into corn meal mixture. Now, fold in egg whites, leaving islands of unblended white. Pile into ungreased 1 1/2 quart casserole. Set in shallow pan filled with 1/2 inch hot water. Bake at 375 degrees for 50 minutes, or until done. *Serve At Once.* Serves 6.

Mrs. Ellis B. Drew, Jr.

SPOON BREAD

3 cups milk
3/4 cup corn meal
2 tablespoons butter

1 teaspoon salt
2 eggs, separated
1 teaspoon baking powder

Scald two cups milk in top of double boiler. Mix remaining milk with the corn meal, add to scalded milk, and cook stirring frequently for 30 minutes. Cool slightly. Preheat oven to 375 degrees. Add butter, salt, and beaten egg yolks to corn meal mixture and mix well — add baking powder and mix. Fold in stiffly beaten egg whites. Bake in greased casserole for 30 minutes. Serves 6.

Mrs. J. Gary Early

SOUR CREAM COFFEE CAKE

1 pound butter
2 cups sugar
4 eggs
2 teaspoons vanilla
4 cups plain flour

2 teaspoons baking powder
2 teaspoons soda
1 pint sour cream
Juice of 1 lemon

Cream butter and sugar. Add eggs one at a time, then vanilla. Sift flour, baking powder and soda. Mix sour cream and lemon juice gently, then add to butter mixture alternately with the flour mixture. Pour 1/4 of the batter into a greased and floured steeple pan. Prepare topping.

NUT MIXTURE

1 heaping cup brown sugar	1 teaspoon cinnamon
1 cup nuts	

Sprinkle on 1/2 nut mixture. Add remaining batter and put nut mixture on top. Swirl topping slightly into batter. Bake at 350 degrees for 40 to 50 minutes. Loaf pans may be used.

Mrs. Lafayette Cromer
Mrs. Chris Suber
Mrs. Samuel R. Moorhead, Jr.

SOUR CREAM COFFEE CAKE

1/2 cup butter	2 1/2 cups flour
1/4 cup Crisco	3 teaspoons baking powder
1 cup white sugar	1 teaspoon baking soda
3 eggs	1 teaspoon salt
1 cup sour cream	1 teaspoon almond flavoring

Cream butter and Crisco. Add sugar gradually. Add eggs one at a time beating thoroughly after each. Sift dry ingredients and add alternately with sour cream mixture (sour cream and flavoring mixed). Mix thoroughly.

FILLING

3/4 cup chopped pecans	1 cup brown sugar (light)
2 teaspoons cinnamon	

In greased and floured 10 inch tube pan, pour 1/3 batter, then 1/2 of filling. Then pour remaining batter and remaining filling. Bake at 350 degrees for 50 to 60 minutes. Serves 10 to 12.

Mrs. Warren F. Harris

SOUR CREAM COFFEE CAKE

2 sticks butter
1 cup sugar
3 eggs
1 cup sour cream
1 teaspoon lemon extract

2 and 1/2 cups flour
3 teaspoons baking powder
1 teaspoon baking soda
1/4 teaspoon salt
1 teaspoon vanilla

Cream butter and sugar; add eggs one at a time. Add sour cream and mix in flour which has been sifted with dry ingredients. Add flavorings.

TOPPING

1 cup chopped nuts
1 tablespoon melted butter

1 teaspoon cinnamon
1/2 cup sugar

Place 1/2 of mixture in a greased 9 x 13 pan or two 8 inch foil cake pans. Top with 1/2 of topping. Pour remaining batter and sprinkle nut mixture on top. Bake at 375 degrees for 25-30 minutes. Serves 8 to 10.

Mrs. Richey Ramseur

SOUR CREAM COFFEE CAKE

2 sticks margarine
1 1/4 cups sugar
2 eggs
1 cup sour cream
1 teaspoon vanilla

2 cups plain flour
1/2 teaspoon baking soda
1 teaspoon baking powder
1/2 cup sugar
1 teaspoon cinnamon

Cream margarine and sugar. Add eggs, sour cream and vanilla, beating thoroughly. Sift together flour, baking soda and baking powder. Gradually add flour mixture to sour cream mixture. Pour half of batter into greased 9 x 13 pan. Mix together 1/2 cup sugar and 1 teaspoon cinnamon. Sprinkle half of cinnamon mixture over batter. Carefully spread remaining batter and sprinkle rest of cinnamon mixture on top. May be served hot, or frozen and reheated. Bake at 350 degrees for 30-40 minutes. Serves 12.

Mrs. Kirk Oglesby

STREUSEL COFFEE CAKE

1 1/2 cups sifted flour
3 teaspoons baking powder
1/4 teaspoon salt
3/4 cup sugar

1/4 cup shortening
1 egg
1/2 cup milk
1 teaspoon vanilla

Sift dry ingredients. Cut in shortening with hands until it looks like coarse corn meal. Blend in egg, milk, and vanilla. Put half the batter in a greased 9 inch pan. Prepare topping.

FILLING AND TOPPING

3/4 cup brown sugar
3 tablespoons flour

3 teaspoons cinnamon
3 tablespoons melted butter

Sprinkle half the topping on batter. Spread remaining batter on and add remaining topping. Bake at 375 degrees until lightly browned, about 25 or 30 minutes. Serves 8 to 10.

Mrs. Richard Pruitt

CREOLE CORN MUFFINS

2 1/2 cups flour
2 tablespoons baking powder
1 teaspoon salt
4 tablespoons cornmeal plus
   1 teaspoon cornmeal
1 tablespoon sugar
3/4 cup cheese, grated

2 tablespoons pimento, chopped
2 tablespoons onion, chopped
2 tablespoons pepper, chopped
3/4 cup shortening, melted
1 1/2 cups milk
2 eggs, beaten

Combine dry ingredients and sift together. Add cheese, pimento, onion, and green pepper. Combine shortening, milk, and beaten eggs then add to dry mixture, stirring only until moistened. Spoon into greased muffin tins and bake in a hot oven 425 degrees for about 20 minutes until done. Serve immediately. Serves 8.

Mrs. Samuel R. Moorhead, Jr.

OLIVE MUFFINS

1/4 cup shortening
2 tablespoons sugar
1 egg
4 teaspoons baking powder

1/2 teaspoon salt
1 1/2 cups flour
1 cup milk
1 small bottle olives

Cream shortening; add sugar gradually. Add egg. Sift flour, baking powder, and salt; add alternately with milk to creamed mixture. Place in muffin pan and add several olives to each muffin. Bake at 425 degrees for 20 minutes(until golden brown). Serves 12.

Mrs. Beaty Jackson

SWEDISH PANCAKES

1 1/3 cups sifted flour
3 tablespoons sugar
1/2 teaspoon salt
3 eggs

2 cups milk
2 tablespoons margarine
  (melted and cooled)

Blend first 3 ingredients in bowl. Beat eggs; blend in milk and butter. Combine egg mixture and dry ingredients and beat until smooth. Pour batter onto hot grill, turning once.

Mrs. William V. McAbee

ICE BOX ROLLS

1 package yeast
4 cups plain flour
1 1/4 cups water

4 tablespoons lard
1 teaspoon salt
4 tablespoons sugar

Put one cup of hot water in mixing bowl and add lard, salt, and sugar. Let cool. Stir in flour. Dissolve yeast in 1/4 cup of luke warm water and add to mixture. Mix thoroughly, and cover. Place in ice box and let stand 1 1/2 hours. Knead lightly. Form rolls and let stand in warm place about an hour. Bake at 400 degrees. If desired, you may knead dough and then store for 5 to 7 days in ice box.

Mrs. J. D. Thrasher

REFRIGERATOR ROLLS OR LOAVES — NEVER FAIL

1 cup margarine or shortening
1 tablespoon salt
3/4 cup sugar
1 cup water

2 packages dry yeast
1 cup warm (not hot) water
2 slightly beaten eggs
6 cups unsifted flour

Mix together margarine, salt, and sugar. Boil 1 cup water and pour over this mixture. Dissolve yeast in warm water and allow to stand 10 minutes. Add to above, then add 2 beaten eggs. Add flour gradually. Cover and leave in refrigerator overnight.

The next day divide into 3 portions. (I usually make 2 loaves and 1 portion rolls.) Knead. Place loaves in greased loaf pans. Allow to rise in warm place. Bake 5 minutes at 400 degrees, then 20 minutes at 350 degrees or until desired brownness is reached.

For rolls: Knead and roll out on floured dough board. Cut out with biscuit cutter, fold in half, and place on greased cookie sheet, barely touching. Brush with melted margarine. Bake at 350 degrees about 10 minutes. Yields 100 rolls or 3 loaves.

Mrs. Robert Gallant

REFRIGERATOR ROLLS

1/2 cup shortening
1/2 cup boiling water
1/4 cup sugar
1 1/2 teaspoons salt

1 egg, unbeaten
1 package yeast
1/2 cup warm water
3 cups unsifted flour
(loosely packed)

Dissolve yeast in warm water. Pour boiling water over shortening. Add sugar, salt, and egg. Add yeast mixture. Add flour one cup at the time, working after each addition. Cover and place in refrigerator over night. Roll out and cut on floured board. Place on greased baking sheet and allow to rise until double in size. Bake at 425 degrees until brown.

Mrs. Sam Earle, Jr.

YEAST ROLLS

1 package yeast
1/2 cup warm water
1/2 cup lard
1 cup boiling water

1 teaspoon salt
4 tablespoons sugar
4 cups flour, sifted
1 egg, beaten

Dissolve yeast in warm water and let stand for 1/2 hour. Melt lard in boiling water and let cool. Sift flour, salt and sugar in large bowl. Make a well in mixture and pour yeast, fat, and beaten egg. Beat and mix well. Let rise for 1 hour. Knead a little and make rolls. Put in warm place to rise double their size. Bake at 375 degrees for 12 to 14 minutes or lightly brown. Makes 50 medium rolls.

Mrs. Robert Mayfield

FRENCH TOAST

1/4 cup pancake flour
2 eggs
1/4 cup milk

1/2 teaspoon vanilla
Dash of nutmeg
6 slices of bread

Mix ingredients. Dip bread slices in mixture and fry on medium heat. Yields 6 slices.

Mrs. Henry Beatty
Lexington, North Carolina

He may live without books — what is knowledge
but grieving?
He may live without hope — what is hope but
deceiving?
He may live without love — what is passion
but pining?
But where is the man that can live without
dining?   — Owen Meredith

SALADS

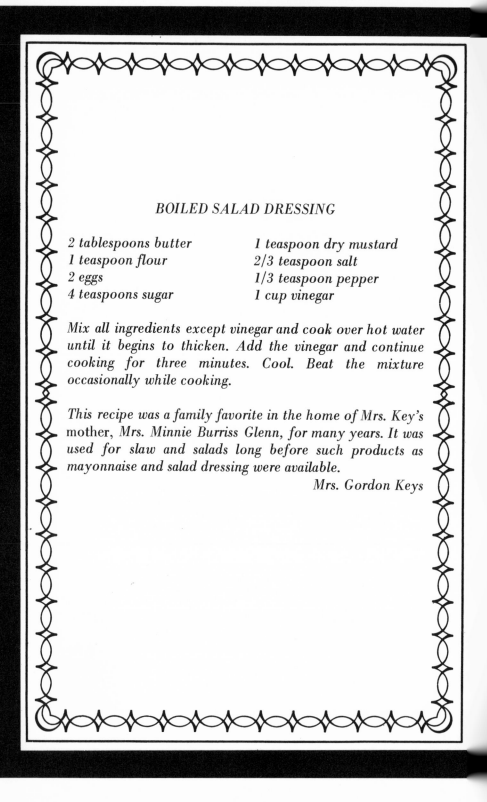

BOILED SALAD DRESSING

2 tablespoons butter
1 teaspoon flour
2 eggs
4 teaspoons sugar

1 teaspoon dry mustard
2/3 teaspoon salt
1/3 teaspoon pepper
1 cup vinegar

Mix all ingredients except vinegar and cook over hot water until it begins to thicken. Add the vinegar and continue cooking for three minutes. Cool. Beat the mixture occasionally while cooking.

This recipe was a family favorite in the home of Mrs. Key's mother, Mrs. Minnie Burriss Glenn, for many years. It was used for slaw and salads long before such products as mayonnaise and salad dressing were available.

Mrs. Gordon Keys

CHERRY JELLO SALAD

2 3-ounce boxes cherry gelatin
3 bananas, sliced
2 cups small marshmallows

1 cup dairy sour cream
1/2 cup chopped nuts

Prepare cherry gelatin as directed on the package. Chill until almost firm. Fold in bananas. Pour into 8 inch square pan. Chill until firm. Combine marshmallows and sour cream. Spread on gelatin. Top with nuts. Chill. Serves 6.

Mrs. Robert E. McNair
Columbia, South Carolina

APPLESAUCE SALAD

1 small can applesauce
1 small box lime gelatin

1 7-ounce 7-UP

Heat applesauce, add gelatin and stir until dissolved. Add 7-UP. Chill until congealed. Serves 6.

Mrs. James H. Barton

AVOCADO-ORANGE SALAD

1 cup hot water
1 package 3-ounce lime
   gelatin
1 cup cottage cheese
1 peeled, pitted avocado

1 tablespoon lemon juice
2 tablespoons mayonnaise
1/2 teaspoon salt
1/2 cup diced orange

Pour hot water over gelatin. Stir until dissolved. Refrigerate until syrupy. With fork, mash half of avocado. Cut other half into small thin slices. To gelatin add mashed avocado, cheese, lemon juice, mayonnaise and salt. Beat with egg beater until well blended. Fold in diced orange and sliced avocado. Turn into 1 quart mold. Refrigerate until firm. Garnish with crisp lettuce. Serves 6.

Mrs. D. Carroll Brown

BLUEBERRY SALAD

3 3-ounce boxes black
  cherry gelatin
1 15-ounce can blueberries
  (drained)

1 can crushed pineapple
  (drained)
1 cup orange juice

Follow directions on gelatin package using 3 cups of juice (pineapple, blueberry, and orange juice) instead of water. Cool and add blueberries and pineapple. Serves 8.

Mrs. Douglas McDougald

BLUEBERRY-PINEAPPLE SALAD

1 large box black
  cherry gelatin

1 large can crushed pineapple
1 15-ounce can blueberries

Drain liquid from fruit and add water or fruit juice to make 3 cups. Make gelatin with the 3 cups heated liquid. When it starts to congeal, add blueberries and pineapple.

TOPPING

1 large package cream cheese
  softened with 1 teaspoon milk

1/4 cup sugar
1 cup sour cream

Mix ingredients and spread on congealed salad. Serves 8 to 10.

Mrs. William L. Thompson

CHERRY SALAD

2 packages lemon gelatin
Juice of 1/2 lemon
1 cup sugar
Juice and rind of 1 orange

1 cup finely chopped celery
1 can sour pie cherries
1 cup chopped nuts

Mix lemon juice, orange juice and grated rind with syrup from cherries. Add water, if necessary, to make 3 1/2 cups liquid. Add sugar and boil 5 minutes. Pour over gelatin and let set. Add celery, nuts and cherries and congeal. Serves 12.

Mrs. Theo L. Burriss

COCA-COLA SALAD

2 cups hot water
2 boxes cherry gelatin
1 8-ounce package cream cheese
1 large can crushed pineapple

1 12-ounce Coca-cola
1 cup nuts
1 cup maraschino cherries

Mix gelatin and water. Add cream cheese and mix well. Add pineapple, Coke, nuts and cherries. Mix and chill 4 or 5 hours. Serves 9 to 12.

Mrs. Dan Chamblee

CONGEALED LIME SALAD

1 3-ounce package lime gelatin
12 large marshmallows, cut up
1 small can crushed
   pineapple

1/2 pint whipping cream
1 teaspoon vanilla flavoring
1/2 cup granulated sugar
3/4 cup chopped pecans

Make gelatin using the pineapple juice to help make up the two cups of liquid needed. Melt marshmallows in the gelatin while it is still hot. Let gelatin and marshmallows cool and begin to thicken. Whip the cream, adding vanilla and sugar. Add whipped cream, crushed pineapple and pecans to gelatin and marshmallows. Pour mixture into a flat 8 inch glass container and let congeal. Cut into squares and serve on lettuce. Serves 4 to 6.

Mrs. Walter Duffie

CRANBERRY WALDORF SALAD

2 cups raw cranberries
3 cups marshmallows
3/4 cup sugar
2 cups diced unpared tart
  apple

1/2 cup broken California
  walnuts
1/4 teaspoon salt
1/2 cup seedless green grapes
1 cup whipped cream

Grind cranberries and combine with marshmallows and sugar. Cover and chill overnight. Add apple, grapes, walnuts and salt. Fold in whipped cream. Chill. Serve in large bowl or individual lettuce cups. Garnish with clusters of grapes if desired. Serves 8 to 10.

Mrs. Wilburn Gable

CURRIED FRUIT

1 large can peach halves
1 medium can pineapple chunks
1 small bottle maraschino
  cherries
1 large can pear halves

1 medium can apricots
1 can plums or prunes
1/2 cup butter
1 cup brown sugar
3 teaspoons curry powder

Drain fruit. Place butter, sugar, curry powder in flat casserole and arrange fruit over it. Bake 1 hour at 325 degrees. Serves 4 to 6.

Mrs. William B. Royster

FROZEN FRUIT SALAD

1 1-pound can fruit cocktail
1 tablespoon butter
1 tablespoon flour
1 tablespoon sugar

1 tablespoon lemon juice
1 egg
1 cup heavy whipping cream

Melt butter in double boiler. Add flour and stir until blended. Add juice from fruit cocktail, sugar, lemon juice and egg. Cook and stir these ingredients until smooth. Cool. Fold in whipped cream; fold in fruit. Freeze and keep frozen until 5 or 10 minutes before serving. Serves 4 to 6.

Mrs. William P. Lowe
Louisville, Ky.

FROZEN HEAVENLY SALAD

1 8-ounce package cream cheese
3/4 cup mayonnaise
1 large can crushed pineapple
1 large bottle maraschino
  cherries

1 large package miniature
  marshmallows
1 cup chopped nuts
1/2 pint whipping cream

Mix together all ingredients except cream. Whip cream and fold the other ingredients into cream. Pour mixture into pyrex dish and freeze. Serves 8.

Mrs. Robert S. Owens, Jr.

FROZEN STRAWBERRY SALAD

2 3-ounce packages cream cheese
3 tablespoons mayonnaise
2 tablespoons pineapple juice
1 Number 2 can pineapple chunks

2 small bananas, diced
1 pint frozen strawberries
1 cup heavy cream (add sugar)

Soften cream cheese and blend with mayonnaise. Add pineapple juice and mix in bananas, pineapple and strawberries. Whip cream and fold into first mixture. Pour into refrigerator tray and freeze until firm. Serves 8 to 10.

Mrs. D. D. Gillespie

FRUIT CURRY

10 slices pineapple
10 pear halves

10 peach halves
10 maraschino cherries

Drain fruit and blot well. Place a pineapple slice, a peach half, a pear half, then a cherry in pyramids in a baking dish.

SAUCE

1 stick butter
2/3 cup brown sugar

1 tablespoon curry powder

Mix until melted. Cover fruit with sauce and bake at 325 degrees for 1 hour. Serves 10.

Mrs. James H. Barton

FRUIT DELIGHT

1 package lemon gelatin
1 package orange gelatin
2 diced bananas

1 large can crushed pineapple
  drained
1 cup small marshmallows

Dissolve gelatin in 2 cups boiling water. Add 1 1/2 cups cold water. Add bananas, pineapple and marshmallows. Congeal.

TOPPING

1 egg
2 tablespoons butter
2 tablespoons flour

1 cup Cool Whip
1/2 cup shredded cheese

Cook egg, flour and butter until thick. Cool. Fold in Cool Whip. Spread over top of congealed salad. Sprinkle with grated cheese. Serves 8.

Mrs. Sidney Harper
Westminister, South Carolina

Mrs. Ralph Dodson
Ware Shoals, South Carolina

GELATIN SALAD

1 box strawberry gelatin
1 box mixed fruit gelatin
1 small can crushed pineapple

2 or 3 bananas
1 package frozen strawberries
1 cup sour cream

Mix strawberry and fruit gelatin with 1 cup boiling water. Crush bananas and strawberries with a fork. Mix the crushed pineapple and juice with other fruit, and mix in dissolved gelatin. Pour half of mixture into glass dish and put in refrigerator. When congealed spread sour cream on top. Add remaining gelatin mixture. Serves eight.

Mrs. Charles K. Jackson

*When a man is invited to dinner, he is
disappointed if he does not get something
good. — Samuel Johnson*

GRAPEFRUIT CONGEALED SALAD

1 large can grapefruit
  sections
1 small can crushed pineapple
1/2 cup slivered almonds

1 1/2 envelopes Knox gelatin
1/2 cup sugar
Juice of 1 lemon

Dissolve gelatin in 1/2 cup cold water. Heat juice from grapefruit with 1/2 cup water. Pour over gelatin. Add fruit, almonds, sugar and lemon juice. Pour into individual molds. This will congeal in about 1 hour. Serves 8.

Mrs. James B. Cox
Columbia, S. C.

HEAVENLY ORANGE FLUFF

2 packages orange gelatin
2 cups hot water
1 small can frozen orange juice
  (undiluted)

2 cans mandarin oranges
1 large can crushed pineapple

Mix gelatin with hot water. Stir in juice and cool. Add drained oranges and pineapple. Congeal.

TOPPING

1 package lemon instant
  pudding mix

1 cup milk
1/2 pint whipping cream

Beat pudding with milk until slightly firm. Whip cream. Fold into pudding mixture. Spread over gelatin. Good for company because a dessert is not needed with this salad. Serves 10 to 12.

Mrs. Harold L. Murray

*There is no love sincerer than the
love of food. — Bernard Shaw*

ICE CREAM SALAD

1 package lime gelatin
1 cup boiling water
1 pint vanilla ice cream

1 cup crushed pineapple
1 cup grated sharp cheese

Dissolve gelatin in boiling water. Add ice cream and stir until melted. Mix in pineapple and cheese. Chill until firm. Do not freeze. Serves 8.

Mrs. Pat B. Harris

MARILUS SALAD

2 small boxes orange gelatin
1 1/2 cups boiling water
1 1/2 cups fruit syrup (from
apricots and pineapple)

2 small cans crushed pineapple
2 small cans apricots, mashed
1 cup whipping cream

Dissolve gelatin in boiling water. Add fruit syrup. Chill until partially set. Take out of refrigerator and beat until fluffy. Fold in fruit and whipped cream. Pour into individual molds. Serves 12.

Mrs. A. Owen Meredith

It is dazzling to discover smorgasbord at a South Carolina inn or a Caesar salad in Arkansas. Surely, we think, such internationalism is a good sign, rather like the Daughters of the American Revolution voting for an increase in foreign aid. — Eleanor Perenyi

MARSHMALLOW SALAD

1 package marshmallows
2 large bananas
1 can crushed pineapple, drained

1 pint whipping cream
1 tablespoon salad dressing
2 teaspoons sugar

Chop bananas, pineapple and marshmallows, add salad dressing and whipped cream. Fold together, adding sugar to mixture. Place each serving on lettuce and top with a cherry. Serves 6.

Mrs. Julian Bannister

PEACH PICKLE SALAD

2 packages lemon gelatin
1 envelope gelatin dissolved
  in 1/4 cup water
1 can mandarin oranges

1 8-ounce jar maraschino
  cherries (cut)
1 jar pickled peaches (chopped)
1 cup broken pecan meats

Dissolve gelatin in heated pickle juice. Add dissolved gelatin and enough water to make 4 cups. Chill well and add other ingredients. Chill. Serves 8.

Mrs. G. Carey Hayes

PEAR DELIGHT

1 large can pears
1 small package lime gelatin

1 3-ounce package cream cheese
1 small box Dream Whip

Heat pear juice and dissolve gelatin. Cool. Mash (or blend) pears and cream cheese together. Whip Dream Whip and add to pear mixture. Mix with gelatin and refrigerate. Serves 6 to 8.

Mrs. Needham Long

RASPBERRY SALAD

1 small box raspberry gelatin
1 1/2 cups water
1 package frozen raspberries
1 cup applesauce

1 cup marshmallows
1 cup sour cream
1 teaspoon sugar

Mix gelatin with 1 cup boiling water, 1/2 cup cold water. Add raspberries and applesauce. Congeal in oblong dish. Mix sour cream, marshmallows and sugar. Spread over top of salad 1 hour or longer before serving. Serves 6 to 8.

Mrs. Klugh Fooshe
Greenwood, S. C.

RED TOP SALAD

1 3-ounce box lemon gelatin
1 3-ounce box cherry gelatin
10 marshmallows
1 small can crushed pineapple

1 cup chopped pecans
1/4 cup salad dressing
1/2 pint cream, whipped
1/2 pound grated cheese

Dissolve lemon gelatin in 1 3/4 cups boiling water. Add marshmallows and let melt. When cold, add other ingredients (except cherry gelatin). Mix well. Pour into square pyrex dish and chill. Dissolve cherry gelatin in 2 cups hot water. When cool, pour over the congealed lemon mixture. Let congeal. Serves 8.

Mrs. Carl G. Oehmig, III

A man is in general better pleased when he
has a good dinner upon his table than when
his wife talks Greek. — Samuel Johnson

RUSSIAN SALAD

1 3-ounce package cream
   cheese
1 3-ounce box lime gelatin
1/2 cup broken pecans

1 cup diced celery
1 small can crushed pineapple
1 3/4 cups hot water

Whip softened cheese. Blend in pineapple. Add nuts and celery. Dissolve gelatin in water. Cool. Add to cheese mixture and pour into small molds. Refrigerate several hours or until firmly molded. Unmold on lettuce leaves. Top with mayonnaise or sour cream dressing. Serves 6 to 8.

Mrs. James B. Pruitt, Jr.

SHERRY-BING CHERRY SALAD

2 large boxes red gelatin
2 Number 2 cans black bing
   pitted cherries

2 cups sherry wine
1 1/2 cups cherry juice
Pecans

Stuff cherries with pecans halved lengthwise. Heat juice and dissolve gelatin in it. Cool slightly, then add sherry wine and stuffed cherries. Pour into greased mold. This recipe makes 1 large ring mold and 2 individual molds or 12 individual molds.

Mrs. Marion Talley
Atlanta, Ga.

SOUR CREAM SALAD

1/2 pint sour cream
2 cups marshmallows

1 can (15-ounce) fruit cocktail
2 bananas

Mix sour cream, marshmallows, fruit cocktail and sliced bananas. Freeze until firm. Serves 8.

Mrs. William M. Dillard, Jr.

SOUR-CREAM CUCUMBER SALAD

1 small package lime gelatin
3/4 cup hot water
1/4 cup lemon juice

1 teaspoon onion juice
1 cup sour cream, whipped
1 cup unpeeled cucumber
   finely chopped

Dissolve gelatin in hot water. Add lemon juice and onion juice. Place in refrigerator to chill. When partially set, fold in whipped sour cream and cucumbers. Pour into molds and chill until firm. Unmold on lettuce leaf. Serves 6.

Mrs. Cliff W. Bryant

STRAWBERRY-NUT SALAD

2 small boxes strawberry gelatin
3 tablespoons sugar
1 cup boiling water
1 10-ounce package frozen
  strawberries

1 Number 2 can crushed
  pineapple, drained
3 medium bananas, mashed
1 cup chopped pecans
2 cups sour cream

Dissolve gelatin and sugar in boiling water. Fold in thawed strawberries with juice, pineapple, bananas, and nuts. Pour half of mixture into 12 x 8 x 2 baking dish and chill until firm. Spread top with sour cream. Gently spoon on remaining gelatin mixture. Chill until firm. Serves 12.

Mrs. Charles J. Riddle, Jr.

STRAWBERRY SALAD

2 small boxes strawberry gelatin
1 1/2 cups boiling water

1 large package frozen strawberries
1 cup sour cream

Dissolve gelatin in water. Add strawberries. Pour 1/2 mixture in mold. Let partially congeal. Spread sour cream over this. Add remaining mixture and congeal. Serves 6.

Mrs. Robert Clyde

SUNSHINE SALAD

1 package lemon gelatin
2 tablespoons vinegar
1 cup grated carrots

1 cup crushed pineapple, drained
1/3 cup chopped nuts

Make gelatin with 1 cup hot water, juice from a can of crushed pineapple, and vinegar. (If there is not a cup full of juice, finish with water). When gelatin begins to congeal, combine other ingredients with it. Serves 6.

Mrs. W. S. McDevett
Durham, N. C.

ASHEVILLE SALAD

2 cans tomato soup
2 3-ounce packages cream cheese
4 tablespoons plain gelatin
1 tablespoon lemon juice
Salt to taste

1 cup minced vegetables
  (onion, celery, green pepper)
1 cup mayonnaise
1/2 cup chopped pecans

Dissolve gelatin in 1/3 cup cold water. Combine cheese and soup over low heat to melt and mix well. Add gelatin and stir until dissolved. Let cool, then add nuts, vegetables, salt and lemon juice. Add mayonnaise last. Pour into mold to congeal. Serve on lettuce with small portion of mayonnaise. Serves 12 to 14.

Mrs. Edna Sewell

CHEF'S SALAD

1 head of lettuce
2 tomatoes
2 chopped carrots
2 stalks chopped celery
1/2 cup grated red cabbage

1/2 cup crumbled bacon or
  sausage
3/4 cup grated cheddar cheese
Good Seasons Italian dressing
Salt and pepper

Combine the above ingredients. Top with Good Seasons Italian dressing. Toss well and serve. Serves 6.

Mrs. Allan P. Sloan, Jr.

COLE SLAW GELATIN SALAD

1 package lime gelatin
1 cup boiling water
1/2 cup cold water
1 tablespoon vinegar
1/2 cup Miracle Whip

1 cup chopped cabbage
1/2 cup shredded carrot
1/3 cup chopped celery
1/2 cup raisins

Dissolve gelatin in water. Stir in cold water and vinegar. Gradually add gelatin to Miracle Whip, mixing until well blended. Chill until slightly thickened. Fold in cabbage, carrots, celery and raisins. Pour in 1 quart mold and chill until firm. Serves 6.

Mrs. Martin Chapman

COUNTRY POTATO SALAD

5 pounds potatoes, pared
1 cup mayonnaise
1/2 cup chopped green onions
1/2 cup sour pickle relish

1/2 cup mustard
1/2 cup chopped pimento
1/2 teaspoon salt

Cook potatoes in boiling, salted water about 15 minutes or until tender. Drain. Cool. Slice potatoes 1/4 inch thick into large bowl. Mix remaining ingredients in small bowl. Pour over potatoes. Toss gently. Serve with barbecued ribs. Serves 10-12.

Mrs. Ernest Garrison

CUCUMBER ASPIC

1 package gelatin
1/2 cup vinegar
1 lemon (juice)
6 or 8 cucumbers
1 pint chicken stock

1/2 teaspoon sugar
1 teaspoon salt
1 medium onion grated
1/2 cup cold water

Soften gelatin in cold water. Have chicken stock boiling hot. Add sugar, salt, vinegar and lemon juice. Add gelatin. When beginning to congeal, add onion and cucumber grated or chopped fine. Add enough green coloring to make a pale green.

Mrs. Beaty Jackson

GUACAMOLE

6 large ripe avocados
2 medium tomatoes, peeled
and finely chopped
1/4 teaspoon salt

1 Jalapeno pepper
1/2 cup Jalapeno pepper juice
1/4 teaspoon black pepper

Place skinned and seeded avocados in a large mixing bowl. Mash with a fork (*do not beat, grind or use blender*) add tomatoes, salt, and pepper. Mash thoroughly. Blend Jalapenos and Jalapeno juice in a blender with 1/2 cup of the above mixture. Add blended mixture to mashed mixture. Place several avocado seeds in the bowl to prevent discoloration. Serve on crisp lettuce. Note: This salad is mildly hot to the taste. If you prefer it Mexican-peppery-hot, use three Jalapeno peppers and 1/2 cup of juice. Serves 4 to 6.

Mrs. Wilton Hall, Jr.

GERMAN SLAW

1 4 to 5-pound cabbage
1 large onion sliced thin
1/2 cup sugar
1 tablespoon salt
2 teaspoons sugar

1 teaspoon dry mustard
1 teaspoon celery seed
1 cup vinegar
3/4 cup oil

Soak cabbage in cold water before shredding. Mix cabbage, onion slices, and 1/2 cup sugar in a large bowl. Mix salt, 2 teaspoons sugar, dry mustard, celery seed, vinegar and oil in sauce pan. Boil for three minutes and pour over raw cabbage, onion and sugar. Put in a covered bowl and store in refrigerator overnight. This slaw will keep in refrigerator for several weeks. Serves 10 to 15.

Mrs. Hugh E. Vincent, Jr.

MARINATED SALAD

1 can French cut beans
1 can tiny English peas
1 can bean sprouts
1 can water chestnuts (diced)

1 medium onion (sliced)
1 green pepper
1 cup (3-4 stalks) celery

Drain canned vegetables. Mix together with onion, pepper and celery.

MIX IN JAR

1 1/2 cups wine vinegar
1/2 cup water
1/2 cup salad oil

1 cup sugar
3 teaspoons each salt
and pepper

Cover and shake. Pour over above mixture. Chill overnight. Keeps well. Serves 8.

Mrs. James H. Young

SAUERKRAUT SALAD

1 can chopped Kraut
1 cup diced onion
1 cup diced celery

1 cup diced green pepper
1 small can pimento

DRESSING

3/4 cup sugar
1/4 cup corn oil

1/4 cup vinegar

Mix dressing in above order. Add other ingredients. Keeps in refrigerator indefinitely. Delicious with all green vegetables. Serves 6 to 8.

Mrs. W. R. Phillips, Jr.

SLAW

2 large heads of cabbage
1 small can pimento pepper
1 can tomatoes
1 pod sweet pepper
1/2 pint sweet pickle relish

1 cup sugar
1 cup vinegar
3 tablespoons salt
1/2 teaspoon black pepper

Mix well. Will keep for 2 months or longer in refrigerator.

Mrs. Adger Hiott

TOMATO AND CREAM CHEESE SALAD

1 can cream of tomato soup
1 envelope gelatin
1 8-ounce package cream cheese
1/2 cup diced celery

1 teaspoon diced onion
1 tablespoon diced green pepper
1 cup mayonnaise
1 small bottle chopped olives

Heat soup. Dissolve gelatin in 2 tablespoons cold water, and add to boiling soup. Mash cream cheese with fork and add soup gradually. Be sure all lumps are out. Add other ingredients. Congeal. Serves 12.

Mrs. James Marchbanks

TOMATO ASPIC VEGETABLE SALAD

1 16-ounce can tomato juice
2 envelopes gelatin
1/2 cup chopped celery
1/2 cup shredded cabbage
1 tablespoon white vinegar

2 teaspoons minced onions
1 small bottle stuffed olives,
  sliced
2 teaspoons Worcestershire
1 tablespoon lemon juice.

Dissolve gelatin in 1 tablespoon white vinegar and 1 tablespoon lemon juice. Heat tomato juice and dissolve gelatin. Let stand until cold. Add salt, red pepper, and Worcestershire. Cool and add vegetables. Spoon into heart shape molds and refrigerate for 6 hours.

Mrs. Virginia Sloan

TUNA-ENGLISH PEA SALAD

1 can drained English peas
1 large can flaked tuna
1/2 cup chopped stuffed olives
3/4 cup chopped celery
2 tablespoons chopped onion
1/8 teaspoon pepper

2 tablespoons lemon juice
2 tablespoons mayonnaise
1 cup sour cream
2 cups cooked, drained macaroni
1/2 teaspoon salt

Cook macaroni and drain. Set aside. Combine tuna, peas, olives and celery. Make a dressing of sour cream, mayonnaise, salt, pepper, onion, lemon juice. Mix with other ingredients, add macaroni and mix well. Chill 1 hour or over night before serving. Serves 8.

Mrs. J. Frank Parnell

VEGETABLE SALAD

2 Number 2 cans cut green
beans (drained)
1 can (16-ounces) English
peas (drained)
1 tablespoon sugar
1/2 teaspoon salt
2/3 cup salad oil

1/3 cup vinegar
1 white onion sliced
1 can (8-ounce) sliced beets
1 cup chopped carrots
1 cup chopped celery
1 small red onion sliced
2 tablespoons mayonnaise

Put drained beans and peas into large bowl. Sprinkle sugar and salt over them. Place sliced onion over top. Combine oil and vinegar and pour over beans well. Cover and store in refrigerator overnight. Remove from refrigerator and discard onions on top. Drain well. Pat with paper towels making sure to remove all liquid. Combine with beets, carrots, celery and red onion. Toss with mayonnaise. Serves 6 to 10.

Mrs. Newton Newell, Jr.

*Tell me what you eat and I will tell you
what you are. — Brillat-Savarin*

BLEU CHEESE DRESSING

1/4 pound bleu cheese
3/4 cup salad oil
1 teaspoon grated lemon peel
1/4 cup fresh lemon juice

1 cup sour cream
Minced garlic bud
1 teaspoon salt
1/2 teaspoon Accent

Mash cheese in mixer, add oil and beat. Stir in the rest of the ingredients. Keeps several weeks stored in refrigerator. Yields 2 cups.

Mrs. Sam T. Haddock

CREAMY LEMON MAYONNAISE

1 cup mayonnaise
3 tablespoons lemon juice
1 teaspoon grated lemon peel

1/3 cup whipping cream
3 tablespoons powdered sugar

Mix together mayonnaise, lemon juice and lemon peel. Whip cream to medium consistency and add powdered sugar. Fold whipped cream mixture into lemon mayonnaise mixture. Serve over chef's salad or shrimp salad. Serves 12.

Mrs. Robert Speakman

FRENCH DRESSING

1/2 cup sugar
2/3 cup salad oil
1/3 cup catsup

1/3 cup vinegar
3 tablespoons sweet pickle juice
Salt and pepper to taste

Mix all ingredients well and chill before serving. May be kept indefinitely in the refrigerator. 12 to 16 servings.

Mrs. Max Kent

FRENCH DRESSING

2/3 cup salad oil
2/3 cup vinegar
1 cup chili sauce
1 cup sugar

1 small onion, minced
2 teaspoons Worcestershire
2 teaspoons salt
2 teaspoons garlic salt

Mix ingredients thoroughly. Chill to blend ingredients and mix before using. Yields about 3 cups.

Mrs. Douglas Glenn
Greenville, S. C.

MAYONNAISE

2 egg yolks
2 tablespoons vinegar or
    lemon juice
1 tablespoon Worcestershire

1 teaspoon each dry
    mustard, salt and sugar
2 cups salad oil

Put egg yolks in small chilled bowl. Add vinegar and Worcestershire. Then add dry ingredients and beat at high speed until well-mixed. Add chilled oil slowly, beating at high speed, until oil is thoroughly combined. This makes slightly more than a pint of mayonnaise which is delicious on salads and tomatoes. Store in covered jar in refrigerator.

Mrs. Arthur E. Holman, Jr.

ROQUEFORT CHEESE DRESSING

1/3 cup evaporated milk
1 1/2 tablespoons lemon juice
1/4 teaspoon garlic powder

1 cup mayonnaise
4 ounces Roquefort cheese

Put milk and lemon juice in blender. Blend briefly. Add garlic powder and mayonnaise. Blend briefly. Crumble 3 ounces Roquefort cheese and blend until almost smooth. Add 1 ounce crumbled Roquefort. Stir. *Do Not Blend.* Chill well.

Mrs. Charles J. Riddle, Jr.

ROYAL FRENCH DRESSING

1/2 cup sugar
1/4 cup vinegar
1 small onion (chopped)
1/2 cup salad oil

1 teaspoon salt
1 teaspoon paprika
1 tablespoon lemon juice
2 tablespoons catsup

Mix in a blender and refrigerate.

Mrs. William C. Hill
Winston Salem, N. C.

LOMAGE DRESSING

1 pint mayonnaise
1 pint chili sauce
1/2 cup India Relish
1 chopped egg
1 teaspoon chopped chives
1 chopped green pepper

2 tablespoons chopped celery
1 tablespoon mustard
1 tablespoon A-1 sauce
Dash of paprika
Salt and pepper to taste

Mix all ingredients well, and chill. Serve on tossed salad. Yields 1 quart.

Mrs. Charles J. Riddle, Jr.

When the waitress puts the dinner on the
table, the old men look at the dinner.
The young men look at the waitress.
—Gelett Burgess

MAYFAIR DRESSING

1 button garlic
1 stalk celery
1/2 medium onion
1 2-ounce can anchovies
3 whole eggs
2 cups salad oil

1 teaspoon ground pepper
1 teaspoon Accent
1/2 teaspoon sugar
1/4 teaspoon mustard
1 tablespoon lemon juice

Peel and slice garlic, celery, and onion. Mix these together with anchovies, mustard, lemon juice and all other ingredients *except eggs* in blender and whirl for about 2 to 3 seconds. Add eggs and blend again. Add 2 cups of salad oil, 1/4 of a cup at a time, blending between additions. Blend a few seconds more after all oil has been added. Can be used on head lettuce salad. Yields 1 quart.

Mrs. V. E. Merchant, Jr.

THOUSAND ISLAND DRESSING

1 pint mayonnaise
1/3 cup catsup
1 teaspoon vinegar
3 drops Tabasco
1 teaspoon Worcestershire

1 teaspoon onion juice
2 hard boiled eggs
3 strips crisp bacon
3 tablespoons green pepper
3 tablespoons pimento

Chop eggs, bacon, pepper and pimento. Combine all ingredients. Let stand at least 6 hours before using.

Mrs. James Smith

*Part of the secret of success in life
is to eat what you like and let the
food fight it out inside. — Mark Twain*

NOTES

DESSERTS

QUICK FREEZER

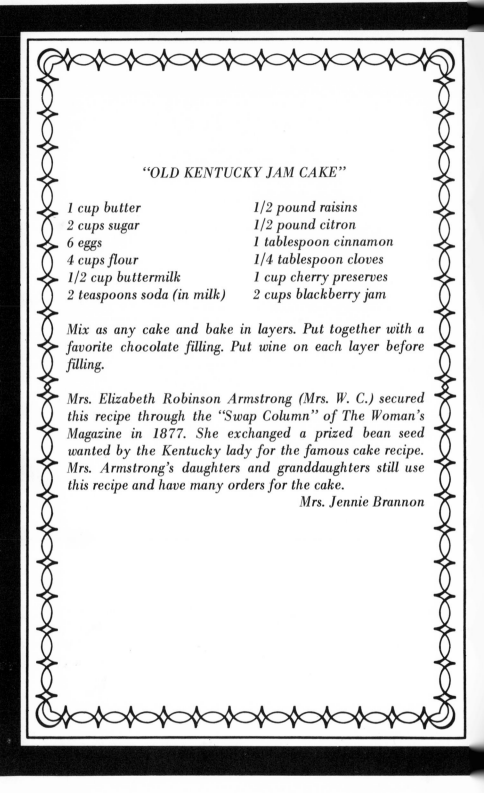

"OLD KENTUCKY JAM CAKE"

1 cup butter	1/2 pound raisins
2 cups sugar	1/2 pound citron
6 eggs	1 tablespoon cinnamon
4 cups flour	1/4 tablespoon cloves
1/2 cup buttermilk	1 cup cherry preserves
2 teaspoons soda (in milk)	2 cups blackberry jam

Mix as any cake and bake in layers. Put together with a favorite chocolate filling. Put wine on each layer before filling.

Mrs. Elizabeth Robinson Armstrong (Mrs. W. C.) secured this recipe through the "Swap Column" of The Woman's Magazine in 1877. She exchanged a prized bean seed wanted by the Kentucky lady for the famous cake recipe. Mrs. Armstrong's daughters and granddaughters still use this recipe and have many orders for the cake.

Mrs. Jennie Brannon

CAKES

APPLESAUCE CAKE

4 cups sifted flour
4 teaspoons soda
1 1/4 teaspoons salt
2 teaspoons cinnamon
1/2 teaspoon nutmeg
1/2 teaspoon cloves

2 tablespoons cocoa
1 cup vegetable oil
2 cups sugar
3 cups unsweetened applesauce
1/2 cup chopped walnuts
1/2 cup raisins

Sift together dry ingredients and set aside. Blend vegetable oil and sugar, and add hot applesauce. Add dry ingredients, blending well. Stir in raisins and walnuts. Turn batter into well greased and floured 9-inch cake pan. Bake at 400 degrees for 15 minutes. Reduce temperature to 375 degrees and bake 15 minutes longer. Let stand in pan 5 minutes. Remove and cool on rack. Fill and frost with Caramel Frosting.

CARAMEL FROSTING

1/2 cup butter
1 cup dark brown sugar

1/4 teaspoon salt
2 cups confectioners sugar

Melt butter in saucepan over low heat. Stir in brown sugar and salt. Bring to a boil over medium heat, boil hard 2 minutes stirring constantly. Remove from heat, cool to lukewarm. Stir in confectioners sugar and beat until smooth. If frosting is too thick, add a little milk.

Mrs. Darwin H. Wright

179

STUFFED ANGEL FOOD CAKE

1 cup chopped marshmallows
1 cup chopped pecans
1 small can crushed pineapple
2 cups whipped cream

1 4-ounce bottle maraschino
  cherries
1 round angel food cake

Remove inside of cake to within 1 inch thickness of the sides and bottom. Combine whipped cream and bits of cake taken from whole cake. Add remaining ingredients. Place mixture loosely into hollowed out cake. Refrigerate overnite. Slice and serve with sweetened whipped cream topped with cherry. Serves 12 to 16.

Mrs. Mary Evelyn Jolly

APPLE NUT CAKE

2 cups sugar
1 cup vegetable oil
3 eggs
3 cups diced raw apples
3 cups plain flour

1 teaspoon salt
1 teaspoon soda
2 teaspoons vanilla
1 cup chopped nuts

Cream sugar and oil. Add eggs one at a time. Sift flour, salt, and soda. Add to mixture. Add apples, nuts, and vanilla. Mix well. Pour in greased square cake pan. Bake at 350 degrees for 35 or 40 minutes.

ICING FOR APPLE NUT CAKE

1 stick butter
8 ounces cream cheese

1 box confectioners sugar
1 teaspoon vanilla

Soften cream cheese, then cream with butter. Add remaining ingredients and blend until smooth. Spread on cake.

Mrs. Harold L. Murray

180

CHEESE CAKE

2 cups graham cracker crumbs
2 8-ounce cream cheese
3/4 cup sugar

4 eggs, separated
1 teaspoon lemon juice
1 teaspoon vanilla

Spread cracker crumbs very lightly in pie plate. Blend cheese and sugar well with an electric mixer. Add egg yolks and mix well. Add lemon juice and vanilla; blend well. Beat egg whites until they are stiff; fold into cheese mixture. Spread filling over crumbs. Bake for 30 minutes at 350 degrees (will rise high in oven and flatten while cooling).

TOPPING

1/2 pint sour cream
2 tablespoons sugar

1/2 teaspoon vanilla

Mix ingredients with a spoon and spread over warm cheese cake. Return cake to oven and bake at 350 degrees for 5 minutes.

Mrs. Robert Mayfield
Mrs. Max Kent

TROPICAL CHEESE CAKE

1/2 cup graham cracker crumbs
2 tablespoons butter
8-ounce cream cheese

1/2 cup confectioners sugar
4 1/2-ounce can pineapple
1 package Dream Whip

Mix crumbs and melted butter, reserving two tablespoons. Press on bottom of 8-inch cake pan and chill. Whip cream cheese and confectioners sugar until fluffy and stir in crushed drained pineapple. Prepare Dream Whip according to package directions and fold into pineapple mixture. Spread over crust and sprinkle with reserved crumbs. Chill well. Serves 6.

Mrs. W. Ray Thompson

181

CHEESE CAKE

2 1/2 cups graham cracker
  crumbs
1/3 cup sugar
1 stick margarine
3 eggs

2 8-ounce cream cheese
1 cup sugar
1/4 teaspoon salt
3 cups sour cream
1 teaspoon vanilla

Mix first 3 ingredients and press in bottom and sides of spring-form pan. Bake at 350 degrees. Cool. Blend cream cheese, sugar and salt. Add egg yolks one at a time. Add sour cream and fold in beaten egg whites and vanilla. Pour in baked crust. Bake at 350 degrees for 55 minutes. Serves 8.

Mrs. Paul K. Rogers

It is the hope of a good dinner
that beguiles you. — Juvenal

CHEESE CAKE

2 cups vanilla wafer crumbs
6 tablespoons butter
3 8-ounce packages
  cream cheese

5 eggs
1 cup sugar
1/2 teaspoon vanilla
1 teaspoon lemon juice

Mix crumbs with butter and press into pie pan. Beat egg yolks with cheese. Add sugar and vanilla. Beat egg whites until stiff. Fold into egg and cheese mixture. Pour into crust. Bake for 1 hour at 300 degrees.

TOPPING

1 cup sour cream
1/4 cup sugar

1 1/4 teaspoon vanilla

Mix ingredients and pour over top of warm cake. Bake 5 minutes at 475 degrees. Cool to room temperature and chill for 24 hours.

Mrs. Joseph C. Yarbrough, Jr.

CARROT CAKE

2 cups flour
2 teaspoons baking powder
1 1/2 teaspoons soda
2 teaspoons salt
2 cups sugar
4 eggs

1 1/2 cups vegetable oil
2 cups grated carrots
1 8 1/4-ounce can crushed
  pineapple
1 cup chopped pecans

Mix flour, baking powder, soda, salt and sugar. Add eggs and oil. Mix in carrots, pineapple, and pecans. Pour into 2 greased and floured cake pans. Bake at 350 degrees for 30 to 40 minutes.

FILLING

8 ounces cream cheese
1 stick butter

1 box powdered sugar
1 teaspoon vanilla

Mix together. Ice layers.

Mrs. James F. White
Columbia, S. C.

The greatest animal in creation,
the animal who cooks. — Douglas Jerrold

LEMON PUDDING CAKE

3 tablespoons soft butter
1 cup sugar
3 tablespoons flour
2 egg yolks

Juice of one lemon
Rind of one lemon (grated)
1 cup milk
2 egg whites, beaten stiff

Cream sugar and butter. Add flour, beaten yolks, grated rind, juice and milk. Mix well. Fold egg whites into mixture. Pour into greased 1 quart casserole; set in pan of hot water. Bake at 325 degrees 1 hour. Serves 4.

Mrs. Needham Long

LEMON CAKE

1 1/2 cups sugar
1/4 cup butter
1 tablespoon Crisco
  (heaping)
5 eggs

1/8 teaspoon salt
3 cups flour
1 teaspoon baking powder
1 cup milk

Cream sugar and butter thoroughly. Add eggs one at a time, beating thoroughly as added. Sift flour — then measure and sift again with salt and baking powder. Add flour and milk to egg and shortening mixture. Cook in layer cake pans at 350 degrees until done when tested. Fill with the following:

FILLING

2 lemons (grated
  rind and juice)
2 eggs

1 cup sugar
2 tablespoons water
3 tablespoons butter

Beat all ingredients together. Let boil for one to two minutes. Use as filling. Double filling recipe in order to obtain sufficient quantity for top and sides.

Mrs. Wilton E. Hall

JAM CAKE

3/4 cup butter
1 cup sugar
3 eggs
1 cup jam
1 teaspoon allspice

1 teaspoon cloves
1 teaspoon cinnamon
3 cups flour
1 cup buttermilk

Cream butter and sugar. Beat eggs into butter mixture. Add jam. Sift together spices and flour. Add the flour mixture to the batter, alternating with buttermilk. Pour batter into greased tube pan. Bake at 350 degrees for 1 hour.

Mrs. Joseph W. Black

Other men live to eat, while I eat to live.
— Socrates

GERMAN CHOCOLATE CAKE AND FROSTING

1 teaspoon vanilla
1 4-ounce package sweet
   chocolate
1/2 cup boiling water
1 cup butter
2 cups sugar

4 eggs separated
2 1/2 cups cake flour
1/2 teaspoon salt
1 teaspoon soda
1 cup buttermilk

Melt chocolate in boiling water and put aside. Cream butter and sugar until fluffy. Add egg yolks, one at a time. Add chocolate and vanilla and mix well. Sift together salt, soda, and flour. Add to chocolate mixture, alternately with buttermilk. Beat until smooth. Fold in beaten (stiff) egg whites. Pour into 3 (8 or 9 inch) paper lined pans. Bake at 350 degrees for 35 minutes.

FILLING AND FROSTING

1 teaspoon vanilla
1 cup evaporated milk
1 cup sugar
3 egg yolks

1/2 cup butter
1 1/3 cups flaked coconut
1 cup chopped pecans

Combine ingredients and cook over medium heat stirring until thick. Add coconut and pecans. Beat until thick. Cool a few minutes and spread on cake.

Mrs. Earle Maxwell

Success may go to one's head,
but the stomach is where it
gets in its worst work. — Kin Hubbard

OLD FASHIONED CHOCOLATE LAYER CAKE

1 stick butter
1 1/4 cups sugar
2 eggs
3 squares chocolate
2 cups sifted cake flour

1/2 teaspoon salt
2 teaspoons baking powder
1/4 teaspoon soda
1 cup milk
1 teaspoon vanilla

Sift flour, salt, baking powder, and soda. Cream butter and sugar. Add eggs one at a time. Then add melted chocolate. Alternate flour mixture and milk to creamed mixture. Add vanilla. Pour into two 9 inch or three 8-inch greased and waxed paper lined pans. Cook at 350 degrees for 30 minutes. Serves 20.

GOLDEN CREAM FILLING

1/2 cup sugar
3 tablespoons flour
1/4 teaspoon salt

1 1/2 cups milk
2 beaten egg yolks
1 teaspoon vanilla

Combine in top of double boiler sugar, flour and salt. Add milk gradually, stirring until blended. Cook, stirring constantly for ten minutes. Blend small amount with egg yolks and add to mixture. Cook 2 minutes longer, add vanilla and cool. Fill between layers.

FROSTING

1/2 stick butter
1 1/2 cups powdered sugar
1 teaspoon vanilla

2 egg whites
1/2 teaspoon salt
3 squares melted chocolate

Cream butter and 3/4 cup sugar. Add vanilla, salt, and melted chocolate. Mix well. Beat egg whites until stiff. Add remaining 3/4 cup sugar, 2 tablespoons at a time. Beat until mixture stands in peaks. Fold the two mixtures together. Frosts top and sides of cake.

Mrs. James Glenn

SCOTT CHOCOLATE CAKE

2 cups sugar	1 stick margarine
2 cups flour	1/4 cup cocoa
1/4 teaspoon salt	1/2 cup buttermilk
1 teaspoon soda	1/2 cup water
1 egg	1 teaspoon vanilla

Combine sugar, flour, salt and soda in large mixing bowl. Add egg. Melt margarine in saucepan. Add cocoa, buttermilk, water, and vanilla. Pour into dry mixture, mix and bake in a loaf pan about 30 minutes at 325 degrees. Serves 12.

FILLING

1 stick margarine	1 teaspoon vanilla
1/4 cup cocoa	3/4 cup chopped nuts
6 tablespoons milk	3/4 cup coconut
1 pound box powdered sugar	

Melt margarine and add other ingredients and spread over cake while hot.

Mrs. Adger Hiott
Mrs. L. E. McGaha

COCONUT POUND CAKE

3 sticks margarine	1 cup evaporated milk
3 cups sugar	1 tablespoon lemon flavoring
5 eggs	1 can coconut
3 cups sifted flour	

Cream margarine and sugar. Add eggs one at a time, and beat. Combine milk and flavoring. Add flour alternately with milk, beginning and ending with flour. Fold in coconut. Grease a stem pan with margarine and flour. Bake at 325 degrees for about 1 hour. Serves 16.

Mrs. Forest Suggs, Jr.

DATE NUT CAKE

3/4 stick margarine
1 cup sugar
4 eggs, separated
1 teaspoon vanilla
1 cup flour

3 teaspoons baking powder
1/2 teaspoon salt
16 ounces dates
3 1/2 cups nuts

Cream margarine, sugar, egg yolks, and vanilla. Sift flour, baking powder, and salt. Roll nuts and dates in flour mixture. Beat egg whites until stiff and add to other ingredients. Put in greased loaf pan. Bake at 300 degrees 1 hour. Serves 8 to 10.

Mrs. Jack Caulkins
St. Petersburg, Florida
Mrs. Lena Wright

FRUIT COCKTAIL CAKE

2 cups sugar
2 cups flour
2 teaspoons soda

Pinch of salt
1 Number 303 can fruit cocktail
1 egg

Sift dry ingredients together. Add fruit cocktail and egg. Beat with electric mixer for 2 minutes. Bake at 350 degrees 45 minutes.

TOPPING

1 stick margarine
1 cup sugar
1 cup evaporated milk

1 cup shredded coconut
1 cup chopped pecans
1 teaspoon vanilla

Blend margarine, sugar and milk. Boil 10 minutes or until thickened. Remove from heat and add coconut, pecans and vanilla. Stir well. Pour over cake while still in pan. Cut cake into squares. Serves 12.

Mrs. Douglas McDougald, Jr.

ICE BOX FRUIT CAKE

1 pound dates
1/2 pound pecans
1/2 pound walnuts
1 can sweetened condensed milk
1 box graham crackers

1 fresh coconut or
  1 package frozen coconut
1 pound candied cherries
  (1/2 red and 1/2 green)

Chop dates, nuts, and cherries. Mix with crumbs. Add coconut and milk. Blend thoroughly. Pack tightly in wax paper or foil.

Mrs. Joe D. Ivester

Many excellent cooks are spoiled by going into the arts.
—Paul Gauguin

WHITE FRUIT CAKE

3/4 pound butter ·
2 cups sugar
6 eggs
5 cups flour
2 teaspoons baking powder
Rind of 1 lemon
Juice of 1 lemon

Juice of 1 orange
1 1/2 teaspoons vanilla
1 1/2 teaspoons lemon extract
1/2 pound candied pineapple
1/2 pound candied cherries
1/2 pound citron
3 cups pecans

Cream butter and sugar. Add eggs, one at a time. Use 1 cup flour on fruits and nuts. Sift remaining flour and baking powder and add to creamed mixture. Add grated rind, lemon and orange juice and extracts. Add fruits and nuts. Bake 275 degrees for approximately 2 hours.

Mrs. Julian M. Smith, Jr.
Charleston, S. C.
Mrs. Joe C. Prevost, Jr.

ORANGE SLICE CAKE

1 cup margarine
1/2 cup buttermilk
3 1/2 cups flour
2 cups sugar
4 eggs

1 small can coconut
1 pound orange slice candy
1 teaspoon soda
7 1/4-ounce package dates
2 cups pecans

Prepare the fruit, candy and nuts by cutting up finely and rolling in a portion of the flour. Cream margarine with sugar and add eggs, one at a time, blending well. Add buttermilk. Sift together all remaining flour with soda and add to mixture. Fold in chopped nuts, dates and orange slices; add coconut. Bake for 3 hours at 250 degrees. Leave cake in pan and while still hot, glaze.

GLAZE

2 cups confectioners sugar   1 cup orange juice

Mix sugar and orange juice well and pour on cake while cake is still in pan and hot. Leave cake in tube pan until well cooled and all juice is absorbed.

Mrs. Ralph Dodson

PINEAPPLE-NUT ICE BOX CAKE

1 1/2 cups powdered sugar
1 cup margarine
1 cup pecans
1 1/2 cups crushed pineapple

2 egg whites
1 pint whipping cream
Vanilla wafers

Cream butter and sugar. Add nuts and drained pineapple. Blend thoroughly. Fold in stiffly beaten egg whites. Line oblong dish with vanilla wafers. Cover with layer of mixture. Continue layers until all ingredients are used. Chill for approximately 12 hours. Top with whipped cream and serve. Serves approximately 12.

Mrs. Wesley Strong

PLAIN CAKE WITH STRAWBERRIES

3 sticks butter or margarine
2 1/2 cups sugar
5 eggs
1 teaspoon strawberry extract
3 1/2 cups all-purpose flour

1 teaspoon baking powder
1/4 teaspoon salt
1 cup crushed strawberries
1/4 cup milk

Cream margarine until light and fluffy. Add sugar and cream well. Add eggs one at a time, beating well after each addition. Add extract. Sift dry ingredients together and add to sugar mixture alternately with strawberries (to which the milk has been added). Pour into greased 10-inch tube pan and bake at 325 degrees for 1 1/2 hours. Let stand in pan on wire rack for 10 minutes after removing from the oven. Place on rack until cold.

Mrs. Fred Compton

BLACK WALNUT POUND CAKE

3 sticks margarine
1 box confectioners sugar
1 box flour
  (measure with sugar box)

6 eggs
1 teaspoon lemon flavoring
1 teaspoon vanilla
1 small can black walnuts

Cream margarine and sugar. Add eggs one at a time. Add sifted flour a little at a time. Add lemon and vanilla flavoring. Add chopped walnuts. Bake 1 hour and 10 minutes at 300 degrees.

GLAZE

1/4 cup butter
1 cup packed brown sugar

1/4 cup milk

Boil 1 minute and pour over cake while hot.

Mrs. W. A. Thompson

VANILLA-BUTTERNUT CAKE

2 sticks margarine
2 cups sugar
3 cups sifted plain flour
1 cup buttermilk
1 teaspoon soda

1/4 teaspoon salt
3 eggs, separated
3 teaspoons vanilla-butternut
   flavoring

Cream margarine and sugar. Mix soda and salt in milk until foamy. Add milk alternately with flour to cream mixture. Add egg yolks one at a time. Stir in flavoring. Fold in stiffly beaten egg whites. Pour into a greased 10 inch tube pan. Bake at 350 degrees for 1 hour.

CREAM CHEESE FROSTING

2 3-ounce packages cream
   cheese
4 teaspoons milk

Dash of salt
1 1/2 teaspoons vanilla
1 pound confectioners sugar

Cream milk and cheese. Blend in salt and vanilla. Gradually add sugar beating for about 1 1/2 minutes. Spread on cake.

Mrs. Fred Bolt, Jr.
Charlotte, North Carolina

CHOCOLATE POUND CAKE AND ICING

1 box yellow cake mix
1 box instant chocolate
   pudding

1/4 cup cooking oil
4 eggs
1 cup plus 2 tablespoons water

In large bowl, pour cake mix and chocolate pudding. Add eggs, oil and water; beat thoroughly. Grease and flour cake pan. Bake at 325 degrees for 50 minutes.

192

ICING

1 stick butter
3 tablespoons cocoa

1 box powdered sugar
1/4 cup milk

Cream butter well, then add cocoa, powdered sugar and milk. Spread on cake.

Mrs. Larry King

CHOCOLATE POUND CAKE

2 sticks margarine
1/2 cup shortening
3 cups sugar
5 eggs
3 cups flour

1/2 teaspoon baking powder
1/2 teaspoon salt
4 tablespoons cocoa
1 cup milk
1 tablespoon vanilla

Cream together margarine and shortening. Add eggs and sugar. Sift dry ingredients together. Add ingredients alternately with milk to creamed mixture. Add vanilla. Bake in 9 or 10-inch greased tube pan at 325 degrees about 80 minutes.

Mrs. Robert E. Padgett, Jr.
Mrs. Bill Metz
Mrs. Robert Gallant

CHOCOLATE ICING

1/2 stick butter
2 squares chocolate
1-pound confectioners sugar

1 teaspoon vanilla
3 tablespoons milk

Melt butter and chocolate. Add sugar and vanilla. Spread on cake. Add enough milk to reach desired consistency.

Mrs. Bill Metz

193

CRISCO POUND CAKE

1 cup Crisco
2 1/2 cups sugar
1 cup milk
5 eggs
3 cups plain flour

1/2 teaspoon baking powder
1/4 teaspoon salt
1 teaspoon vanilla
1 teaspoon lemon flavoring

Cream Crisco and sugar. Blend in milk. Add eggs one at a time, and flour a little at a time. Add remaining ingredients and bake for 1 hour and 15 minutes at 300 degrees.

Mrs. Joe Garvin

Condiments are like old friends — highly thought of, but often taken for granted.
— Marilyn Kaytor

GINGER ALE POUND CAKE

1/2 cup shortening
2 sticks butter
2 1/2 cups sugar
5 eggs

2 teaspoons lemon extract
3 cups cake flour
6-ounce bottle ginger ale

Cream sugar, shortening, and butter. Add eggs one at a time and beat. Add lemon extract. Alternate flour with ginger ale. Bake in greased, floured tube pan at 325 degrees for 1 hour and 30 minutes. Glaze while still hot.

GLAZE

1/2 stick butter
1 1/2 cups sifted powdered sugar

2 to 3 tablespoons milk

Cream butter and sugar. Add enough milk to reach cream consistency.

Mrs. Snead Schumacher
Walhalla, S. C.

ENGLISH POUND CAKE

1 cup Crisco
2 cups sugar
5 egg whites
3 cups flour

1 teaspoon almond flavoring
1 teaspoon baking powder
1 cup milk
1/4 teaspoon salt

Cream Crisco and sugar. Add 3/4 cup milk and mix well. Add flour and flavoring; fold in egg whites. Blend in baking powder with 1/4 cup milk and add to batter. Bake at 325 degrees 1 hour.

Mrs. Norman Wayne Wham

LEMON POUND CAKE

1/4 pound butter
1/2 cup shortening
2 cups sugar
3 eggs
3 cups flour
1/2 teaspoon soda

1/2 teaspoon salt
1 cup buttermilk
1 teaspoon vanilla
1 teaspoon lemon juice
1 teaspoon lemon rind

Cream butter, shortening and sugar. Add eggs, one at a time. Add flour sifted with salt and soda, then buttermilk. Add flavorings. Bake at 350 degrees 1 hour.

Mrs. E. C. Sanders

POUND CAKE

2 sticks butter
3 cups sugar
6 eggs
3 cups sifted flour

1 teaspoon lemon, vanilla or
    almond flavoring
1/2 pint whipping cream

Cream butter and sugar. Add eggs one at a time, then flavoring. Add flour and cream alternately. Bake at 350 degrees for 1 hour and 30 minutes or until cake springs back.

Mrs. John C. Edwards

POUND CAKE

1 box powdered sugar
1 box cake flour (measure
  with sugar box)
6 eggs

3 sticks butter
1 teaspoon vanilla
1 teaspoon lemon flavoring
1 teaspoon almond flavoring

Cream butter and sugar. Add eggs, one at a time, beating each time. Fold in flour gradually. Beat 3 minutes. Add flavorings and mix. Line steeple pan with waxed paper and grease. Bake at 300 degrees 1 hour.

Mrs. William Lowe
Louisville, Kentucky
Mrs. Sam Taylor

RUM POUND CAKE

2 sticks butter
1/2 pint sour cream
3 cups sifted flour
3 cups sugar, sifted

6 eggs
1/4 teaspoon soda
2 tablespoons rum extract

Cream butter and sugar. Add eggs one at a time, beating well. Sift flour and soda. Add alternately with sour cream. Stir in rum extract. Grease and line bottom of tube pan with two layers of waxed paper. Bake at 325 degrees 1 hour and 15 minutes.

Mrs. Richard J. Willis
Mrs. Sam Fretwell, Jr.

SOUR CREAM POUND CAKE

1 cup butter or margarine
3 cups sugar, sifted
1 cup sour cream
6 eggs

3 cups flour, sifted 3 times
1/4 teaspoon soda
1 1/2 teaspoons vanilla
  almond, or lemon flavoring

Cream butter well, and add sugar gradually, continuing to mix. Add eggs, one at a time, mixing well after each, then add sour cream. Sift dry ingredients, and add gradually to mixture. Stir in flavoring. Pour batter into stem pan. Bake at 325 degrees 1 hour and 30 minutes. Be careful not to overcook; this cake is much better moist. Let cool for fifteen minutes before removing cake from pan. Serves about fifteen.

Mrs. Milton Simonton
Brighton, Tennessee
Mrs. Robert Owens, Jr.
Mrs. W. C. McGregor
Mrs. Everett Newman
Mrs. Athen R. Morris, Jr.

POPPY SEED CAKE

1 1/2 cups milk
1 cup poppy seeds
1 stick butter
1 1/2 cups sugar

2 teaspoons baking powder
2 cups flour
4 egg whites, beaten
1 teaspoon vanilla

Heat 1/2 of the milk. Pour over poppy seeds and let stand 1 hour. Cream sugar and butter. Add remaining milk, sugar, flour and baking powder. Blend in poppy seed, milk, and vanilla. Beat egg whites and fold into batter. Bake in 2 nine-inch layer pans at 350 degrees 25 to 30 minutes. Cool layers and frost.

FROSTING

1/2 stick butter
2 cups sifted confectioners sugar

1 teaspoon vanilla
1 tablespoon cream

Beat softened butter and sugar. Soften with cream, and add vanilla.

Mrs. James B. Pruitt, Jr.

PRALINE CAKE

1 package yellow cake mix
1/2 cup butter or margarine
1 pound light brown sugar
2 tablespoons flour

2 eggs, beaten
1 teaspoon vanilla
1 1/2 cups coarsely chopped
  pecans

Prepare cake mix according to package directions. Pour batter into 2 greased and floured 13x9x2 inch pans. Bake in 350 degree oven 20 to 30 minutes. Remove from oven. Melt butter in skillet. Mix brown sugar, flour and eggs. Add to butter in skillet and cook 3 minutes over low heat. Remove from heat and stir in vanilla and pecans. Spread evenly over cooled cakes. Return cakes to oven and bake at 400 degrees for 8 minutes. Cool, and cut into 1 1/2 inch strips for party service. Yields 60.

Mrs. Wilburn Gable

"Fate cannot harm me; I have dined. . ."
— Sydney Smith

PRUNE CAKE

3 eggs
1 cup cooking oil
1 1/2 cups sugar
1 cup buttermilk
1 cup prunes, cooked and cut
  or 1 baby food jar, junior
  prunes

1 teaspoon vanilla
1 cup chopped nuts
2 cups self-rising flour
1 teaspoon soda
1 teaspoon cinnamon
1 teaspoon nutmeg
1 teaspoon allspice

Combine sugar and oil. Add eggs. Add sifted dry ingredients and buttermilk, beginning and ending with flour mixture. Add vanilla, nuts and prunes. Bake in tube or oblong pan, well greased and line bottom with waxed paper. Bake at 350 degrees for 1 hour and 30 minutes.

SAUCE FOR PRUNE CAKE

1 cup sugar
1/2 cup buttermilk
1/2 teaspoon soda

1/4 cup butter
1 tablespoon corn syrup
1/2 teaspoon vanilla

Combine in saucepan and boil to soft ball stage, stirring frequently.
Pour sauce over hot cake.

Mrs. William Seabrook
Gastonia, N. C.
Mrs. William D. McClellan
Manchester, Ga.
Mrs. Paul L. Embler
Mrs. Carl G. Oehmig, III

STRAWBERRY CAKE

1 box yellow cake mix
4 eggs
1 cup cooking oil
1/2 cup boiling water

1 regular box strawberry
gelatin
5-ounces frozen strawberries

Combine cake mix, eggs, one at a time, and oil. Add strawberry
gelatin with 1/2 cup boiling water. Mix well and add the strawberries.
Cook in a stem pan at 325 degrees, 1 hour.

Mrs. Charles A. Brown
Mrs. Wallace Reid

VANILLA WAFER CAKE

1 cup butter
2 cups sugar
6 eggs
1/2 cup milk

7-ounce package coconut
1 cup chopped nuts
12-ounce box vanilla wafers

Cream butter and sugar; add eggs one at a time. Add milk, coconut,
nuts, and crumbled vanilla wafers. Pour into greased and floured tube
pan. Bake at 275 degrees for 1 hour and 30 minutes.

Mrs. W. Clayborn Hatcher

BLACK WALNUT CUPCAKES

1/2 cup Crisco
1 cup sugar
2 eggs (separated)
1 cup milk
32 graham crackers

1 teaspoon vanilla or
1 teaspoon black walnut
flavoring
1 teaspoon baking powder
1 cup black walnuts or pecans

Cream Crisco and sugar. Add beaten egg yolks. Break crackers and pour milk over them. Add to creamed mixture. Add flavoring, baking powder and nuts. Beat egg whites until stiff and fold into batter. Fill paper lined cupcake pan to about 1/2 full. Bake at 350 degrees for 12 minutes.

TOPPING

1 small can crushed pineapple   1 cup sugar

Boil pineapple and sugar together slowly for 10 minutes and pour over cupcakes while still hot. Yields 24 cupcakes.

Mrs. James Marchbanks, Jr.

CHOCOLATE CHIP CUPCAKES

2 cups flour
1 tablespoon cocoa
1 teaspoon salt
1 teaspoon soda
1 teaspoon vanilla

1 cup water
1 1/4 cups sugar
3/4 cup Crisco
2 eggs
1 package chocolate chips

Cream sugar and Crisco. Add eggs. Alternately add dry ingredients with water to sugar and Crisco. Put batter into cupcake tins and sprinkle chocolate chips on top of batter. If desired, may also sprinkle nuts on batter. Bake at 350 degrees for 25 minutes. Yields 24 cupcakes.

Mrs. E. L. Menees
Columbia, S. C.

ORANGE CUPCAKES

1 cup butter	Juice of 1 orange
2 eggs	1 teaspoon vanilla
1 cup sugar	1 cup nuts
3 cups flour	3/4 cup buttermilk
1 teaspoon baking powder	1/2 cup chopped raisins
1 teaspoon baking soda	(optional)

GLAZE

2 oranges   2 cups sugar

Before starting on cake, mix juice of oranges and sugar for the glaze. Stir often while mixing batter. Cream butter, sugar, and eggs. Add dry ingredients, then remaining ingredients. Grease muffin tins and fill each about 2/3 full. Bake at 375 degrees for 12 to 15 minutes. Yields 3 dozen.

Mrs. Michael Glenn

All that's sweet was made,
but to be lost when sweetest.
—Moore

AMALGAMATION FILLING

8 egg yolks	1 cup nuts, chopped
2 cups sugar	1 cup raisins
1 cup butter	1 cup citron
1 teaspoon vanilla	1 cup fresh coconut

Cook first three ingredients in double boiler until thick, stirring constantly. Remove from heat and add remaining ingredients. Spread on two-layer oblong white cake.

Mrs. H. S. Sullivan

CARAMEL ICING

1/4 cup sugar
3 cups sugar
1 cup milk
1/4 cup margarine

1/4 teaspoon salt
1/4 teaspoon soda
1 teaspoon vanilla

Brown 1/4 cup sugar. Bring to boil 3 cups sugar and milk. Add browned sugar and next three ingredients. Cook until soft ball forms. Add vanilla. Cool and spread on cake. (Use a large pan as the soda causes the mixture to boil up very high.)

Mrs. H. S. Sullivan

Would the cook were of my mind! — Shakespeare

CREAM CHEESE ICING

3-ounces cream cheese
1 tablespoon milk
2 1/2 cups sifted
   confectioners sugar

1 square unsweetened chocolate
1 teaspoon vanilla
Dash of salt

Beat cream cheese with milk in mixer. Add remaining ingredients and spread on cake.

Mrs. Robert Gallant

ONE MINUTE CHOCOLATE FROSTING

2 cups sugar
1/2 cup whole milk

1 stick butter
1/2 cup cocoa

Combine all ingredients, stir and bring to a rolling boil. Continue boiling for one minute. Remove from heat and cool. Beat and frost cake.

Mrs. T. Ed Garrison

COOKIES

ACCORDION COOKIES

3/4 cup butter
3/4 cup sugar
2 eggs
1 teaspoon vanilla

1/4 teaspoon salt
1 1/4 cups cake flour
1/2 cup nuts

Cream butter. Gradually add sugar, creaming well. Blend in unbeaten eggs, vanilla and salt. Beat well. Add sifted cake flour and chopped nuts. Mix thoroughly. Fold one yard of heavy-duty aluminum foil lengthwise, fold the foil crosswise into 1 inch pleats to make an "accordian-pleated pan." Place on baking sheet. Drop a rounded teaspoon of dough into each fold of foil (dough spreads during baking). Bake at 325 degrees for 25 to 30 minutes. Cool. Yields 48.

Mrs. J. C. Yarbrough, Sr.

APRICOT BALLS

11 ounces dried apricots
2 1/2 cups flaked coconut
1/2 orange
1 cup nuts, if desired

3/4 cup condensed milk
1 to 4 tablespoons
    graham cracker crumbs
Sesame seeds

Blend apricots, coconut, orange (with juice and seeds removed) and nuts by grinding very fine. Add milk. If too soft to make into balls, add graham cracker crumbs. Roll balls in toasted sesame seeds. Season 3 to 4 days. Yields 60.

Mrs. Pat B. Harris

BOURBON BALLS

2 tablespoons cocoa
1/4 cup bourbon
1 cup powdered sugar
1/2 cup powdered sugar

2 tablespoons light corn syrup
2 1/2 cups vanilla wafers
1 cup broken pecans

Sift together cocoa and sugar. Combine and stir in bourbon and syrup. Add crushed wafers and pecans. Mix thoroughly. Roll mixture into small balls. Dredge in 1/2 cup powdered sugar. Yields 24 to 36 balls.

Mrs. Robert Hunt

BLONDIES (BROWN SUGAR BAR COOKIE)

3/4 cup shortening
2 1/2 cups brown sugar
3 eggs
1 cup nuts
2 3/4 cups flour

1/2 teaspoon salt
2 1/2 teaspoons baking powder
1 small package chocolate
   chips

Melt shortening and cool. Add brown sugar and eggs, beating with mixer until well blended. Sift flour, baking powder and salt. Add to sugar mixture, blending with mixer. Stir in chocolate chips and nuts. Pour into pan. Bake at 350 degrees for 30 minutes. Cool 10 minutes. Cut in bars. Remove from pan with metal spatula. Yields 40 to 50 cookies.

Mrs. Richard Christopher, III

FUDGE BROWNIES

2 ounces bitter chocolate
1/2 stick butter
1/4 teaspoon salt
1 teaspoon vanilla

1 cup sugar
2 eggs
1/2 cup flour
1 cup nuts

Melt chocolate and butter. Add sugar, flour, and salt. Beat well. Add eggs, vanilla and nuts. Bake in a pyrex dish 25 minutes in 350 degree oven until firm, but still moist. Yields 24.

Mrs. W. M. Dillard

The difference between a rich man and a poor man, is this — the former eats when he pleases, and the latter when he can get it. — Sir Walter Raleigh

GLORIFIED BROWNIES

1/2 cup butter	2 tablespoons cocoa
1 cup sugar	1 cup nuts
2 eggs	1/4 teaspoon salt
3/4 cup flour	Marshmallows

Cream butter and sugar. Add eggs. Sift flour, cocoa and salt together. Blend with egg mixture. Add nuts. Bake in shallow pan at 350 degrees for 20 minutes or until firm on top. Cover with marshmallows and put back into warm oven until marshmallows melt. Spread marshmallows and cover with icing. To vary, cut a large marshmallow in half. Place on warm brownie and ice without spreading marshmallow. Each brownie has a mound on top. Yields 12 to 24.

ICING

1/4 cup butter	2 tablespoons cocoa
2 cups confectioners sugar	4 tablespoons evaporated milk

Heat butter, add milk. Sift cocoa and sugar into mixture and stir until creamy.

Mrs. Averett Taylor
Mrs. James P. Clamp

CARAMEL CHEWS

36 vanilla caramels
3 tablespoons light cream
1 cup corn flakes

1 cup flaked coconut
1 cup chopped nuts
1 cup Rice Krispies

Melt vanilla caramels in light cream in the top of a double boiler. Toss together corn flakes, Rice Krispies, flaked coconut, and chopped nuts. Pour caramel over mixture. With buttered spoon, drop by teaspoon on wax paper. Yields 24.

Mrs. Thomas E. Garvin

"...the last taste of sweets, is sweetest last..."
— Shakespeare

CHEWY BUTTERSCOTCH BARS

1/2 cup butter
1 1/2 cups brown sugar
2 eggs
1 teaspoon vanilla

1 1/2 cups flour
1 teaspoon baking powder
1/2 cup chopped nuts
Semi-sweet chocolate bits

Melt butter in a saucepan. Add brown sugar, packed, and bring to a boil over low heat, stirring constantly. Cool slightly. Add eggs, one at a time, and mix well. Add vanilla, sifted flour, and baking powder. Stir in nuts, if desired. Grease pans and add batter. Sprinkle the top with semi-sweet chocolate bits before baking. Bake at 350 degrees for about 30 minutes. Cut into bars when cool. Yields 48.

Mrs. John A. Holman

CHINESE CHEWS

1 cup sugar	1 cup chopped dates
1 teaspoon baking powder	1 cup English walnuts
3/4 cup flour	2 eggs
1/4 teaspoon salt	1 box powdered sugar

Mix sugar, flour, baking powder and salt. Add chopped nuts and dates. Add beaten eggs. Spread thinly on a lightly greased cookie sheet. Bake in 300 degree oven about 25 minutes. Be sure edges do not harden. Cover with foil to help prevent crusty edges. When cool enough to handle, make into balls and roll in powdered sugar. Good for drop-ins. Yields 36.

Mrs. Harold L. Murray

Young children and chickens would ever be eating.
—Thomas Tusser

CHOCOLATE BALLS

1/2 cup peanut butter	1 box powdered sugar
2 sticks margarine	1 teaspoon vanilla
1 1/2 cups graham cracker crumbs	1 large package chocolate chips
1 can coconut	2/3 cup grated parafin wax
1 cup nuts	

Melt margarine and mix with peanut butter, crumbs, sugar, coconut and nuts. Make into balls. Chill in refrigerator several hours or overnight. Melt chocolate chips and parafin wax over hot water. Dip balls into mixture with fork or toothpick. Place on wax paper. Yields 100 small balls.

Mrs. A. A. Ellison
Greenville, S. C.

CHOCOLATE DIPPED CANDY

2 boxes powdered sugar
1 can condensed milk
1 stick margarine
1 can flake coconut

1 large bag chocolate chips
1 block of parafin
1 cup pecan halves

Mix sugar, milk, margarine and coconut together and form into small balls. Place in refrigerator about one hour or overnight. Remove and dip in chocolate. Melt chocolate chips and parafin in double boiler. Dip candy very rapidly. Top with nuts (pecans). Yields 36 to 48.

Mrs. Bill Metz

CHOCOLATE-COCONUT COOKIES

2 egg whites
1/2 cup sugar
1 small package chocolate bits

1 small can flake coconut
1 cup chopped nuts
1 teaspoon vanilla

Melt chocolate bits in double boiler. Beat egg whites until frothy. Add sugar and beat until whites form peaks. Pour chocolate over egg mixture. Add vanilla and mix. Fold in coconut and nuts. Drop from spoon on greased sheet and bake at 325 degrees for 12 to 15 minutes.

Mrs. M. L. Propp

CHRISTMAS TREE KUCHEN

1 egg
3 cups packaged biscuit mix
3/4 cup milk
2 tablespoons softened butter
3 tablespoons sugar

2 teaspoons cinnamon
1/4 cup seedless raisins
  or dates
2 tablespoons chopped walnuts

Beat egg. Add biscuit mix and milk. Stir to make a stiff dough. Turn onto lightly floured board. Knead lightly until smooth. Pat out into a 12 by 8 inch pan. Spread with butter. Sprinkle with mixture of sugar and cinnamon. Top with raisins and walnuts. Then roll up in pinwheel fashion. On ungreased cookie sheet, arrange slices in shape of tree. Bake at 400 degrees for 20 minutes. Cool.

GLAZE

1/4 cup confectioners sugar 1 tablespoon milk

Glaze with mixture of sugar and milk. If desired, sprinkle with green colored sugar and maraschino cherries.

Mrs. Thomas E. Garvin

COCONUT DATE BALLS

2 eggs	6 ounces dates (chopped)
1 cup sugar	2 cups Rice Krispies
1/8 teaspoon salt	Confectioners sugar or
1 teaspoon vanilla	shredded coconut
2 tablespoons butter	

Beat eggs, sugar, salt and vanilla. Add butter and dates. Cook over low heat for 10 minutes and add Rice Krispies. Allow to cool and roll into balls. Roll in sugar or shredded coconut.

Mrs. D. S. Ellis

CHOCOLATE COOKIES

12 ounces chocolate chips	1 can sweetened condensed
1/2 stick butter	milk
1 cup flour	1 teaspoon vanilla
1 cup nuts	

Melt chocolate, milk and butter in double boiler. Blend in flour, vanilla and nuts. Drop by teaspoon on greased cookie sheet. Bake at 350 degrees for 8 to 10 minutes. Yields 60.

Mrs. T. Frank Sutherland
Greenville, S. C.

CRANBERRY SQUARES

1 cup quick oats
2/3 cup light brown sugar
1/2 cup flour
1/2 cup coconut
1/4 teaspoon salt

1/3 cup shortening
1 can whole cranberry sauce
1 tablespoon orange juice
2 teaspoons grated orange
  rind

Mix first six ingredients. Spread half of this mixture in a greased 8 inch square baking dish. Over this spread the cranberry sauce, orange juice and grated rind. Top with remainder of first mixture. Bake in 350 degree oven for 30 to 40 minutes. Cut in squares and serve warm, topped with whipped topping or vanilla ice cream. Serves 10 to 12.

Mrs. Walter Walker

DATE-NUT BARS

3 eggs
1 cup sugar
1 teaspoon vanilla
1 cup flour

1 teaspoon baking powder
1/4 teaspoon salt
1 pound pitted dates
1 quart pecan halves

Mix eggs, sugar, and vanilla. Add dry ingredients. Quarter and dredge dates in additional flour and mix with pecans. Bake in two 13 by 9 inch well greased and floured pans at 300 degrees for 30 minutes. Cool and cut into bars. Yields 40 bars.

Mrs. Robert Waldrep

DATE NUT TARTS

CRUST

8 ounces cream cheese
1 cup flour

1 stick margarine

Cream together and mold into small tart pans.

FILLING

1 cup chopped dates	1 stick butter
1 cup chopped nuts	2 eggs
1 cup sugar	1 teaspoon vanilla

Cream sugar, butter and egg yolks. Add dates and nuts. Beat egg whites and fold into cream mixture. Add vanilla. Spoon into uncooked tart shells. Bake at 350 degrees for 20 minutes. Yields 24.

Mrs. Robert Owens, Sr.
Orangeburg, S. C.

All human history attests that happiness
for man — the hungry sinner —
Since Eve ate apples, much depends on
dinner! — Byron

LIZZIES

1/4 cup margarine	1 pound white raisins
1/2 cup light brown sugar	1/2 cup bourbon
2 eggs	1 pound pecans
1 1/2 cups flour	1 pound candied cherries
1 1/2 teaspoons soda	1/2 pound candied citron
1 1/2 teaspoons cinnamon	1/2 pound candied pineapple
1/2 teaspoon cloves	

Soak raisins in bourbon overnight. Cream margarine with sugar. Add eggs one at a time. Beat well. Sift flour with soda and spices. Add raisins, chopped nuts, and chopped candied fruit mixture. Mix all together. Drop from teaspoon onto a greased cookie sheet. Cook at 325 degrees for 15 minutes. Yields 100 to 120.

Mrs. William D. McClellan
Manchester, Georgia

Mrs. Larry Kowalski
Mrs. Richard Anderson

MASHED POTATO DOUGHNUTS

1 cup potatoes
4 tablespoons butter
2 cups sugar
1/2 cup milk
3 eggs well beaten

1 teaspoon vanilla
6 cups flour
6 teaspoons baking powder
1 teaspoon salt

Cook potatoes and mash. Stir butter and sugar into hot potatoes. Add milk, eggs and vanilla flavoring. Cool. Add dry ingredients (will keep for one week in refrigerator). Roll out dough on floured pastry sheet and cut doughnuts. Let stand at room temperature 10 to 15 minutes before dropping in hot grease. They will rise to the top when done. Take care not to have cooking oil too hot or they will not cook inside. Yields 60.

Mrs. Milton Simonton
Brighton, Tennessee

And I'm sorry for people, whoever they are,
Who live in a house where there's no cookie jar.
—Edgar A. Guest

NUTTY FINGERS

1 1/3 sticks butter
5 tablespoons powdered sugar
2 cups flour

2 or 3 tablespoons ice water
1 teaspoon vanilla
1 cup nuts

Cream butter and powdered sugar. Add flour, ice water and vanilla. Blend in nuts. Form small balls and shape into finger rolls. Place on cookie sheet and bake at 300 degrees for 45 minutes. Roll in granulated or powdered sugar when cool enough to handle.

Mrs. Don Nix

OATMEAL COOKIES

3/4 cup shortening
1 cup brown sugar
1/2 cup white sugar
1 egg
1/4 cup water

1 teaspoon vanilla
1 cup sifted flour
1/2 teaspoon soda
3 cups oatmeal

Cream shortening with sugar. Blend in eggs. Add dry ingredients. Mix and drop by teaspoon on a greased cookie sheet. Bake at 350 degrees for 12 to 15 minutes. Yields 36-48.

Mrs. Theo L. Burriss

CANDIED ORANGE SLICE COOKIES

1 1/2 cups brown sugar
2 cups flour
2 eggs
Pinch of salt

1 tablespoon baking powder
9 orange slices (cut up)
1/2 cup nuts (chopped)
1/2 teaspoon vanilla

Sift together flour, baking powder, salt and brown sugar. Add remaining ingredients. Drop from teaspoon onto greased cookie sheet. Bake 10 minutes at 350 degrees. Yields 24.

Mrs. Marshall Kowalski

FROZEN ORANGE JUICE COOKIES

1 12-ounce box vanilla wafers
1 cup powdered sugar
1/4 cup melted margarine
3/4 cup chopped pecans

1/2 cup coconut
1 small can frozen orange
  juice (undiluted)

Mix all above ingredients, and roll in small balls. Dust with powdered sugar. These keep real well in the refrigerator and can be frozen. Yields 60.

Mrs. Marshall Kowalski

OREO DELIGHT

12 cream filled Oreo cookies
8 ounces dates
3/4 cup plus 2 tablespoons
   water
1/4 teaspoon salt

2 cups small marshmallows
1/2 cup chopped nuts
1 cup whipping cream
1/2 teaspoon vanilla

Sprinkle Oreo crumbs (reserve 1/4 cup) in round pie pan. Combine cubed dates, water and salt in pan. Bring to boiling. Reduce heat, and simmer four minutes. Add marshmallows. Stir until melted. Add nuts and vanilla. Spread over crumbs and chill. Then spread whipped cream over top and sprinkle with remaining crumbs. Refrigerate 24 hours before serving. Yields 8 servings.

Mrs. Preston Jones

Feast and your halls are crowded;
Fast, and the world goes by. — Ella Wheeler Wilcox

PARTY SNOWBALLS

1 cup granulated sugar
1 tablespoon white Karo syrup
1 stick margarine
1 egg, well beaten
7-ounces flaked coconut

3/4 cup pecans
1 cup chopped dates, packed
1 teaspoon vanilla
2 cups Rice Krispies

Melt margarine in a saucepan and add sugar, syrup, egg, vanilla, chopped nuts, and chopped dates. Cook this over low heat for 10 minutes, stirring constantly. Pour mixture over Rice Krispies and let cool. Roll into balls about 1 inch in diameter and then roll the balls in flake coconut. Yields 36.

Mrs. Walter Duffie

PEANUT BUTTER BALLS

1/2 cup peanut butter   1 cup powdered milk
1/2 cup honey

Combine ingredients. Roll into balls and refrigerate.

Mrs. Pat Killen

PECAN LOGS

1 tablespoon butter   2 cups sifted powdered sugar
1/4 cup light corn syrup   1 cup chopped pecans
1/2 teaspoon vanilla   14-ounces vanilla caramels
3 tablespoons dry milk   2 tablespoons cream
1/4 teaspoon salt   2 cups pecan halves

Blend butter and corn syrup. Stir in vanilla. Combine dry milk, salt and sugar. Add syrup mixture. Stir and knead until thoroughly mixed. Divide mixture into 3 equal portions and shape into rolls 6 inches long. Wrap in wax paper and chill 1 hour. Heat caramel and cream in a small saucepan over low heat until melted. Place candy roll on wax paper. Spread roll with caramel and press pecans on sides.

Mrs. James A. Smith, Jr.

PRALINE COOKIES

1/2 cup butter   1 beaten egg
1 1/2 cups brown sugar   1 1/2 cups flour
1/2 teaspoon soda   1 teaspoon vanilla

Cream butter, sugar and egg. Beat until fluffy. Add flour, baking soda and vanilla. Drop by teaspoon on greased cookie sheet. Bake at 350 degrees for 12 minutes or until golden. Yields 48.

Mrs. T. Frank Sutherland
Greenville, S. C.

PECAN TARTS-CREAM CHEESE PASTRY

3 ounces cream cheese   2 cups flour
1 stick butter

Cream cheese, butter and flour for a stiff dough. Chill in refrigerator. Cut pastry into circles. Press pastry circles inside muffin cups or tart pans.

FILLING

2 eggs   1 cup chopped nuts
1 cup sugar   1 cup raisins
1 stick butter   1 teaspoon vanilla

Cream butter and sugar and add yolks of eggs and vanilla. Mix in nuts and raisins. Beat egg whites and fold into mixture. Divide filling into 8 tart shells. Bake at 250 degrees for 1 hour, or until firm. Serves 8.

Mrs. James B. Pruitt, Jr.

PRALINE CONFECTIONS

22 double graham crackers   1 cup brown sugar
2 sticks margarine   1 cup chopped nuts

Line a 15 x 10 x 1 jelly roll pan with aluminum foil. Then line pan with crackers. Bring margarine and sugar to a rolling boil for 2 minutes. Stir and scrape down sides. Remove from heat and add nuts. Spoon over the crackers. Bake in a 325 degree oven for 18 minutes.

Mrs. Theo L. Burriss

SEVEN LAYER COOKIES

1 stick margarine   1 package butterscotch chips
1 cup graham crackers   1 can condensed milk
1 cup coconut   1 cup pecans
1 package chocolate chips

Use a 9 by 13 inch pan. Melt margarine and pour into pan. Make a layer of each of the remaining ingredients in the order listed. No mixing is necessary. Bake in 325 degree oven for 20 to 25 minutes. Cool and cut into squares.

Mrs. Charles K. Jackson

SNICKERDOODLES

2 3/4 cups flour
2 teaspoons cream of tartar
1 teaspoon baking soda
1/2 teaspoon salt
1 cup soft shortening

1 1/2 cups granulated sugar
2 eggs, unbeaten
2 tablespoons granulated sugar
2 teaspoons cinnamon

Sift together first 4 ingredients. Cream shortening with sugar and eggs until light and fluffy. At low speed, beat in flour mixture until batter is dough-like; chill until easy to handle. Start heating oven. Form dough into walnut-sized balls; roll in sugar and cinnamon mixed. Place 2 inches apart on ungreased cookie sheet. Bake at 375 degrees for 15 minutes. Yields 60.

Mrs. M. L. Propp

STIR AND DROP SUGAR COOKIES

2 eggs
2/3 cup Wesson oil
2 teaspoons vanilla
1 teaspoon lemon rind

3/4 cup sugar
2 cups flour
2 teaspoons baking powder
1/2 teaspoon salt

Beat eggs with fork until well blended. Stir in oil, vanilla, and grated lemon rind. Blend in sugar until mixture thickens. Stir flour, baking powder and salt into oil mixture. Drop with a teaspoon about 2 inches apart on ungreased cookie sheet. Flatten with greased glass dipped in sugar. Bake at 400 degrees for 8 to 10 minutes or until delicate brown. Remove immediately from baking sheet. Yields 36.

Mrs. Glenn McGee

THIN NUT WAFER

1 cup sugar
1 cup flour
1 stick margarine

1 egg
1/2 cup grated pecans

Mix sugar, flour and margarine like biscuit dough. Add egg yolk and mix well. Grease cookie sheet. Divide dough into 6 or 8 pieces and pat dough over cookie sheet. Beat egg white slightly and rub over dough. Sprinkle nuts on top. Bake at 275 degrees for around 30 minutes; take out and mark cookies into squares. Put back in oven for five minutes. Take out and remove from pan. You have to work fast!

Mrs. Jesse A. Cobb, Sr.

*"No spectacle on earth is more appealing than
a beautiful woman. . .cooking dinner for someone she loves."
— Thomas Wolfe*

TOFFEE SQUARES

1 cup butter
1 cup sugar
2 cups flour
1 egg

1 tablespoon cinnamon
1/4 teaspoon salt
1 cup chopped pecans

Cream butter, sugar, and egg yolk. Add flour, salt and cinnamon. Mix well. Spread over cookie sheet to 1/4 inch thick. Spread beaten egg white over batter. Cover with chopped nuts. Mash into batter. Bake at 375 degrees for 20 to 25 minutes. Cut while still hot and leave on cookie sheet until cool.

Mrs. Carroll Smith

PIES

FRENCH SILK CHOCOLATE PIE

1 1/2 sticks butter	2 eggs, unbeaten
1 1/2-ounces bitter chocolate	1 teaspoon vanilla
3/4 cup sugar	

Use electric mixer, medium speed. Cream butter, add sugar gradually, creaming mixture thoroughly. Blend in chocolate (melted and cooled). Add vanilla. Add eggs, one at a time, beating 5 minutes after each addition. Pour into 8" pie shell. Chill. Top with whipped cream. Serves 8.

Mrs. Strom Thurmond
Washington, D. C.

DATE-NUT ICE CREAM PIE

1 1/2 cups vanilla wafer crumbs	1/2 cup water
6 tablespoons butter	1/2 cup chopped pecans
1 cup snipped dates	1 tablespoon lemon juice
1/2 cup sugar	1 quart soft vanilla ice cream

Mix crumbs with butter. Press into 9-inch pie pan. Chill. In saucepan, combine dates, sugar, and water. Heat to boiling. Simmer five minutes. Add pecans and lemon juice to hot date mixture. Chill. Spread half of date mixture in crust. Cover with half the ice cream. Return to freezer to freeze ice cream. Repeat with remaining date filling and ice cream. Freeze. Remove from freezer five minutes before serving.

Mrs. Robert E. McNair
Columbia, S. C.

LEMON CREAM

3 eggs
2 egg yolks
1 cup plus 2 tablespoons sugar

1/2 cup butter
2 large lemons

Beat eggs and egg yolks in top of double boiler until foamy. Add sugar, butter, grated rind and juice of lemons. Cook until thickness of heavy cream, stirring occasionally. Use as filling for tarts, pie, or as parfait.

TART PASTRY

2 cups sifted flour
5 tablespoons sugar

4 large egg yolks
1/2 cup soft butter

Mound flour on board. Make well in center. Add remaining ingredients and work into a paste. Work in flour. If too dry, add a few drops of water. Knead lightly and put into refrigerator overnight. Roll dough to 1/8 inch thickness. Line tart pans. Bake in 400 degree oven 7 to 10 minutes or until lightly browned.

Mrs. John C. West
Columbia, S. C.

ANGEL PIE

4 egg whites
8 double graham crackers
Scant cup of sugar
1 cup chopped pecans

1/4 teaspoon almond extract
1/4 teaspoon salt
1 heaping teaspoon baking
   powder

Beat egg whites with salt until stiff. Fold in sugar, cracker crumbs, nut meats, flavoring, and baking powder. Grease 8-inch pie plate. Bake at 350 degrees 30 or 40 minutes until golden brown. Serve with whipped cream flavored with sherry or sherry flavoring. Serves 6.

Mrs. William F. Bolt

TANGY APPLE PIE

6 medium-sized apples
1/2 cup sugar
1/8 teaspoon salt
1 1/2 tablespoons cornstarch

1/4 teaspoon cinnamon
1/8 teaspoon nutmeg
1/3 cup orange juice
1 1/2 tablespoons butter

Cut apples into thin slices. Combine and sift dry ingredients over the apples. Stir gently until well covered. Place in 9-inch pie shell. Dot with butter; add orange juice. Cover with pricked upper crust. Bake in hot oven (450 F) for 10 minutes. Reduce to 350 degrees and bake until golden brown (45 minutes to 1 hour). Let pie cool until just warm. Serves 6 to 8.

Mrs. Marshall Walker

APPLESAUCE PIE

1 egg
1/4 cup sugar
1 tablespoon flour

2 cups applesauce
1 unbaked pie shell

Blend egg, sugar and flour in bowl. Add applesauce and blend. Pour into unbaked pie shell. Preheat oven to 350 degrees and cook for 30 minutes. Serves 4 to 6.

Mrs. D. P. Morrow

BANANA CREAM PIE

2 graham cracker crusts
1 large package Dream Whip
Sliced bananas

1 cup sugar
8-ounces cream cheese

Prepare 2 graham cracker crumb crusts. Cover each with 2 layers of sliced bananas. Beat cream cheese and sugar until smooth. Fold in whipped cream and spread over bananas. May be topped with blueberries. Makes two 8-inch pies.

Mrs. Alan Blanchard

BLUEBERRY CREAM PIE

8-ounces cream cheese
1 can condensed milk
1/3 cup lemon juice
1 teaspoon vanilla

1 can blueberry or cherry
   pie filling
1 graham cracker pie shell

Blend all ingredients, except pie filling. Pour into graham cracker shell. Chill two hours. Top with 1 can of blueberry or cherry pie-filling. Serves 4 to 6.

Mrs. Oren Jones

BLUEBERRY PIE

1 envelope Dream Whip
8-ounces cream cheese
1/2 cup sugar

3 bananas
2 baked pie shells
1 can blueberry pie filling

Mix Dream Whip according to directions. Combine cream cheese and sugar and mix with Dream Whip. Pour into baked pie shells lined with bananas. Top with can of blueberry pie filling.

Mrs. Roger Chamblee

BROWNIE PIE

3 egg whites
1/2 cup chopped nuts
Pinch of salt
3/4 cup sugar

1 teaspoon vanilla
3/4 cup chocolate wafer crumbs
1/2 pint whipping cream
1/2 teaspoon vanilla

Have egg whites at room temperature. Beat egg whites and salt until soft peaks form. Add vanilla. Fold in chocolate wafer crumbs and nuts. Put in greased pie pan and build up sides like pie crust. Bake at 325 degrees for 35 minutes. Let cool, then put on sweetened whipped cream and sprinkle chocolate crumbs on top. Chill overnight or all day. Pie will keep for 2 or 3 days. Serves 5 to 6.

Mrs. Jim Gray Watson
Mrs. Everette Newman

CHERRY PIE

1 box vanilla pudding or
  pie filling mix
1/4 cup sugar
1/4 teaspoon salt
1/2 cup water
Whipped cream

2 teaspoons lemon juice
1 pound can pitted red
  sour cherries
6 drops red food coloring
2 tablespoons butter
8-inch pie shell baked

Mix pie filling, sugar, water, salt and lemon juice in sauce pan. Add cherries and juice. Cook over medium heat until mixture comes to full boil. Remove from heat. Stir in butter and food coloring and allow to set 5 minutes. Pour in baked pie shell. Chill at least 3 hours before serving. Top with whipped cream. Serves 6.

Mrs. Robert E. Padgett, Jr.

CHOCOLATE CHESS PIE

1 square chocolate
1 stick margarine
1 cup sugar

2 eggs, beaten
1 teaspoon vanilla
1/4 teaspoon salt

Melt chocolate and margarine. Blend in other ingredients. Pour into 9-inch uncooked pie shell. Bake at 325 degrees for 30 minutes.

Mrs. Furman Walter

CHOCOLATE PIE

1 cup sugar
2 eggs, separated
4 tablespoons flour
2 cups milk

1 teaspoon vanilla
1 tablespoon butter
2 tablespoons cocoa
4 tablespoons sugar

Mix sugar and flour. Beat in egg yolks. Add milk and cocoa. Cook over medium heat until thick. Add butter and vanilla flavoring. Cool and pour into pie crust. Beat egg whites with 4 tablespoons sugar. Bake 10 minutes at 325 degrees.

Mrs. Jerry Gillespie

CHOCOLATE CREAM PIE

3/4 cup sugar
7 tablespoons flour
2 level tablespoons cocoa
3 eggs, separated
1/4 teaspoon salt

2 1/2 cups milk
1 teaspoon vanilla
2 tablespoons margarine
1/4 teaspoon salt
6 tablespoons sugar

Combine sugar, flour, cocoa, salt and milk. Cook over medium heat until thickened. Add small amount to beaten egg yolks. Return to chocolate mixture: Cook until thick. Add margarine and put into cooked pastry. Beat egg whites and salt until frothy. Beat in 6 tablespoons sugar, one at a time. Beat until the meringue is stiff and glossy. Bake in 350 degree oven for 12 to 15 minutes. Serves 8.

Mrs. Gerald Welborn

CHOCOLATE MERINGUE PIE

3 1-ounce squares unsweetened
  chocolate
1 tablespoon butter
6 tablespoons flour
1 cup sugar
1 teaspoon vanilla

1/4 teaspoon salt
1 1/2 cups hot water
1 cup evaporated milk
3 well beaten egg yolks
1 baked pastry shell
Whipped cream or meringue

Melt chocolate over hot, not boiling water, in top of double boiler. Add butter, flour, sugar and salt. Blend. Gradually stir in hot water. Add milk. Cook until mixture is thick and smooth, about 20 minutes, stirring constantly. Add small amount of hot chocolate mixture to egg yolks. Stir into remaining hot chocolate mixture. Cook 2 or 3 minutes. Cool. Add vanilla. Pour filling into cooled baked pastry shell. Cover with whipped cream or meringue. Make meringue with 3 egg whites and 6 tablespoons sugar. Serves 6.

Mrs. J. Roy Martin, Jr.

CHOCOLATE-NUT ANGEL PIE

1/2 cup sugar
1/8 teaspoon cream of tartar

2 egg whites
1/2 cup chopped nuts

Sift sugar and cream of tartar together. Beat egg whites until stiff but not dry. Add sugar mixture until meringue is stiff. Fold in nuts. Butter a 9-inch pie plate and fill with meringue. Bake at 275 degrees 1 hour. Cool.

FILLING

3/4 cup semi-sweet chocolate
3 tablespoons hot water

1 teaspoon vanilla
1 cup whipping cream

Melt chocolate pieces in double boiler. Add hot water and cook until thickened. Cool slightly. Mixture will become thick. Add vanilla. Fold whipped cream into chocolate. Combine well but do not beat. Pour into meringue shell and chill 2 to 3 hours. Serves 8 to 10.

Mrs. E. L. Menees
Columbia, S. C.

BLACK BOTTOM PIE

1 1/2 squares chocolate
2 cups milk
1/4 teaspoon salt
1/4 teaspoon cream of tartar

1 1/4 tablespoons cornstarch
1 cup sugar
4 eggs, separated
1 tablespoon gelatin

Melt chocolate. Scald milk. Mix 1/2 of the sugar with the cornstarch and salt. Add to scalded milk. Cook 15 minutes. Add yolks and cook until thick. Add one cup of the filling to the melted chocolate and add the rest to the gelatin. Strain. Cool until nearly set. Beat egg whites with cream of tartar and sugar until stiff. Fold into the yellow mixture. Put a layer of the chocolate filling into a pie shell made of ginger snaps and butter, then a layer of the yellow mixture. Top with whipped cream and grated chocolate.

Mrs. Bob King

COCONUT PIE

3 beaten eggs
1 1/2 cups sugar
1/2 cup butter
4 teaspoons lemon juice

1 teaspoon vanilla
3 1/2-ounces or 1 1/3
  cups flaked coconut
1 unbaked pastry shell

Combine eggs, sugar, melted butter or margarine, lemon juice and vanilla. Stir in coconut. Pour into unbaked shell. Bake in moderate oven (350 degrees) for 40 minutes or until a knife inserted just off center comes out clean. Cool before serving.

Mrs. J. C. Yarbrough, Sr.

COCONUT CREAM PIE

1 1/2 cups sugar
1 stick margarine
4 eggs beaten
1 teaspoon vanilla

1 cup canned milk
1 cup whole milk
1 cup coconut

Melt margarine and blend in sugar and eggs. Add vanilla, milk and coconut. Mix well. Pour into 2 unbaked pastry lined pie pans. Cook in 350 degree oven for 30 to 35 minutes.

Mrs. James P. Clamp

CROWN JEWEL JELLO PIE

1 box black cherry Jello
1 box raspberry Jello
1 box lime Jello
1/4 cup sugar

1 cup pineapple juice
1 box strawberry Jello
1 pint cream
2 or 3 packages Lady Fingers

Prepare separately 1 package raspberry, lime and black cherry Jello, using 1 cup hot water and 1/2 cup iced water for each package. Pour into 3 shallow pans and congeal until firm (overnight if possible). Cut into cubes. Make filling by heating 1/4 cup sugar with 1 cup pineapple juice to boiling point. Dissolve 1 package strawberry Jello in hot liquid. Add 1/2 cup cold water to filling mixture. Chill until syrupy. Whip one pint cream. Fold in Jello mixture. Fold in Jello jewels (cubes). Line 2 10-inch pie plates with lady fingers and fill with mixture. Serves 16.

Mrs. Robert S. Owens, Jr.

VIRGIN ISLANDS DAIQUIRI PIE

1 cup sugar	1 tablespoon butter
3 tablespoons cornstarch	9-inch pie shell baked
1/8 teaspoon salt	4 egg whites
1 cup water	1/4 teaspoon salt
1/4 cup lime juice	1/2 cup sugar
1/4 cup rum (Myer's Jamaican)	Green food coloring
4 egg yolks	Pastry shell

Combine 1 cup sugar, cornstarch and salt. Add water, juice, and beaten egg yolks. Stir constantly until thick and smooth. Add rum toward last. Tint delicate green. Cool and spoon into pastry shell. Beat egg whites with 1/4 teaspoon salt until foamy. Drizzle sugar gradually. Top pie and bake in oven (350 degrees) about 15 minutes.

Miss Carolyn Hodges

EXQUISITE PIE

1 cup sugar	1 teaspoon vinegar
1/2 cup butter	1 cup nuts (pecan)
1/2 teaspoon cinnamon	1 cup raisins
1/2 teaspoon nutmeg	2 eggs
Whipped cream	Pie shell

Cream butter with sugar. Add 1 egg at a time while beating. Add other ingredients. Pour in unbaked pie shell. Bake in a slow oven (300 degrees) for 45 minutes to 1 hour. Serve warm with whipped cream. Serves 6 to 8.

Mrs. Curtis Gillespie

BUTTERMILK LEMON PIE

2 cups sugar
3 tablespoons flour
1/4 teaspoon nutmeg
1/2 cup melted butter

1 cup buttermilk
3 large eggs
Rind and juice of lemon
1 unbaked pie crust

Mix sugar, flour and nutmeg. Add melted butter and beat until creamy. Add eggs, one at a time. Mix in milk and lemon. Pour in uncooked 10-inch crust. Bake at 400 degrees for 10 minutes and at 325 degrees for 30 minutes. Serves 6.

Mrs. Sam T. Haddock

LEMON MERINGUE PIE

1 baked pie shell
1 1/4 cups sugar
6 tablespoons cornstarch
1/8 teaspoon salt
2 cups boiling water

1 teaspoon grated lemon rind
1/4 cup margarine
3 eggs, separated
1/2 cup lemon juice

Mix sugar, cornstarch, salt, boiling water and lemon rind. Heat slowly, stirring until smooth. Cook over low heat until thickened and no taste of cornstarch remains — about 15 minutes. Remove from heat and add margarine. Beat egg yolks slightly and add lemon juice. Add hot mixture slowly. Return to heat and cook, stirring constantly for 5 to 7 minutes. Do not boil. Fill pie shell and cover with meringue. Bake at 425 degrees for 5 minutes or until brown. Serves six.

Mrs. Joe Prevost, Jr.

MERINGUE ANGEL PIE

1 3/4 cups sugar
2 lemons
1 pint whipping cream
4 eggs
1/2 cup sugar

1 teaspoon vanilla
1 teaspoon vinegar
1 pint strawberries
3 tablespoons lemon juice
1 tablespoon lemon rind

Separate eggs and beat the whites until stiff, but not dry. Slowly add 1 3/4 cups sugar. Add 1 teaspoon vinegar and 1 teaspoon vanilla. Beat until meringue forms stiff peaks. Grease brown paper and place on cookie sheet. Place about 1/2 cup meringue on paper. Scoop out center. Bake in oven for 1 hour at 275 degrees or until light brown (may be stored in oven until convenient to prepare filling). Beat egg yolks in double boiler, stir in 1/2 cup sugar, lemon juice and lemon rind. Cook until thickened. Cool. Whip 1 cup of cream. Fold into lemon mixture. Place filling in shells. Refrigerate (overnight if possible). Just before serving, top with whipped cream and strawberries.

Mrs. Richard G. Christopher III

MINCE WHIP PIE

1 package Whip 'n Chill
Vanilla dessert mix
1/2 cup cold milk
1/3 cup cold water

1/2 cup cold sour cream
1 cup moist mincemeat
1 unbaked 9-inch crumb crust
1 envelope Dream Whip

Combine dessert mix and milk. Blend thoroughly. Whip at high speed for 1 minute. Blend in water and sour cream. Whip at high speed about 2 minutes. If necessary, chill until mixture will mound, about 10 minutes. Fold in mincemeat. Spoon into crust. Chill 2 hours or more. Top with prepared Dream Whip.

Mrs. Douglas McDougald, Jr.

LIME JELLO PIE

16 graham crackers
1 stick butter
1 package lime Jello
1/2 pint whipping cream

1 cup sugar
2 lemons
1 can evaporated milk

Mix crackers and butter and press into pie plate. Dissolve Jello in 1 cup boiling water. Add sugar and juice from lemons. Cool. Pour into crust. Chill until firm. Top with whipped cream. Serves 9.

Mrs. Newton J. Newell, Sr.

MUSCATEL PIE

22 large marshmallows
1/2 cup muscatel wine
1/2 pint whipping cream

Fresh nutmeg
Slivered almonds
8 pastry shells

Melt marshmallows and muscatel wine in a double boiler, and let cool. Whip the cream and fold into marshmallow mixture. Sprinkle with freshly ground nutmeg and slivered almonds. Refrigerate. Prepare a day ahead. Serves 8.

Mrs. Ted Owen

OATMEAL PIE

3 eggs
2/3 cup sugar
1 cup brown sugar
2/3 cup uncooked oatmeal

2/3 cup flaked coconut
2 tablespoons butter
1 teaspoon vanilla
1 unbaked pie shell

Mix well beaten eggs, sugar, brown sugar, oatmeal, coconut, butter, and vanilla. Pour this mixture into unbaked pie shell. Bake 45 minutes at 350 degrees.

Mrs. Charles K. Jackson

FRESH PEACH PIE

2 eggs
1/2 cup brown sugar
3/4 cup sugar
Favorite pastry crust

1/4 cup butter
2 tablespoons flour
1/2 teaspoon vanilla
3 cups fresh sliced peaches

Bake crust in oven a few minutes until it looks glazed. Cover bottom of pastry with fresh sliced peaches and sprinkle with 1/2 cup sugar. Cook until tender (about 15 minutes). Beat eggs. Add sugar, butter, flour and vanilla. Mix well and pour over peaches. Bake at 350 degrees for 25 minutes or until set. Serves 6.

Mrs. Athen R. Morris, Jr.

PECAN PIE

1/2 cup margarine
1/2 cup granulated sugar
3/4 cup white corn syrup
1/4 cup maple syrup

3 eggs slightly beaten
1 teaspoon vanilla flavoring
2 cups pecans
1 unbaked pie shell

Cream margarine and sugar together until light and creamy (adding sugar slowly to margarine). Stir in syrups. Beat eggs and add to mixture. Add vanilla and blend well. Add chopped nuts. Stir well. Pour into unbaked pie shell (9-inch). Bake at 325 degrees for 1 hour. Cool and serve with ice cream.

Mrs. James Halford, Jr.

PECAN PIE

3 egg whites
1 teaspoon baking powder
1 cup sugar
1 teaspoon vanilla

12 graham crackers
1 cup broken pecans
1/2 pint whipping cream

Beat egg whites until stiff. Add sugar and baking powder slowly. Add vanilla, crushed crackers, and nuts. Pour into 9-inch pie plate. Cook at 350 degrees for 30 minutes. Cool and top with 1/2 pint cream, whipped. Place in refrigerator for at least 2 hours before serving. Serves 6.

Mrs. William M. Dunn, Jr.

SUMMER PECAN PIE

20 Ritz crackers
1 cup sugar
1 cup chopped pecans

3 egg whites
1 teaspoon vanilla
1/2 pint whipping cream

Mix the cracker crumbs, nuts and half of the sugar. Beat the eggs until stiff and add the remaining sugar and vanilla; fold into cracker, nut and sugar mixture. Pour into buttered pie pan and bake at 350 degrees for 20 to 25 minutes. Chill and top with whipped cream.

Mrs. Foster F. McConnell

PINEAPPLE CHIFFON PIE

1 cup sugar	1 package lemon Jello
2 cups pineapple juice	1 large can Pet milk
2 eggs	2 cracker crumb crusts

In saucepan bring to boil: 1 cup sugar, 2 cups pineapple juice, 2 eggs slightly beaten. Then add 1 package lemon Jello and let cool. Have 1 large can Pet milk chilled. Whip canned milk and add to other ingredients. Pour into crusts. Chill. Makes 2 large pies.

Mrs. W. L. Hendrix
Greenwood, South Carolina

What moistens the lip,
And what brightens the eye,
What calls back the past
Like rich pumpkin pie?
—John Greenleaf Whittier

NEW JERSEY PUMPKIN PIE

2 eggs	1/4 teaspoon allspice
1/8 teaspoon mace	1/2 teaspoon salt
1 cup sugar	1/2 teaspoon cinnamon
1/8 teaspoon ginger	1/4 teaspoon nutmeg
1 tablespoon butter (heaping)	2 cups canned pumpkin
1/2 cup milk	

Line 1 large pie plate or 2 small aluminum foil pie plates with pastry (frozen pie crust shells may be used). Beat eggs well. Add mace, sugar, ginger, allspice, salt, cinnamon, nutmeg and soft or melted butter. Mix these well with canned pumpkin (fresh pumpkin is too watery). Add milk last. Bake in moderate oven (350 to 375 degrees) in same manner as custard pie and test in same way with silver knife. Crust should be medium brown when done. Yields 1 large or 2 small pies.

Mrs. Sam J. Fretwell

MILE HIGH RASPBERRY PIE

1 stick soft butter	10 ounces frozen raspberries
1/4 cup brown sugar	1 cup sugar
1 cup all-purpose flour	3 unbeaten egg whites
1/2 cup chopped almonds	1 cup whipping cream

Mix and spread first four ingredients in an 8-inch square pan and bake at 400 degrees for 15 minutes. Cool, crumble and press into pie pan. Beat the next 3 ingredients at high speed for 15 minutes. Fold in whipped cream. Pour in pie shell and freeze overnight. Serves 8.

Mrs. William Rutledge

RUM CREAM PIE WITH GRAHAM CRACKER CRUST

6 egg yolks	1/4 cup cold water
3/4 cup sugar	1 pint heavy cream (whipped)
1 tablespoon gelatin	1/2 cup rum

Beat egg yolks and sugar until light. Put gelatin in cold water and place over boiling water, until melted. Pour into egg mixture. Add rum and fold in whipped cream. Pour into graham cracker crust. Place in refrigerator to set.

Mrs. Robert Gallant
Mrs. Richard Shawn

QUICK AND EASY PIE

1/2 gallon vanilla ice milk	1 graham cracker pie crust
1 small can frozen lemonade	

Soften ice milk. Blend in lemonade. Pour into pie crust. Put in freezer until frozen. Makes one pie.

Mrs. Jack Cobb

STRAWBERRY PIE

Two pie shells
1 can condensed milk
1/3 cup lemon juice
2 packages Dream Whip

1 small package frozen
  strawberries
1/2 teaspoon vanilla

Add lemon juice to condensed milk. Fold in strawberries (keep out a few of the best ones to put on top of pie). Fold in one package of Dream Whip (whipped). Add 1/2 teaspoon vanilla. Pour into cooled pie shells. Top with remaining package of Dream Whip. Chill and serve. Makes 2 pies.

Mrs. Marshall C. Kowalski

STRAWBERRY CREAM CHEESE PIE

9-inch baked pie shell
1/2 pint strawberries
1/2 cup sugar

1 1/2 tablespoons cornstarch
2 teaspoons butter
10 drops red food color

In medium saucepan crush strawberries with potato masher or fork. Combine sugar and the cornstarch. Stir into crushed strawberries. Add 1/4 cup water. Cook over medium heat until thick, stirring constantly. Strain. Add butter and food coloring. Cool at room temperature.

FILLING

1/2 pint strawberries
8-ounce cream cheese
1/3 cup sugar
1 teaspoon orange peel

2 tablespoons orange juice
2 tablespoons cream
1 cup heavy cream

In medium bowl with electric mixer beat softened cream cheese, sugar, orange peel and juice and cream well until well combined and smooth. Spread in baked, cooled pie shell. Refrigerate 1 hour. Arrange strawberries, stem end down, evenly over cream cheese mixture. Pour cooled glaze over berries. Refrigerate until well chilled, about 3 hours. Top with whipped cream and refrigerate until served. Serves 6.

Mrs. Cliff Bryant

PEACH ALMOND UPSIDE DOWN PIE

2 tablespoons soft butter
2/3 cup almonds
1/3 cup brown sugar
5 cups fresh peaches
3/4 cup sugar

1/4 cup brown sugar
4 tablespoons flour
1/2 teaspoon nutmeg
1/4 teaspoon cinnamon

Line 9-inch pie pan with 12 inch foil. Spread butter. Press nuts and 1/3 cup brown sugar into butter. Mix rest of ingredients; pour into pastry shell. Brush lightly with milk. Bake at 450 degrees for 10 minutes; turn oven to 375 for 35 to 40 minutes. Cool slightly and turn. Serves 6.

Mrs. Larry Kowalski

ENGLISH WALNUT PIE

3 egg whites
1 cup sugar
1 teaspoon vanilla
1/2 cup whipping cream

3/4 cup crushed saltines
3/4 cup walnuts or pecans
1 teaspoon baking powder

Butter pie pan. Beat egg whites until stiff. Slowly add sugar and continue beating until stiff. Add crushed saltines and remaining ingredients. Put in pie pan and bake at 325 degrees for 35 minutes. Allow to cool and top with whipped cream. Garnish with chocolate slivers and refrigerate. Serves 6.

Mrs. James H. Barton

NEVER FAIL PIE CRUST

1 1/2 cups sifted flour
1/2 cup shortening

1/2 teaspoon salt
5 tablespoons cold water

Blend ingredients together until crumbly. Roll out. Bake at 350 degrees for 7 minutes or until brown. Makes 2 pie crusts.

Mrs. Marshall Kowalski

MISCELLANEOUS DESSERTS

APPLE SQUARES

1 1/2 cups Wesson Oil
2 cups sugar
3 well beaten eggs
3 cups chopped fresh
  apples (not too fine)

1 cup nuts chopped
3 cups plain flour (sifted)
1 teaspoon salt
1 teaspoon soda
2 teaspoons vanilla

Combine oil and sugar. Add eggs, apples and nuts. Mix well, then add flour, salt, soda and vanilla. Bake in 13x9x2 pan for 45 minutes at 325 degrees.

TOPPING

1/2 cup margarine
1 cup brown sugar

1/4 cup canned milk
1 teaspoon vanilla

Mix margarine and sugar over heat. Beat until melted. Add milk and bring to a full boil. Cool, add vanilla and pour over warm cake.

Miss Sylvene King
Mrs. Mabel Marshall

CREAMY CHOCOLATE FUDGE

2 cups sugar
3 tablespoons cocoa
1/2 cup light corn syrup
1 cup cream

2 tablespoons butter
1/2 teaspoon vanilla
1 cup chopped nuts
2 tablespoons marshmallow creme

Combine sugar, cocoa, corn syrup, cream and butter. Boil to soft ball stage (238 degrees). Remove from heat. Add vanilla and marshmallow creme. Cool without stirring 10 to 15 minutes. Beat. Add nuts, and pour into greased pan. Cool and cut. Yields 24 pieces.

Mrs. Julian M. Smith, Jr.
Charleston, S. C.

"I have been sent to procure an angel to do cooking."
—Emerson

CHOCOLATE FUDGE

2 cups light brown sugar
2 cups white sugar
1/2 cup dark Karo syrup
1 cup evaporated milk
2 1/2 squares bitter chocolate

1/4 teaspoon salt
1 stick margarine
1/2 cup nuts
1 teaspoon vanilla

Mix sugar, syrup, milk and chocolate in saucepan. Stir until chocolate begins to melt over medium heat. Allow to cook without stirring until mixture reaches 240 degrees on candy thermometer. Remove from heat and add margarine. When cooled, add nuts and vanilla. Beat at high speed for several minutes until mixture is creamy. Pour into a well greased pan, about 8 by 12 inches. Cut into squares when hard. Yields 40 pieces.

Mrs. Robert F. Coble, Jr.

FUDGE

5 cups sugar
2 sticks margarine
1 large can Carnation milk
1/4 teaspoon salt

1 jar marshmallow creme
3 packages chocolate chips
2 teaspoons vanilla

Combine first four ingredients, stirring constantly. Boil 6 minutes. Remove from heat and add marshmallow creme, chocolate chips and vanilla. Blend until smooth. Pour into 2 greased pans. Cool and cut. Yields 5 pounds.

Mrs. Ben J. Smith

MRS. KING'S ORANGE CANDY

3 cups sugar
1/2 cup milk
1/2 cup orange juice
4 cups pecan halves

3 orange rinds cut into
  small strips
1 tablespoon vanilla

Boil sugar, milk and orange juice to soft boil stage. Add chopped nuts. Cut orange rind into small strips and add. Beat all together. Add vanilla. Drop by spoonsful onto buttered pan or waxed paper. Yields 48.

Mrs. T. Ed Garrison

CHOCOLATE ECLAIRS

PASTRY

1 cup water
1 stick oleo

1 cup sifted flour
4 eggs

Heat water and oleo to boiling point. Add flour and stir constantly until mixture forms a ball. Remove from heat and let cool. Beat in eggs one at a time. Drop dough from teaspoon to form small eclairs on ungreased cookie sheet. Cook at 400 degrees for 30 minutes or until lightly browned. Cool slowly away from draft.

FILLING

3 cups rich milk
3/4 cup sugar
1/2 teaspoon salt

6 tablespoons flour
3 whole eggs
2 teaspoons vanilla

Combine milk, sugar, salt and flour. Cook slowly until thick. Add beaten eggs and cook until even thicker. When cool, add vanilla. Cut off the tops of puffs and add the custard mixture. Replace tops.

ICING

2 1-ounce squares baking
   chocolate

2 cups sugar
1 cup cream

Melt chocolate; add sugar and cream. Cook over medium heat until soft ball stage is reached. Cool, then beat. Put icing on the eclairs. Yields 12 large eclairs or 60 to 70 miniature eclairs.

Mrs. Arthur Klugh

HEAVENLY CHOCOLATE DESSERT

1 large angel food cake
2 packages chocolate chips
4 egg yolks
4 egg whites

1 pint cream
Nuts, if desired
1/2 cup sugar

Melt chips in double boiler. Remove when entirely melted and add well beaten egg yolks. Whip cream stiff and add 1/2 cup sugar. Beat egg whites stiff. Add cream to chocolate mix gradually. Fold in egg whites. Break up cake into bite size cubes. Add nuts if desired. Place in large buttered casserole dish and chill. May be made several days ahead and can be topped with whipped cream when served, if desired. Serves 8.

Mrs. Bruce Salley

CHOCOLATE SAUCE

1 1/2 cups sugar
2 tablespoons butter
4 1-ounce squares chocolate

1 cup heavy cream
1 teaspoon vanilla or
2 teaspoons cognac

Combine sugar, butter, and chocolate in the top of a double boiler. When chocolate is melted, add cream and flavoring. Serve hot. Yields about 2 1/2 cups.

Mrs. W. F. Bolt

BAKED ALASKA

1 8-inch layer cake
3 egg whites

1/2 cup sugar
1 quart firm ice cream

Beat egg whites until foamy. Add sugar and beat until stiff, but not dry. Place cake on heavy unfinished wooden tray or heat proof platter. Spoon ice cream on the cake leaving a one inch border all around. Cover ice cream and cake completely with egg white meringue. Brown meringue lightly in a hot oven (500 degrees) for 2 minutes. Serves 8.

Mrs. Fritz Waidner

FLUMMERY

1 large package cherry gelatin
1 cup wine or sherry

1/2 pint whipping cream

Mix gelatin according to directions on box, omitting one cup of water and substituting one cup of wine or sherry. Put gelatin in refrigerator; when it begins to congeal, whip in 1/2 pint whipping cream. Return to refrigerator until firm. Serves 8.

Mrs. Allan P. Sloan, Jr.

240

HOMEMADE ICE CREAM

1 1/2 cups sugar
3 eggs
1 large can evaporated milk

2 quarts homogenized milk
2 teaspoons vanilla flavoring

Mix sugar and eggs until creamy. Add cream, milk and flavoring. Peaches, strawberries, bananas or pineapples may be added for flavors. Freeze until firm following churning instructions. Yields 1/2 gallon.

Mrs. Bobby W. McAlister

PEACH ICE CREAM

1/2 pint whipping cream
1 quart milk
1 Number 303 can
    evaporated milk

1 teaspoon vanilla
3 eggs
2 cups sugar
4 cups peaches

Put cream, milk and vanilla in bowl. Beat eggs and sugar until fluffy. Add peaches to eggs and mix well. Blend egg and peach mixture with milk. Chill in refrigerator and then place in ice cream churn. Finish in accordance with churn instructions. Yields 1 gallon.

Mrs. Earle Maxwell

MINT PARFAIT

16 marshmallows
3/4 cups milk
3-ounce bottle creme
    de menthe cherries

5 drops peppermint extract
1/2 pint whipping cream

Steam marshmallows and milk over hot water until smooth. Add chopped cherries, juice and peppermint. Cool. When slightly stiffened, combine carefully with beaten cream. Pour into tray and freeze without stirring. Serve in parfait glasses. Serves 4 to 6.

Mrs. Bill Holloway
Mobile, Alabama

ORANGE HALVES WITH ORANGE SHERBET

Cut oranges in half, removing juice and pulp. Fill with orange sherbet. The halves may be fitted together and left in deep freeze for a few days. Serve with meal.

Mrs. Beaty Jackson

FLAMING PEACHES

12 canned peach halves   1 cup brandy

Preheat top pan of chafing dish. Arrange drained peach halves, cut side down, in the pan. Pour brandy into ladle, light, and flame peaches with it. Serves 6.

Mrs. Fritz Waidner

FRENCH PINEAPPLE DESSERT

1 pound vanilla wafers   1 cup pecans
1/2 cup butter   1 cup crushed pineapple
2 cups powdered sugar   1 small bottle
4 eggs   maraschino cherries
1/2 pint whipping cream

Crush wafers and put 1/2 of the crumbs in 9 by 13 pan. Cream butter with powdered sugar. Add the eggs one at a time, beating well. Pour mixture over the wafer crumbs and smooth out. Whip cream. Drain pineapple and chop cherries and nuts. Mix fruit and nuts with cream and pour over sugar and egg mixture. Sprinkle wafer crumbs over the top. Refrigerate for 24 hours. Serves 8 to 12.

Mrs. James W. Smith

FROSTY STRAWBERRY SQUARES

1 cup all-purpose flour	2 egg whites
1/4 cup brown sugar	1 cup granulated sugar
1/2 cup chopped walnuts	2 cups sliced fresh
1/2 cup butter	strawberries
1 cup whipping cream	2 tablespoons lemon juice

Stir together first 4 ingredients. Spread evenly in shallow baking pan. Bake in 350 degree oven for 20 minutes, stirring occasionally. Sprinkle 2/3 of the crumb mixture in 13 x 9 x 2 inch baking pan. Combine egg whites, sugar, berries and lemon juice in large bowl. With electric mixer, beat at high speed to stiff peaks, about 10 minutes. Fold in whipped cream. Spoon over crumbs; top with remaining crumbs. Freeze 6 hours or overnight. Cut in squares, trim with whole strawberries. One 10-ounce package partially thawed strawberries may be used; cut sugar to 2/3 cups. Serves 12.

Mrs. Wilburn Gable

FROZEN DATE DELIGHT

8 1/2 ounces crushed pineapple	8 ounces cream cheese
2 tablespoons sugar	8 ounces imported dates
1/2 cup pecans	1 cup whipping cream

Drain pineapple and reserve 1/4 cup of juice. Gradually add juice and sugar to softened cream cheese. Beat until fluffy. Chop dates and nuts. Blend nuts, pineapple and dates and add to cream cheese mixture. Whip cream and fold into date cream mixture. Spoon into 8 by 8 inch pan or 8 individual molds. Cut into squares or unmold to serve. Omit sugar if used as a salad. Serves 7 to 9.

Mrs. F. Spencer Shirley

HOT FRUIT CASSEROLE

1 cup sliced pineapple
1 cup pears
1 cup peaches
1 cup apricots
1 jar apple rings

1/4 cup butter
1/2 cup sugar
2 tablespoons flour
1 cup sherry

Drain fruit. Put in casserole. In double boiler,heat butter, sugar, flour and sherry until thick as cream. Pour over fruit and let stand at least overnight. Heat when ready to serve. (You might use any fruit.) Serves 12.

Mrs. V. E. Merchant, Jr.

APPLE CRISP

6 tart cooking apples
1/8 teaspoon salt
1 teaspoon lemon rind
1 tablespoon lemon juice
1/2 cup flour

1/2 cup brown sugar
1/4 cup shortening
1/4 teaspoon salt
1/2 teaspoon cinnamon
1/2 pint whipping cream

Pare, core and slice apples into thin slices. Place in greased 8 x 8 inch pan. Sprinkle with salt, grated lemon rind and juice. Blend flour, sugar and shortening until crumbly. Add salt and cinnamon. Sprinkle crumbly mixture over apples. Bake at 350 degrees for 45 minutes until apples are tender and top brown. Serve warm with whipped cream.

Mrs. Thomas R. Gaines

APRICOT JAM STRUDEL

2 sticks butter
2 1/2 cups flour
1/2 teaspoon salt
1 cup sour cream

10-ounces apricot jam
1 cup shredded coconut
2/3 cup nuts
2/3 cup powdered sugar

Cream butter, flour and salt. Add sour cream. Put in refrigerator overnight. Let stand until room temperature, then cut dough in half and roll each piece in rectangle, measuring 10 x 15. Spread with jam, sprinkle with coconut and nuts. Roll like jelly roll. Place on greased baking sheet with powdered sugar. Cut and serve. Yields 24.

Mrs. Reuben Seigel

CHERRY DESSERT

1 Number 303 can sour cherries
1 package cherry gelatin
1 cup sugar

2 eggs
2 cups graham cracker crumbs
1/2 cup nuts

Drain juice from cherries and heat. Dissolve gelatin in juice. Beat egg whites until stiff. Set aside. Add sugar to beaten yolks. Add yolks to juice mixture. Stir in graham cracker crumbs, nuts, beaten egg whites and cherries. Place in refrigerator until firm. Cut in squares. Serve with Dream Whip. Serves 6 to 8.

Mrs. Robert C. Herndon

CHERRIES JUBILEE

2 cans Bing cherries
1/2 jar currant jelly
3/4 cup brandy

Salted toasted almonds
1/2 gallon ice cream

Remove pits from cherries. Heat cherries and jelly. Add brandy. Light match and let it flame for a minute. Spoon over ice cream and sprinkle almonds on top. Serves 8.

Mrs. Don King

EASY FRUIT COBBLER

1 cup flour
2 teaspoons baking powder
3/4 cup sugar
3/4 cup milk

1 stick butter
2 cups sweetened fruit
(peaches, cherries, etc.)

Melt butter in baking dish. Mix flour, baking powder, sugar, and milk. Pour batter in baking dish, but do not stir. Pour fruit in middle of batter. Bake for 1 hour at 325 degrees. Serves 4.

Mrs. Iola Patterson

EASY PEACH DESSERT

1 cup sugar
1 stick butter
2 eggs

3/4 cup flour
1 teaspoon vanilla
2 cups peaches

Cream sugar and butter. Add eggs and stir. Blend in flour and vanilla. Slice peaches and place in casserole dish. Cover with batter. Bake at 300 degrees for 1 hour. Serves 8.

Mrs. Patrick Killen

LEMON BISQUE

1 cup evaporated milk
1 package lemon gelatin
1 cup boiling water
1/2 cup sugar

1/8 teaspoon salt
Juice and rind of 2 lemons
2 1/2 cups vanilla wafer crumbs

Chill milk in refrigerator. Dissolve gelatin in boiling water. Add sugar, salt, lemon juice and rind. Place in refrigerator until slightly congealed. Beat milk until stiff and whip gelatin mixture into it. Spread half of crumbs in a large pan (10" by 13 1/2"). Pour lemon mixture over it. Top with remaining crumbs and put in refrigerator or freezer to chill. Serves 12.

Mrs. Vic Chapman

LEMON DELIGHT

1 large angel cake
1/2 pint whipping cream

10 tablespoons lemon juice
1 can sweetened condensed milk

Mix lemon juice and condensed milk. Crumble cake and mix with 3/4 of the milk mixture. Whip cream and fold 3/4 of it into cake mixture. Spread in a 9 by 9 inch pan. Spread remaining milk mixture on top. Then cover with remaining whipped cream. Cut into squares and top with a cherry. Serves 12.

Mrs. H. G. Anderson

*Tis an ill cook that cannot lick
his own fingers. — Shakespeare*

LEMON TORTE

8 egg whites
1 1/2 cups sugar
3 teaspoons vinegar
1 teaspoon vanilla

8 egg yolks
1 cup sugar
1/2 cup butter
Juice and rind of 3 lemons

Beat egg whites until very stiff. Fold sugar gradually into egg whites. Add vinegar and vanilla. When thoroughly mixed, spoon into torte pan with removable side and bake at 350 degrees until mixture reaches top of pan. Reduce heat to about 250 degrees and bake 40 minutes. Top should be light brown when done. Let cool in pan and cover with following, cooked together: egg yolks, sugar, butter, juice and grated rind of lemons.

Mrs. V. E. Merchant, Jr.

ARAAC PUDDING

12 almond macaroons
1/2 cup butter
1/2 cup sugar
3 eggs

1 teaspoon unflavored gelatin
1 1/2 teaspoons rum flavoring
1 teaspoon vanilla
1/2 pint whipping cream

Crumble macaroons. Melt sugar and butter in a double boiler. Add beaten egg yolks and stir until thick. Add gelatin and stir until dissolved. Then add macaroons. Remove from heat and cool. Fold in well beaten egg whites. Add rum and vanilla. Place in glass dish and refrigerate. Serve small helpings as this is very rich. Top with whipped cream. Serves 8.

Mrs. Joe Ben McGill

BOILED CUSTARD

2 eggs
1/2 cup sugar

2 cups milk

Beat eggs until frothy, then add sugar. Heat milk and add to eggs. Stir until it thickens and coats the spoon. Do not overcook or it will lump. To be used over Jello or cake, etc., or drunk warm. Yields 2 cups.

Mrs. Robert E. Jones

BUTTERSCOTCH ICE BOX SURPRISE

2 cups chocolate crumbs
4 tablespoons melted butter
2 tablespoons sugar

1 box butterscotch pudding mix
2 1/2 cups milk
1/2 pint whipping cream

Mix first three ingredients. Press into pie shell. Bake at 350 degrees for 5 minutes. Cook pudding with milk. Cool and pour over crumb mixture. Chill. Top with whipped cream to serve. Serves 8.

Mrs. Ellis McClelland

CHERRY PUDDING

1/2 pound graham crackers
2 eggs
1 cup sugar

1 package cherry gelatin
1/2 cup nuts, pecans
1 can sour pitted cherries

Mix sugar, egg yolks and juice from cherries. Bring to a boil and pour over cherry gelatin. Mix in graham cracker crumbs, nuts and cherries. Beat egg whites and fold into mixture. Refrigerate until firm. Top with whipped cream if desired. Serves 12.

Mrs. Bobby W. McAlister

An undisputed queen am I
My realm I proudly rule;
A rolling pin's my scepter and
My throne's a kitchen stool.
—Betty Heisser

CHOCOLATE PIE OR PUDDING

1 cup sugar
4 tablespoons flour
4 tablespoons cocoa
2 cups milk

3 egg yolks
1 teaspoon vanilla
2 tablespoons butter
1/2 pint whipping cream

Mix sugar, flour and cocoa. Beat egg yolks and add to mixture. Beat until well blended. Slowly add milk, butter and vanilla. Cook in double boiler over medium heat. Pour into baked pie crust. For pudding, blend in an additional 1/2 cup of milk. Using a glass baking dish, alternate layers of vanilla wafers with pudding. Serve pudding or pie with whipped cream. Serves 6.

Mrs. Wilton Williamson

FUDGE PUDDING

1 cup flour	1/2 cup milk
2 teaspoons baking powder	2 tablespoons shortening
1/2 teaspoon salt	1/2 cup nuts
1 teaspoon vanilla	3/4 cup brown sugar
3/4 cup sugar	1/4 cup cocoa
2 teaspoons cocoa	2 cups hot water

Sift together flour, baking powder, salt, sugar and cocoa. Add milk, vanilla, and melted shortening. Mix until smooth. Add nuts. Pour into greased 8-inch square pan. Mix brown sugar and cocoa. Sprinkle over top. Pour hot water over entire batter. Bake in 350 degree oven 40 to 45 minutes. Serve hot with ice cream. Serves 6 to 8.

Mrs. R. B. Fretwell

That all-softening, overpowering knell,
The tocsin of the soul — the dinner bell.
—Byron

HONEY COMB PUDDING

1 cup sugar	1/2 cup butter
1 cup flour	1/2 cup lukewarm milk
1 cup molasses	1 teaspoon soda
4 eggs, well beaten	

Mix sugar and flour, then add molasses. Melt butter in milk and add soda. Combine mixtures, beat thoroughly and add eggs. Turn into buttered baking dish and bake in moderate oven (350 F.).

Mrs. Bob King

BEVERAGES

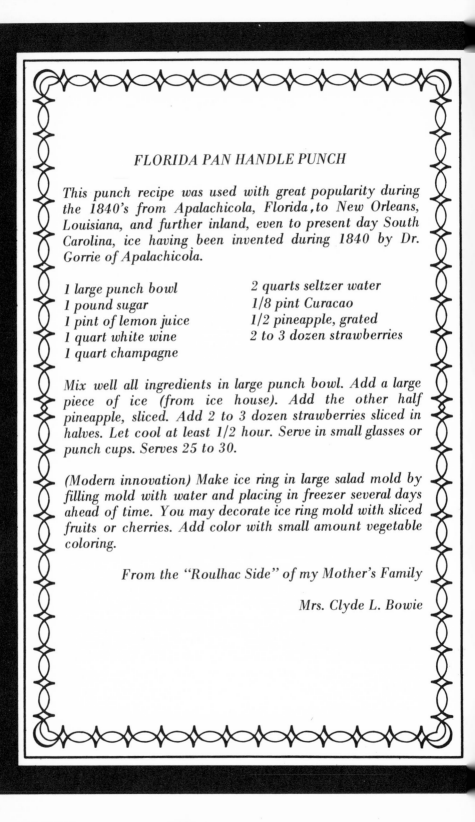

FLORIDA PAN HANDLE PUNCH

This punch recipe was used with great popularity during the 1840's from Apalachicola, Florida, to New Orleans, Louisiana, and further inland, even to present day South Carolina, ice having been invented during 1840 by Dr. Gorrie of Apalachicola.

1 large punch bowl
1 pound sugar
1 pint of lemon juice
1 quart white wine
1 quart champagne

2 quarts seltzer water
1/8 pint Curacao
1/2 pineapple, grated
2 to 3 dozen strawberries

Mix well all ingredients in large punch bowl. Add a large piece of ice (from ice house). Add the other half pineapple, sliced. Add 2 to 3 dozen strawberries sliced in halves. Let cool at least 1/2 hour. Serve in small glasses or punch cups. Serves 25 to 30.

(Modern innovation) Make ice ring in large salad mold by filling mold with water and placing in freezer several days ahead of time. You may decorate ice ring mold with sliced fruits or cherries. Add color with small amount vegetable coloring.

From the "Roulhac Side" of my Mother's Family

Mrs. Clyde L. Bowie

CHRISTMAS PUNCH

5 quarts cranberry juice
1 quart pineapple juice
1 1/2 cups of sugar
4/5 of a quart of
    Taylor's Burgandy Wine

3 5 3/4-ounce cans of
    frozen lemon juice
4 lemon juice cans of water
1 quart gingerale

Combine all of the ingredients, *except* the gingerale. Just before serving, add the gingerale for sparkle. If punch is to be served from a punch bowl, float a small cube of dry ice on top for a special attraction. Serves 25.

Mrs. Jack Ellenberg
Greenwood, S. C.

CRANBERRY PUNCH

4 cups cranberry juice
4 cups pineapple juice
2 quarts gingerale

1 1/2 cups sugar
1 tablespoon almond extract

Mix and chill all ingredients, except gingerale. Add gingerale immediately before serving. Serves 30.

Mrs. Richard G. Christopher III

GOLDEN MEDLEY PUNCH

2 32-ounce bottles apricot nectar
3 6-ounce cans orange juice
2 Number 2 cans of pineapple juice
3 quarts crushed ice

1 8-ounce bottle lemon
    juice (reconstituted)
1 quart gingerale

Mix ingredients and pour over crushed ice in punch bowl. Serves 75.

Mrs. C. J. Canupp

HOT TOMATO JUICE COCKTAIL

4 cups tomato juice
1 tablespoon sugar
1/2 teaspoon salt
1 clove garlic, crushed
1 tablespoon Worcestershire

1/2 cup or less of juice
  from dill pickles
Juice of 1 lemon
1/2 cup whipping cream
1 tablespoon horseradish

Combine all but last two ingredients — bring to a boil and pour into bouillon cups. Garnish each serving with the cream whipped and mixed with the horseradish. Serves 8. May be fixed several days ahead.

Mrs. Samuel R. Moorhead, Jr.

KENTUCKY PUNCH

2 quarts strong tea
8 cups sugar
1 quart lemon juice
1 quart orange juice

1 quart grapefruit juice
1 quart gingerale
10 quarts ice water

For the tea, pour 2 quarts boiling water over 5 tablespoons tea. Allow it to steep 5 minutes, and strain. Then add sugar. Stir until sugar is dissolved, and cool and add fruit juices and ice water. Then add gingerale at serving time. Serves 100 people in punch cups. Makes 4 gallons.

Mrs. Richard Shawn

INEXPENSIVE PUNCH

1 package any flavor Kool-Aid
2 quarts water
2 cups sugar

1 large can pineapple juice
1 large can orange juice

Mix all juices together. Chill until needed, and serve on ice. Serves thirty.

Mrs. Wayne L. McGee

PERKED CRANBERRY PUNCH

2 quarts cranberry juice
2 quarts unsweetened
   pineapple juice
1 quart water
2/3 cup light brown sugar

1 tablespoon whole cloves
1 tablespoon whole allspice
4 cinnamon sticks
2 lemons, quartered

Combine juices in bottom of 30 cup electric percolator. Place remaining ingredients in basket. Perk 30 minutes or until light signals. Makes 5 quarts. Serves 25.

Mrs. D. Bruce Salley

RUSSIAN TEA MIX

1 cup Tang
1 cup sugar
1/4 cup instant tea

1 teaspoon cinnamon
1/2 teaspoon cloves

Mix all ingredients together. Store in glass jar or container. When ready for use, add 2 teaspoons or more to each cup of boiling water.

Mrs. Stuart M. Brown

SPARKLE PUNCH

1 6-ounce can frozen orange juice
1 6-ounce can frozen lemonade
1 12-ounce can apricot nectar

1 Number 2 can pineapple juice
1 large bottle gingerale

Add water to frozen juices as directed on cans. Combine with apricot and pineapple juices. Chill until ready to serve. Add gingerale. Serves twenty-five.

Mrs. M. L. Propp

SPICED TOMATO JUICE

2 quarts tomato juice
1/2 cup vinegar
3 medium white onions, sliced
Salt, Tabasco, red pepper

1/3 cup lemon juice
1 tablespoon sugar
6 to 8 celery tops

Combine all ingredients and boil gently for one hour. Strain and chill thoroughly. Make certain that it is hot enough, pepperwise. This can be made several days ahead of time. Serves 10 to 12.

Mrs. Neil Chamblee

SUPERB LEMONADE

1 cup lemon juice
2 cups sugar

1 orange sliced
1 cup pineapple cubes

Boil 2 quarts water. Add all ingredients and chill. Pour over crushed ice. This is better if it stands overnight before serving. It can easily be doubled or tripled. Serves 8.

Mrs. James Mattison
Belton, S. C.

WHITE GRAPE FLOAT

1 46-ounce can pineapple juice
1 cup white grape juice

1/2 gallon vanilla ice cream
1 bottle gingerale

Chill all ingredients. Combine pineapple and white grape juices. Pour over softened ice cream in punch bowl. Slowly add gingerale. Serves twenty-five.

Mrs. H. G. Anderson, III

I think if I were a woman I'd wear
coffee as a perfume. — John van Druten

256

PICKLES

ATLAS
E-Z
SEAL

ARTICHOKE RELISH

1 peck root artichokes
  well scrubbed
Brine: 2 cups salt to a
  gallon of water
2 quarts onions
1 bunch celery
8 bell peppers
1 tablespoon pimento or
  red pepper

3 3/4 quarts vinegar
3/4 quart water
4 cups sugar
1/4 cup dry mustard
8 tablespoons tumeric
2 cups flour
1/2 teaspoon black pepper

Soak artichokes in brine for several hours or overnight, then grind artichokes, onions, celery and bell peppers. Add to this mixture cut-up pimento or red pepper (do not grind). Put in large kettle and add vinegar, water, sugar and black pepper, except save enough water to make a smooth paste of the flour, mustard and tumeric before putting these in. Cook, stirring constantly to prevent burning for about an hour or until it thickens and tastes done. Take up in small glass jars, pouring paraffin over each jar to keep out the air, or use self-sealing jars.

This recipe was used each year for many years by Harriet Yarbrough's grandmother, Mrs. Frances Marion Dwight of Stateburg who raised her own artichokes in the back yard, often using the yellow flowers in the house for decorations while the tubers were maturing.

Many of these little jars of artichoke relish found their way into the homes of the neighborhood where Mrs. Dwight's husband practiced medicine around the turn of the century.

Mrs. Joseph C. Yarbrough, Jr.

ARTICHOKE PICKLE

1 quart onions
1 quart cucumbers
2 small cabbages
1 quart green tomatoes
1 cauliflower

6 large green peppers
3 large red peppers
1/2 gallon Jerusalem artichokes
Hot peppers (optional)
1 cup salt

Chop fine everything but artichokes. Cover with water and salt and let soak overnight. Next morning, press water out. Clean and chop artichokes, keeping separate.

DRESSING

2 quarts vinegar
1 scant cup flour
1 small box dry mustard
6 cups sugar

1/4 box tumeric
1 small box celery seed
1 small box mustard seed

Mix dry ingredients and add to hot vinegar stirring constantly until thickened. Add vegetables to dressing, bring to boil, then drop in artichokes. Pack and seal.

Mrs. Robert Gallant

BREAD AND BUTTER PICKLE

1 gallon cucumbers
12 large white onions
1/2 cup salt
4 1/2 cups white sugar
2 teaspoons tumeric

5 cups vinegar
1/2 teaspoon cloves
1 teaspoon celery seed
2 teaspoons mustard seed

Slice cucumbers and onions paper thin (potato slicer is good to use). Put crushed ice over cucumbers and onions mixed in salt. Let stand 3 hours. Drain and cover with the following: sugar, tumeric, vinegar, cloves, celery seed, and mustard seed. Place cucumbers, onions and the above mixture on a slow fire and bring to scalding point (do not boil). Put in sterilized jars and seal.

Mrs. Douglas McDougald

CHOW-CHOW

8 to 10 pounds cabbage
2 quarts green tomatoes
(or 1 quart artichokes)

2 quarts onions (8 or 9)
2 dozen green and red peppers

Sprinkle with salt. Let stand a short while. Strain through colander. Let the following come to a boil:

3 pints vinegar
4 cups sugar (2 brown, 2 white)

1/2 box mustard seed
1/2 box celery seed

MAKE A PASTE OF THE FOLLOWING

1 cup flour
3 to 4 tablespoons mustard

1 or more cups of water
2 tablespoons tumeric

Add vegetables to boiling mixture. Stir in paste, keep stirring until it comes to a rolling boil. Take off heat. Put in jars and seal. Makes about eight quarts.

Mrs. Joe Ben McGill

GREEN TOMATO PICKLE

4 quarts green tomatoes
8 medium onions
Salt
2 cups sugar
1 tablespoon black pepper

1 teaspoon allspice
1 teaspoon ground cloves
1 tablespoon mustard
1 teaspoon salt
1 pint vinegar

Slice tomatoes and onions. Sprinkle salt over onions and tomatoes. Let stand for 2 hours. Drain off water (juices). Add remaining ingredients to tomatoes and cook on low heat for 1 hour or until peeling begins to come loose on tomatoes. Put into jars and seal.

Mrs. Jack Ellenberg
Greenwood, S. C.

PEACH PICKLE

1 cup brown sugar
  or 1 cup dark Karo Syrup
3 cups white sugar

2 cups vinegar (apple cider)
4 quarts firm ripe peaches
1 tablespoon whole mixed spices

Bring sugar, vinegar and spices to boil in a large open boiler pan. Add peaches and cook until tender. Place in jars and seal while hot. Yields 8 pints.

Mrs. J. Prue Garrison

PICKLED OKRA

1 clove garlic
  per pint jar
1 pod red pepper
  per pint jar
1 teaspoon dill seed
  per pint jar

2 1/4 pounds
  small tender okra
1 quart vinegar
1 cup water
1/4 cup salt

Wash okra and pack in sterilized jars. Bring vinegar, water and salt to hard boil. Pour over okra and seal. Yields 6 pints.

Mrs. John Edwards
Mrs. William L. Thompson

PICKLED ORANGE SLICES

3 medium size navel oranges
Whole cloves
1 cup sugar

1/4 cup light corn syrup
1/2 cup vinegar
3 to 4 sticks cinammon

Boil oranges in enough water to cover for about 30 minutes. Remove from water and cut into 1/2 inch slices. Stick six cloves in peel of each slice. Boil sugar, syrup, vinegar and cinammon together in heavy skillet for about five minutes. Arrange orange slices in syrup and simmer about 10 minutes. Spoon syrup up over slices occasionally. Serve hot or cold as accompaniment to roast turkey. Yields 12 slices.

Mrs. V. E. Merchant, Jr.

WATERMELON PICKLE

1 large watermelon
1 gallon vinegar
10 pounds sugar
1 box (1 1/4-ounce)
   whole cloves

1 box (1 1/4-ounce)
   whole cinammon
Small bottle powdered lime
   (1/2-ounce)

Select melon with thick, tender rind. Cut off thick green skin and remove pink pulp. Cut rind in squares, wedges, or fancy shapes with crinkle french-fry cutter and weigh (there should be about 7 pounds). Cover with water in which lime has been dissolved and soak overnight. Drain, cover with fresh water, bring to boiling point, and drain again. Make spice bag and put cloves and cinammon inside. Cook sugar and vinegar with spice bag until syrup is somewhat thick. Cook rinds in syrup until tender. Pack in jars, fill jars with syrup, seal, label, and store. Yields 8 pints. Note: Save any left-over syrup (store in refrigerator) and use when cooking ham. Also good over pork roast.

Mrs. Lamar Cope

YESTERDAY & TODAY

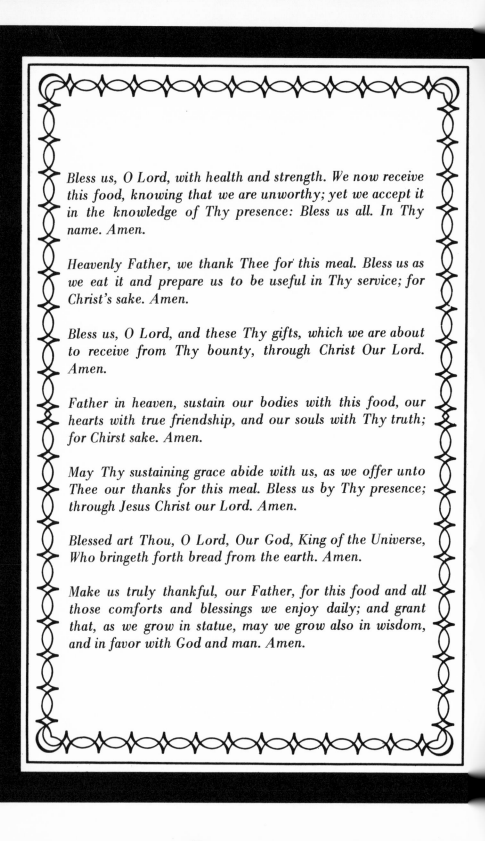

Bless us, O Lord, with health and strength. We now receive this food, knowing that we are unworthy; yet we accept it in the knowledge of Thy presence: Bless us all. In Thy name. Amen.

Heavenly Father, we thank Thee for this meal. Bless us as we eat it and prepare us to be useful in Thy service; for Christ's sake. Amen.

Bless us, O Lord, and these Thy gifts, which we are about to receive from Thy bounty, through Christ Our Lord. Amen.

Father in heaven, sustain our bodies with this food, our hearts with true friendship, and our souls with Thy truth; for Chirst sake. Amen.

May Thy sustaining grace abide with us, as we offer unto Thee our thanks for this meal. Bless us by Thy presence; through Jesus Christ our Lord. Amen.

Blessed art Thou, O Lord, Our God, King of the Universe, Who bringeth forth bread from the earth. Amen.

Make us truly thankful, our Father, for this food and all those comforts and blessings we enjoy daily; and grant that, as we grow in statue, may we grow also in wisdom, and in favor with God and man. Amen.

When the cookstove had to be stoked with wood, grandmother often needed hours to prepare even simple family meals. While today's cook may occasionally prepare time consuming recipes for special occasions, there are other days when she must produce a meal in a matter of minutes. CAROLINA CUISINE found it interesting to compare the following favorite antique recipes, along with those at the beginning of each section, with some of the indespensable modern recipes which allow today's cooks to spend less time in the kitchen.

BLACKBERRY WINE

Wash berries and squeeze out all juice. Boil five minutes or more. Skim well. Put three pounds of sugar to a gallon of juice and keep in jug, well plugged, until October and then bottle. This wine goes well on fruit cake, is excellent for toasting and for many illnesses. It will promote a good appetite and induce a good night's sleep.

Mrs. J. M. Paget

WATERMELON RIND PICKLES

1 large melon rind, cut into squares	1 pint water
1 gallon water	5 pounds sugar
3 tablespoons lime	2 tablespoons whole cloves
1 quart vinegar	2 tablespoons black pepper
	2 sticks cinnamon

Soak rind for 24 hours in 1 gallon of water and lime. Drain, cover with water and cook until tender (1 1/2 to 2 1/2 hours). Drain. Make syrup of vinegar, 1 pint water, sugar, cloves, pepper and cinnamon. Cook 1/2 hour. Add rind and cook 1/2 hour longer. Let stand overnight. Bring to a boil and seal in jars.

Mrs. Marshall Fant, Jr.

BRUNSWICK STEW

2 hens, 5 to 6 pounds each
4 large cans tomatoes
3 pounds chopped onions
1 large potato, chopped

1 kitchen spoon bacon grease
6 cans butter beans or limas
4 cans white creamed corn
Red pepper

This takes at least two days to prepare. The hens must be boiled in salt water in large container or kettle till the meat cooks completely off the bones. (This usually takes one full day.) Add water if necessary, but let water cook nearly out before adding next ingredients. When cool remove all bones. Add 3 pounds chopped onions and 4 large cans tomatoes. Cook for 1/2 a day at least. Everything should cook apart. Add potato, bacon grease, butter beans and red pepper. Cook remainder of day and add corn shortly before serving.

This stew is very thick and can be eaten with a fork. It should not be soupy. It is delicious served with slaw, barbequed or fried chicken livers and corn bread. Serves 20-30 people.

Mrs. Robert E. Jones

Unquiet meals make ill digestions. — Shakespeare

COCONUT CAKE

4 eggs
2 cups sugar
2 cups cake flour, sifted

2 teaspoons baking powder
2 tablespoons butter
1 cup milk

Beat eggs until stiff and lemon colored. Add sugar and beat until well mixed. Add flour and baking powder sifted together. Bring butter and milk to a boil. Add this to the above mixture. Bake in two or three 9 inch cake pans at 350 degrees for 18 to 19 minutes.

FILLING

2 cups sugar
2/3 cup water
2 large coconuts

2/3 cup light corn syrup
2 egg whites

Cook sugar, water and syrup to a soft ball stage or until mixture spins a thread when dropped from a spoon. Beat egg whites until stiff. Add syrup slowly, beat until candy reaches a marshmallow stage, not to a stiff peak stage.

Have prepared 2 large coconuts, peeled and grated by hand. Save the juice.

In a separate bowl, put 1/2 of the coconut and 5 tablespoons of the juice together. Add 7 large tablespoons of icing to this, making a paste type mixture. Put between each layer to which 2 to 3 tablespoons of juice has been put on top. Put remaining icing on cake using the remaining coconut on top and sides.

Mrs. Joe P. Watson

Strange to see how a good dinner and
feasting reconciles everybody. — Samuel Pepys

CORN PUDDING A' LA EMMA

6 ears corn (grated)
2 tablespoons butter
3 eggs, separated
1 cup milk

1 teaspoon salt
1/2 green pepper, chopped
1/2 teaspoon baking powder
1 teaspoon flour

Mix butter well, add the beaten egg yolks, then the corn and other ingredients, adding stiffly beaten egg whites last. Bake at 300 degrees for 30 minutes. Green pepper may be omitted. Grated cheese may be added.

Mrs. J. N. Land

DATE SOUFFLE

1 cup sugar
2 eggs, beaten
1 tablespoon flour

1 teaspoon baking powder
1 cup broken pecans
1 cup dates, halved

Mix all ingredients and pour into greased 1 1/2 quart pyrex baking dish. Bake in 350 degree oven 20 minutes. Serve cold with or without whipped cream. Serves 6.

Miss Emma Major
Miss Frances Major

Soufflé is more important than you think.
If men ate souffle before meetings, life
could be much different. — Jacques Baeyens

EGG CUSTARD PIE

3 large eggs
2 cups sugar
2 tablespoons flour
1/2 teaspoon baking powder
1/8 teaspoon salt

3/4 cup milk
1 teaspoon vanilla
1/2 cup melted margarine
1 unbaked pie shell

Beat eggs. Add sugar mixed with flour, baking powder and salt. Add milk, vanilla and melted margarine. Bake at 425 degrees for 10 minutes — then reduce to 350 degrees and bake until firm.

Mrs. Raymond Fretwell, Jr.

The proof of the pudding is in the eating.
— Proverb from Don Quixote

MEAT LOAF

2 pounds ground beef
1 pound ground pork (sausage)
1/2 cup catsup
2 eggs, mix well

2 handsful rolled cracker
  crumbs
Salt and pepper to taste

Shape in long roll, and roll in more cracker crumbs. Place in baking dish. Serves 12 to 16.

TOPPING

1 can tomato soup
1/4 cup water

Bacon slices

Pour tomato soup and water over loaf. Bake for 1 1/2 hours at 375 degrees. Put bacon slices across top and bake 1/2 hour longer. You may use one half the amount of meats, and same amount of other ingredients and make 6 to 8 servings.

Mrs. Fred Compton

OLD FASHION TEA CAKES

1 stick margarine
1 cup sugar
1 teaspoon soda
5 tablespoons hot milk
1 egg

1 teaspoon vanilla
1 teaspoon lemon extract
4 cups flour
1 teaspoon cream of tartar
Nutmeg

Cream margarine and sugar. Add soda to hot milk, and pour this over creamed margarine and sugar. Add egg. Add flavorings. Blend in flour sifted with cream of tartar and mix well.

Place dough in refrigerator several hours. Take out a small portion of the dough at a time, roll very thin and put on a greased baking sheet about 1/2 inch apart. Sprinkle each tea cake with sugar and nutmeg. Bake at 325 degrees. Place on brown paper to cool. Store in airtight tins and they will keep fresh for several weeks.

You will have to add more flour to roll them out. I use a biscuit cutter.

Mrs. J. R. Keith

PLUM PUDDING

1 pound beef suet
1 pound currents
1 pound seeded raisins
2 cups brown sugar
2 lemons, ground
2 oranges, ground
8 cups bread crumbs

1 cup chopped or ground citron
1 teaspoon cinnamon
1 teaspoon nutmeg
1 teaspoon mace
1 teaspoon allspice
1/2 cup cider or fruit juice
8 eggs

Chop the beef suet very fine and combine with all remaining ingredients *except eggs*. Beat in eggs one at a time. Prepare pudding molds or 4 1-pound coffee cans by greasing lightly, then tossing with a little sugar.

Fill cans or molds 2/3 full. Cover with waxed paper and clamp the lid on tightly. Steam on a trivet in a covered pan, keeping water level half way up side of pan, for about an hour. The pudding may be stored a short while in the refrigerator.

SAUCE OR TOPPING

1/2 stick butter
2/3 cup sugar
Whipped cream

Season to taste with
bourbon or brandy
Sugar to taste

Cream butter with sugar. Season to taste with bourbon or brandy. Serve cold sauce on warm pudding. If preferred, serve whipped cream that has been sugared to taste and spiked with bourbon or brandy.

Pudding may be reheated for serving by dipping out some of the pudding into a double boiler. Cover and steam until warm. Serve with sauce or cream.

This recipe was one used each Christmas at our house by my mother, and before that, by her mother. It has been used by at least three generations of cooks, maybe more.

Mrs. Betty Horton Martin

CHICKEN A LA KING

Preparation time: 15 minutes

1 tablespoon butter or margarine
2 tablespoons chopped green pepper
1 can condensed cream of
  of chicken soup

1 cup diced cooked chicken
1/4 cup chopped pimento
1/4 cup milk
4 baked patty shells

Melt butter in saucepan; add green pepper, and cook until tender. Stir in soup; then milk; add chicken and pimento. Cook over low heat about 5 minutes. Serve in hot patty shells. Serves 4.

Mrs. Norman Wayne Wham, Jr.

CHICKEN ALMOND CASSEROLE

Preparation time: 40 minutes

1 small can boned chicken
1 cup cream of chicken soup
1/2 cup finely chopped onion
2/3 cup cooked minute rice

1/2 cup mayonnaise
1/2 cup sliced almonds
1 cup crushed potato chips

Mix all ingredients (except last) in casserole and bake at 400 degrees for 20 minutes. Sprinkle crushed potato chips on top and cook 15 minutes more. Serves 2.

Mrs. Fred Thackston

DOUBLE QUICK BEAN BAKE

Preparation time: 15 minutes

1 1-pound 5-ounce can pork
  and beans
1 tablespoon minced onion
1/4 cup catsup

2 drops Tabasco sauce
2 tablespoons brown sugar
1/2 teaspoon salt
1/2 teaspoon dry mustard

Combine all ingredients in saucepan. Bring to a boil and simmer for 10 minutes. Serves 4.

Mrs. Newton Newell, Jr.

BEEF STROGANOFF

Preparation time: 15 minutes

1 pound round steak
 1/4 to 1/2 inch thick
2/3 cup water
1 can (3-ounces) broiled
 sliced mushrooms

1 envelope onion soup mix
1 cup sour cream
2 tablespoons flour
Buttered noodles or rice

Trim fat from meat; reserve fat. Cut meat diagonally across grain in strips 1/4 inch thick. Heat fat. When you have 3 tablespoons melted fat, remove trimmings and brown meat quickly. Add water and mushrooms (including liquid). Stir in soup mix. Heat to boiling. Blend sour cream and flour. Cook and stir until mixture thickens. Serve over hot noodles or rice. Serves 5 to 6.

Mrs. James P. Clamp

HEARTY COMBINATION SOUP

Preparation time: 10 minutes

1 can condensed vegetable soup
1 can condensed bean with
 bacon soup

1 can condensed
 beef noodle soup
2 cans water

Combine soups. Add water. Simmer about 5 minutes.

Mrs. Newton Newell, Jr.

MACARONI AND SHRIMP MAIN DISH SALAD

Preparation time: 30 minutes

2 cups shell macaroni
1/2 cup mayonnaise
2 teaspoons prepared mustard
2 tablespoons minced onion
2 cups chopped celery

1/3 cup chopped sweet pickle
1/2 cup chopped green peppers
1/2 cup sliced olives
1 cup shrimp
6 lettuce cups

Cook macaroni as directed on package. Blend mayonnaise and mustard until smooth. Cook shrimp as directed on package. Combine all ingredients and macaroni. Toss until nicely coated with dressing. Serve in lettuce cups. Garnish with pimento and paprika as desired. Serves 6.

Mrs. Marshall Kowalski

MAC O' TUNA CASSEROLE

Preparation time: 30 minutes

1 7-ounce package of elbow macaroni	1 can of tuna
1 can mushroom soup	1/2 cup milk
1 cup grated cheese	Bread crumbs or crushed potato chips
1 tomato, sliced	

Prepare macaroni as directed. Mix with tuna, soup, milk and cheese. Pour into buttered casserole. Garnish with tomato slices and crumbs. Bake 15 to 20 minutes, at 375 degrees. Serves 4.

Mrs. Joe Dent
Lexington, N. C.

SALMON SHORTCAKES

Preparation time: 10 minutes

2 tablespoons minced onion	1/3 cup milk
3 tablespoons butter or margarine	1 can (8-ounces) drained flaked salmon
1 can condensed cream of mushroom soup	4 baking powder biscuits

Cook onion in butter until soft and golden. Blend in soup, milk and salmon; heat. Serve creamed salmon over hot split biscuits. Serves 4.

Mrs. William Cooper
Spartanburg, S. C.

STEAK CASSEROLE

Preparation time: 45 minutes

1 pound ground beef
1 onion chopped
1/2 teaspoon salt
1/2 teaspoon pepper
1 teaspoon Worcestershire

1 can tomato soup
1 can mushroom soup
1 can (8 1/2-ounce) small
English peas
8 to 10 crumbled cheese
crackers or 1 cup
grated cheese

Brown meat and onion. Stir in all remaining ingredients except last. Bake at 350 degrees for 35 minutes. Sprinkle crackers or cheese on top. Return to oven for 5 minutes or until browned. Serves 4.

Mrs. John Horton Smith

People sometimes praise a restaurant by
saying it makes them feel at home. I
don't want to feel at home in a restaurant.
I want to feel that I'm having a night out.
— Alvin Kerr

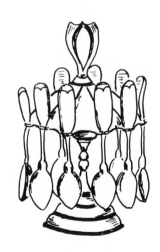

OCCASIONAL
COOKS

BAKLAVA

14 pastry sheets, filo Greek pastry available at delicatessen
4 cups chopped pecans

1 teaspoon cinnamon
Grated rind of one orange
1 cup butter
1 1/4 cups sugar

Mix nuts, sugar, cinnamon and orange rind. Melt butter and brush well a 13 x 9 pan. Place one layer (2 sheets) in bottom of baking pan and allow ends to extend over pan. Sprinkle heavily with nut mixture and place two layers over this. Brush these layers with butter and sprinkle with nut mixture. Alternate layers until all ingredients and sheets have been used, ending with 2 pastry sheets. Brush top with remaining butter and trim edges. Cut through top with diagonal lines to form diamond shapes. Bake in 375 degree oven for one hour until light brown.

GLAZE

2 cups water
3 cups sugar

1 teaspoon lemon juice

While still hot cover with glaze and let stand overnight before serving. Prepare glaze with water, sugar and lemon juice. Boil for 10 minutes. Serves 24. This recipe for Baklava, a favorite Greek pastry used especially for holidays and weddings, has been handed down in the family of Jack Ross for generations.

Jack Ross

Mother may not be the only cook in the family. Occasionally she is dismissed from the kitchen to let someone else try his hand. Knowing that men make the very best cooks, CAROLINA CUISINE asked them to submit their favorite recipes. Children too enjoy concocting goodies and have contributed their recipes.

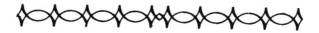

CHILI CON CARNE

2 large onions
2 large green peppers
1 tablespoon cooking oil
2 pounds ground beef
2 1-pound cans tomatoes
2 8-ounce cans tomato sauce

2 cans (1-pound) dark red
  kidney beans, drained
4 teaspoons chili powder
1 1/2 teaspoons salt
2 bay leaves

In heavy skillet, cook chopped onions and chopped peppers in cooking oil until tender. Add ground beef and cook until meat is browned. Stir in remaining ingredients. Cover and simmer for one hour. Serves 8.

Bob Aiken

ESCARGOT DE BOURGOGNE

1 can 24 French snails
  and shells
1/2 cup butter or margarine
2 teaspoons chopped parsley
2 teaspoons chopped onion

1 clove chopped garlic
1/4 teaspoon salt
1/8 teaspoon white pepper
1 teaspoon chopped chives

Drain snails and place 1 in each shell. Mix remaining ingredients well. Place a generous portion of creamed butter sauce in each shell with snail. Place in 300 degree oven for 10 minutes until hot. Serve with hot French bread, soaking up any sauce draining from the snails. Appetizer for 4.

Robert M. Gallant

BARBECUED RIBS

1/3 cup salt
1/3 cup sugar
2 1/2 tablespoons black pepper
2 tablespoons monosodium
  glutamate

1 tablespoon paprika
1 1/2 teaspoon bottled
  dry lemon peel
1/4 teaspoon ground thyme
6 pounds lean spareribs

To Cook In The Oven: Heat oven to 275 degrees. Combine and mix well salt, sugar, pepper, monosodium glutamate, paprika, lemon peel, and thyme. Coat ribs well on all sides with mixture. (Any seasoning mix left over can be stored in a covered jar for use another time). Place ribs in a shallow roasting pan and bake for 3 hours, turning once. Brush with Mop Sauce as needed to keep ribs from drying out. Remove from oven. Cut into single rib portions. Serve with Barbecue Sauce. Serves 10 to 12.

To Cook On The Pit or Grill: Coat ribs with dry seasoning mix as above. Have grill far enough from coals to prevent burning of meat. Place ribs on grill over hot coals to which wood chips have been added to create smoke. Cook 1 1/2 hours or until brown and crisp. Brush with Mop Sauce when ribs start to brown. Brush again if ribs seem dry. Serve with Barbecue Sauce and Country Potato Salad.

MOP SAUCE

1 can (10 1/2 ounce)
  beef consomme'
1 1/3 cups water
3/4 cup Worcestershire
1/3 cup cider vinegar
1/3 cup pure vegetable oil
1 1/2 teaspoons monosodium
  glutamate

1 1/2 teaspoons dry mustard
1 teaspoon hot pepper sauce
1 teaspoon garlic powder
1 teaspoon chili powder
1 bay leaf
1/2 teaspoon paprika

Combine consomme' and water in medium-size saucepan. Bring to boil. Add remaining ingredients and let stand overnight at room temperature. Makes about 2 quarts.

BARBECUE SAUCE

1 1/2 cups water
1 cup catsup
1/2 cup cider vinegar
1/4 cup Worcestershire
1/4 cup margarine
3 stalks celery, chopped
1 teaspoon sugar

1 teaspoon chili powder
1 teaspoon paprika
1 clove of garlic
3 bay leaves
1/4 teaspoon black pepper
1/4 teaspoon salt
2 tablespoons onion, chopped

Combine all ingredients in large saucepan. Bring to a boil and simmer for 15 minutes. Then remove from heat and strain. Serve hot with meat or poultry. Makes about 2 1/2 cups.

Ernest Garrison

WHOPPER-BURGERS

2 pounds ground beef
Salt and pepper

Prepared mustard
5 thin onion slices

Shape patties using a 1/3 cup measure. Divide ground beef into 10 mounds and flatten each mound between squares of waxed paper into a 4 inch patty. Set half the patties aside for *lids*. Sprinkle remaining patties with salt and pepper. Spread with prepared mustard, leaving a 1/2 inch margin for sealing. Top with a mound of pickle filling and an onion slice.

PICKLE FILLING

1 small jar pickle relish

1/2 pound sharp cheese
cut in 1/2-inch cubes

Cover the filling with *lids*. Press together the edges of the burgers all around on top side, then turn and seal the edges again. Place on a greased grill. Season top side with salt and pepper. Broil over hot coals 10 minutes, then turn. Broil 10 minutes more, or until done. Season second side. Slip patties into hot buttered buns. Serves 5.

J. Philip Noury

ORIENTAL STEAK

1 cup soy sauce	1 1/2 inch thick sirloin
1 cup water	steak
Garlic salt	Paprika
Barbecue spice	Onion slices

Soak steak in combined mixture of soy sauce and water for 6 hours. Rub in garlic salt and barbecue spice well. Before broiling and after soaking sprinkle with paprika. Broil in middle of oven for 8 minutes on one side, turn and broil 6 minutes on the other side. After turning add onion slices. Serves 4-6.

Curtis Gillespie

Better is a dinner of herbs where love is, than
a stalled ox and hatred therewith. Proverbs
Men are . . . conservatives after dinner. — Emerson

PIZZA BURGERS

4 hamburger buns	1/2 teaspoon salt
1 cup chili sauce	1/2 teaspoon oregano
1 pound ground beef	1/8 teaspoon garlic powder
1 tablespoon chopped onion	1/2 teaspoon Worcestershire
1 tablespoon parsley flakes	4 slices cheese cut
	into 16 strips

Split buns. Spread with about 1/2 cup of the chili sauce. Mix beef, remaining chili sauce, onion, parsley, salt, oregano, garlic powder, and Worcestershire. Divide into 8 portions; spread on buns evenly, all the way to the edge. Place on rack of broiler pan. Broil 10 minutes. Remove and place 2 strips of cheese criss-cross on top of burgers. Return to broiler and melt the cheese. Makes 8 burgers.

Walter C. Duffie

An empty stomach is not a good
political adviser. — Albert Einstein

FRENCH TOAST

2 eggs
1/4 cup milk
4 slices of bread

Cinnamon
2 tablespoons shortening

Beat eggs with milk. Melt shortening in skillet. Dip bread in egg mixture and sprinkle with cinnamon. Fry in shortening until light brown. Serve with syrup. Yields 4 slices.

Miss Mary Ann Smith

NO BAKE CHOCOLATE COOKIES

2 cups sugar
1/2 cup milk
1 stick margarine
3 tablespoons cocoa
1 teaspoon salt

3 cups raw quick rolled oats
1 teaspoon vanilla
1/2 cup broken nuts
1 cup coconut (optional)

Mix sugar, milk, margarine, cocoa and salt in large saucepan and bring to a boil. Remove from heat and stir in the rolled oats, vanilla, nuts, and coconut. Drop from teaspoon onto waxed paper. Yields 48 cookies.

Miss Katie Klugh

RANGER COOKIES

1 cup shortening
1 cup brown sugar
1 cup white sugar
2 eggs
2 cups cornflakes
2 cups oats

2 cups flour
1 cup coconut, shredded
1 teaspoon baking powder
1/2 teaspoon salt
2 teaspoons soda
1 teaspoon vanilla

Cream shortening and sugars. Beat eggs into mixture. Sift salt, baking powder and soda with flour. Add flour, cornflakes and coconut to cream mixture. Drop cookie dough from a teaspoon on a greased cookie sheet 1 1/2 inches apart. Bake 15 minutes at 350 degrees. Yields 8 dozen.

Miss Pam Shirley

LACE COOKIES

1/2 cup shortening
2 cups oatmeal
1 egg, beaten

3/4 cup sugar
1/2 teaspoon almond flavoring

Heat shortening in skillet; add oatmeal. Mix egg, sugar and almond to oatmeal mixture. Drop from teaspoon onto cookie sheet covered with tin-foil. Bake at 350 degrees for 10 minutes. Cool one minute before removing from sheet. Yields 2 dozen.

Miss Lisa Gallant

No soil upon earth is as dear to our eyes,
As the soil we first stirred in making mud pies.

CHOCOLATE PIE

1 cup sugar
3 tablespoons cocoa
3 1/2 tablespoons flour
1 1/2 cups milk

2 eggs, separated
2 tablespoons butter
1 tablespoon vanilla
1 8-inch baked pie shell

Cook all ingredients together, except eggs, until thickened. Add two beaten egg yolks and cook two or three minutes more. Pour into baked pie shell.

MERINGUE

2 egg whites
4 tablespoons sugar

Pinch salt
1/2 teaspoon vanilla

Beat egg whites until stiff; add sugar gradually and continue beating until the mixture is fine grained and will hold its shape. Add salt and vanilla. Spread on top of chocolate mixture and bake at 350 degrees until meringue browns. Serves 8.

Miss Robin Taylor

COOKING for TWO

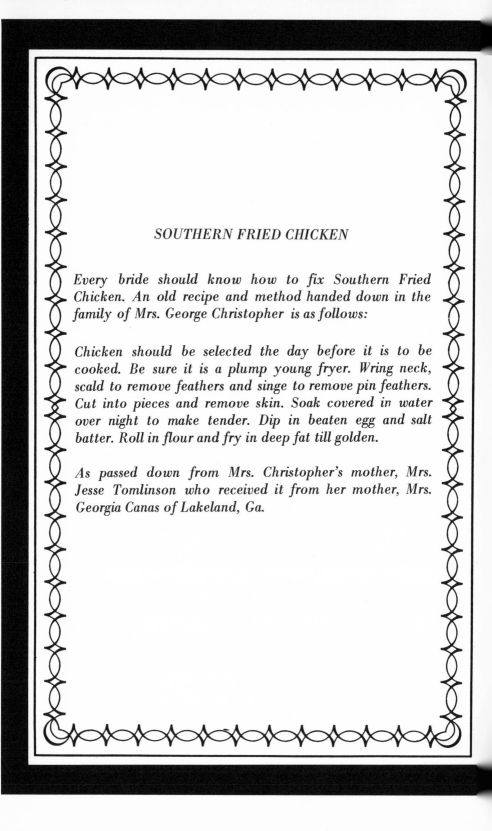

SOUTHERN FRIED CHICKEN

Every bride should know how to fix Southern Fried Chicken. An old recipe and method handed down in the family of Mrs. George Christopher is as follows:

Chicken should be selected the day before it is to be cooked. Be sure it is a plump young fryer. Wring neck, scald to remove feathers and singe to remove pin feathers. Cut into pieces and remove skin. Soak covered in water over night to make tender. Dip in beaten egg and salt batter. Roll in flour and fry in deep fat till golden.

As passed down from Mrs. Christopher's mother, Mrs. Jesse Tomlinson who received it from her mother, Mrs. Georgia Canas of Lakeland, Ga.

When the honeymoon is over, a bride may be somewhat perplexed by her new kitchen. CAROLINA CUISINE presents a bride's bonus, "Cooking for Two," which includes amounts to buy for two, recipes for a couple, "Basic Kitchen Equipment," and suggestions for the bride's "First Day's Marketing."

HAMBURGER AND RICE DISH

1/2 pound ground beef
2 tablespoons butter
1 medium onion, chopped
Salt and pepper to taste

1 cup tomatoes
1/4 cup catsup
1/2 cup instant rice

Brown beef in butter. Add onion, salt and pepper to beef and brown. Stir in tomatoes and cook well on medium heat. Add catsup and rice. If necessary, add enough water to cook rice. Simmer 15 minutes.

Mrs. Marlin S. Sherman

PORK CHOP CASSEROLE

4 pork chops
1 small can sliced pineapple
1 cup uncooked rice

1/4 cup chopped onion
2 tablespoons brown sugar
2 cups boiling water

Brown pork chops in skillet and remove from pan. Brown onion in same grease. Put rice in casserole dish. Add water to rice. Pour onions over rice. Top with pork chops and pineapple slices. Sprinkle brown sugar over pineapple. Bake covered for 30 minutes at 350 degrees. Uncover and bake and additional 10 minutes.

Mrs. Stuart Knobel
Greenville, S. C.

SHRIMP CURRY

1 1/4 teaspoons curry powder
1/8 teaspoon sugar
Dash of ginger

1 cup white sauce
1 7-ounce package frozen
   shrimp, cooked

Blend curry powder, sugar and ginger with a few tablespoons of the sauce; then stir into remaining sauce. Add shrimp; heat to simmering point. Serve on hot rice, biscuits, toast or muffins.

Mrs. W. A. Thompson

QUICK CREAMED VEGETABLE

1/2 package (9 or 10 ounce)
   frozen vegetable
1/4 cup water
1/4 teaspoon salt

1 tablespoon butter
1 1/2 tablespoons flour
1 cup evaporated milk

Add vegetable to water with salt; bring to a boil and cook 3-4 minutes. Add butter; stir until melted. Remove from heat; blend in flour; stir in milk. Cook over low heat until thick.

Mrs. Dan Chamblee

PAN SCALLOPED POTATOES

2 tablespoons butter
Dash of pepper
1/4 cup chopped onion
2 cups cubed raw potatoes

1/2 cup boiling water
1 cup milk
2 tablespoons grated cheese

In a 2 quart saucepan melt butter. Add pepper, onion and potatoes. Cook over low heat until onion is transparent (3-4 minutes) stirring occasionally. Add boiling water and milk; continue cooking over low heat until potatoes are tender, 25-30 minutes, stirring occasionally. Stir in cheese just before serving.

Mrs. Larry Chamblee

HAM STEAK

2 slices cured ham
  1/2 inch thick
2 tablespoons mustard

1 apple, thinly sliced
1/2 cup brown sugar
1/4 cup flour

Rub ham with mustard and roll in flour. Fry ham until lightly browned. Place in broiler pan. Add sliced apples on top of ham. Sprinkle brown sugar on top. Bake 25 minutes at 350 degrees.

Mrs. F. Spencer Shirley

SALMON PATTIES

1 7 3/4-ounce can salmon
12 soda crackers, crushed
  (about 1/2 cup)
2 teaspoons instant minced onion

1 egg
1/3 cup evaporated milk
1 1/2 tablespoons butter

Remove skin and bones from salmon. Flake salmon in liquid. Add crumbs, onions, egg and evaporated milk. Mix well. Shape into 4 balls. Melt butter over low heat in a skillet. Add salmon balls. Cook about 5 minutes on each side.

Mrs. Dan Chamblee

EASY CUP CUSTARD

1 egg
Dash of salt
5 teaspoons sugar
1/2 cup evaporated milk

1/4 cup boiling water
1/8 teaspoon vanilla
Nutmeg (optional)

Beat egg with salt and sugar; stir in evaporated milk, water and vanilla. Pour into custard cups; sprinkle with nutmeg, if desired. Cover cups with foil. Place in saucepan; surround with hot water to within 1/2 inch of top of cups. Bring water to a boil, cover pan with tight fitting lid, turn off heat and let stand undisturbed until custard is set, about 16 minutes.

Mrs. Dan Chamblee

AMOUNTS FOR TWO

VEGETABLES

Cabbage or carrots	1/2 pound
Lima beans or peas, unshelled	1 to 1 1/2 pounds
Onions	1 pound
Potatoes to boil or mash	1 pound
Potatoes, sweet	3/4 pound
String beans	1/2 to 3/4 pound

BEEF

Chopped or ground	3/4 pound
Pot roast	2 1/2 pounds
Sirloin roast	3 pounds
Club steak	1 to 1 1/4 pounds
Porterhouse steak	1 1/2 pounds
Round steak	1 pound
Sirloin or minute steak	1 1/4 pounds

PORK

Canadian bacon	1/4 pound per person
Frankfurters or sausage	1/2 pound
Ham steak or slice	1 pound
Roast loin or spareribs	1 1/2 pounds

VEAL

Cutlet or steak	1 pound
Calf's liver	3/4 pound

SAUSAGE

Bologna, liverwurst, salami	1/4 pound

FISH

Fillets	3/4 pound (approximately)
Steaks	1 pound
Whole fish	1 1/2 pounds

BASIC KITCHEN EQUIPMENT

KITCHEN UTENSILS

Baster
Pastry brush
Corkscrew
Grater
Opener
Rolling pin
Sifter
Meat Thermometer
Pancake turner
Knives: bread, carving
    general utility
    cleaver, paring

Beater
Apple corer
Meat fork (2-pronged)
Masher
Pastry blender
Sieves: 1 coarse, 1 fine
Spatulas: 1 rubber, 1 metal
Tongs
Spoons: measuring (2 sets)
    metal (2)
    slotted metal
    wooden (3, graduated)

COOKWARE

Casseroles (2 quart, 4 quart)
Double boiler (2 quart)
Pot (deep, covered)
Baking sheet
Pans: cake (2, 6x8x2, 10x5x3)
    muffin, pie
    small sauce pan
    sauce (1 pint, 2 quart)
    sauce, covered (2 and 4 quart)
    sauce, enamel (1 pint, 1 quart)

Baking dishes (1 round,
    1 rectangular)
Dutch oven (medium)
Roaster (covered and
    with trivet)
Skillets (10-inch, 5-inch)

MISCELLANEOUS

Pot holders
Containers, covered
    for refrigerator
Matches

Bread tin
Garbage can

CLEANING SUPPLIES

Broom
Dish rack
Pail
Steel wool

Dishcloths
Mops: wet, dry
Sponge
Dish towels

FIRST DAY'S MARKETING

Baking powder
Cream of tartar
Fruits
Tomato sauce
Cheese
Milk: canned, whole
Crackers
Spaghetti
Flavoring, vanilla
Sugar
Shortening
Lemons
Potatoes
Herbs: thyme
    bay leaves

Baking soda
Flour
Juices
Vegetables
Cream
Bread
Noodles
Bacon
Jelly
Oil
Spices and seasonings
Lettuce
Chocolate: sweet
    semi-sweet
Parsley

Cornstarch
Mixes
Soup
Butter
Eggs
Cereal
Rice
Bouillon cubes
Mayonnaise
Salt
Celery
Onions

Cleaning powder
Garbage bags
Steel wool
Tissues: cleansing
    toilet

Detergents
Hand soap
Waxed paper

Light bulbs
Paper towels
Tinfoil

LET'S GO CAMPING

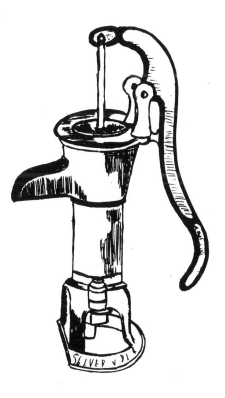

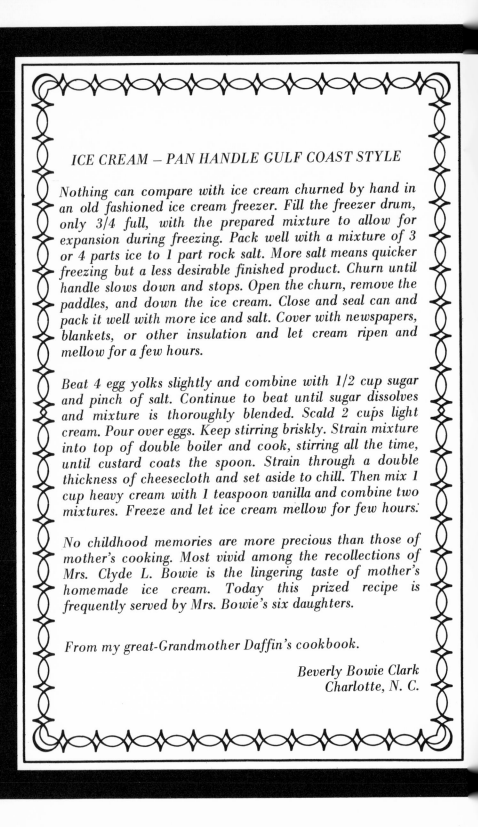

ICE CREAM – PAN HANDLE GULF COAST STYLE

Nothing can compare with ice cream churned by hand in an old fashioned ice cream freezer. Fill the freezer drum, only 3/4 full, with the prepared mixture to allow for expansion during freezing. Pack well with a mixture of 3 or 4 parts ice to 1 part rock salt. More salt means quicker freezing but a less desirable finished product. Churn until handle slows down and stops. Open the churn, remove the paddles, and down the ice cream. Close and seal can and pack it well with more ice and salt. Cover with newspapers, blankets, or other insulation and let cream ripen and mellow for a few hours.

Beat 4 egg yolks slightly and combine with 1/2 cup sugar and pinch of salt. Continue to beat until sugar dissolves and mixture is thoroughly blended. Scald 2 cups light cream. Pour over eggs. Keep stirring briskly. Strain mixture into top of double boiler and cook, stirring all the time, until custard coats the spoon. Strain through a double thickness of cheesecloth and set aside to chill. Then mix 1 cup heavy cream with 1 teaspoon vanilla and combine two mixtures. Freeze and let ice cream mellow for few hours.

No childhood memories are more precious than those of mother's cooking. Most vivid among the recollections of Mrs. Clyde L. Bowie is the lingering taste of mother's homemade ice cream. Today this prized recipe is frequently served by Mrs. Bowie's six daughters.

From my great-Grandmother Daffin's cookbook.

Beverly Bowie Clark
Charlotte, N. C.

Many people who enjoy camping have learned the fun of combining a mass camp-out with a mass cook-out. CAROLINA CUISINE has collected camp-cooking recipes, including a main dish, salad and dessert, which may be used as a menu for a large group. These recipes are followed by basic amounts to serve fifty and by camping tips.

SHRIMP BOIL

1 1-pound box salt with fresh water or salt water only if at beach
1 75-pound sack live shrimp
50 medium, mild, sweet onions

50 medium, white potatoes
2 5-ounce boxes crab boil
4 bay leaves
1 teaspoon Tabasco

Build a fire of driftwood and place iron pot on a brick or stone over it. Fill pot 2/3 full of water and bring to a boil. Add salt if using fresh water. Wash live shrimp by dumping into a tub of water or by leaving in a mesh bag and pouring water over the bag until all sand is removed. Wash onions and remove outer skin. Scrub potatoes with a brush; do not peel or slice. Drop potatoes and onions into boiling water. Tie spices in a piece of cloth and drop in pot. Add Tabasco. Cook until vegetables are almost tender. Pour in live shrimp and push into boiling water quickly with a long-handled paddle. Stir and let boil until they turn red, about 10-15 minutes. Serve from the pot. Allow one potato and one onion per person. Pile shrimp on an extra plate. Pull away potato and onion skins. Break shrimp tails from the body. Remove shell and discard. Provide a cocktail sauce or a tartar sauce if desired. Add bread for a complete outdoor meal. Serves 50.

Mrs. J. Philip Noury

Too many cooks spoil the broth. — Sir Balthazar Gerbier

CABBAGE SLAW

12 pounds green cabbage	2 1/2 tablespoons salt
2 cups celery	1 1/4 tablespoons pepper
1 cup green pepper, chopped	1 1/4 cups vinegar
5 cups sour cream	1 1/4 cups sugar

Toss shredded cabbage, chopped celery, and chopped pepper together. Add sour cream, seasonings, vinegar, and sugar. Yields 2 1/4 gallons.

Mrs. J. Philip Noury

TAKE TO THE LAKE CAKE

2 cups sugar	1 teaspoon salt
1/2 cup shortening	1 teaspoon soda
3 tablespoons cocoa	1/2 cup buttermilk
3 eggs, unbeaten	1 teaspoon vanilla
2 cups flour	1 cup boiling water
1 teaspoon baking powder	

Cream sugar and shortening. Add eggs, one at a time. Mix dry ingredients; add alternately with buttermilk. Mix thoroughly. Add vanilla and boiling water. Bake in a greased (9 x 12-inch) cake pan at 350 degrees for about 30 minutes. Test for doneness.

TOPPING

1 cup plus 2 tablespoons brown sugar	8 tablespoons coffee cream (must use real cream)
6 tablespoons butter (not margarine)	1 cup chopped nuts

Mix all ingredients together and spread over warm cake. Broil until bubbly and brown. Watch carefully.

Mrs. Samuel R. Moorhead, Jr.

BEAN TOSSED SALAD

12 15-ounce can kidney beans
24 hard cooked eggs
3 cups chopped onion
6 cups diced celery

4 cups pickle relish
6 cups shredded sharp cheese
6 cups salad dressing
1/4 cup vinegar

Drain beans and dice eggs. Toss all ingredients together lightly. Garnish with additional hard cooked eggs if desired. Serves 50.

Mrs. J. Philip Noury

"Never camp in ravines and gullies!"

APPLES! FOILED AGAIN!

Core baking apples, taking care not to cut through the bottom. Fill each apple with any of the following: 2 tablespoons sugar with dash of cinnamon, nutmeg, or apple pie spice; 2 tablespoons brown sugar; or 2 tablespoons brown and white sugar mixed. Raisins or chopped nuts may be added to any of the fillings. For a richer flavor fill the apple, then put a small dab of butter on top. Wrap each apple in a square of heavy-duty foil and bake, right side up, for 20 to 35 minutes directly on coals. If baking on a grill close to coals, add at least 20 minutes cooking time. Test by squeezing apples gently, wearing asbestos mitt. If they are soft, they are ready to serve. Use the foil as a serving dish.

Mrs. J. Philip Noury

COOKING FOR A CROWD
(Basic Amounts To Serve Fifty)

MEATS	AMOUNT
Roast beef or baked ham	20 pounds
Meat loaf	13 pounds
Turkey	2 birds (18 to 20 pounds)
Chicken	25 broilers (1 1/2 to 2 pounds)
Frankfurters	12 pounds

VEGETABLES	AMOUNT
Most canned vegetables	10 cans (1 pound, 4 ounces)
Fresh green beans or carrots	10 pounds
White or sweet potatoes (mashed)	15 pounds
White or sweet potatoes (baked)	20 pounds
Slaw or potato salad	6 1/4 quarts
Lettuce for salad	7 large heads
Tomatoes for salad	20 pounds

FRUITS	AMOUNT
Most canned fruit juices	5 cans (46 ounces)
Fresh apples	22 pounds
Watermelon	3 large

BEVERAGES	AMOUNT
Regular coffee (2 cups per person)	2 pounds
Tea bags (2 cups per person)	15 family size bags
Milk	12 1/2 quarts
Half and half for coffee	4 pints
Sugar for coffee	2 pounds
Lemon for tea	6 lemons

CAMPING TIPS

1. – If you boil water to purify it, let it stand for 10 minutes or so to improve the taste.

2. – An army surplus ammunition belt, fitted with "S" hooks and strapped around a tree makes a fine utensil holder.

3. – Tie a string through a roll of paper towels, then tie the string to the table.

4. – Lining the skillet with foil when cooking fish will solve the problem of a "fishy" taste carrying over to the next meal.

5. – If ants are many and persistent, you can keep them off the camp table by setting each leg into an aluminum pie pan and filling it with water. The ants can't make it past the moat.

6. – For weekend camping make hamburgers at home and freeze them. After a day in your camp ice chest, they will be ready to take out, cook and serve.

7. – To protect hands from heat while cooking franks or kabobs over the fire, slit an aluminum pie tin in the center, push skewer or barbecue fork through slit so that it serves as a shield.

8. – Rub detergent on the outside of utensils you plan to use on the open fire. This treatment makes soot easy to wash off later.

9. – Campfires and Dutch ovens go together. To use yours for baking, put wire rack in the bottom, place pan on rack, put on the lid and set oven on bed of coals.

10. – You can cook two foods in one pan, by lining pan with foil and pinching up a ridge in the center to separate them.

I love everything that is old – old friends,
old times, old manners, old books, old wine. – Burns

NOTES

HOMEMAKING HINTS

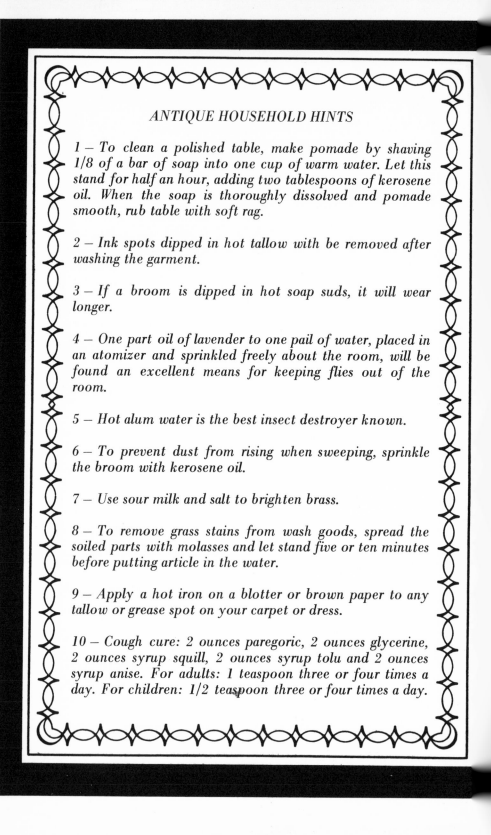

ANTIQUE HOUSEHOLD HINTS

1 – To clean a polished table, make pomade by shaving 1/8 of a bar of soap into one cup of warm water. Let this stand for half an hour, adding two tablespoons of kerosene oil. When the soap is thoroughly dissolved and pomade smooth, rub table with soft rag.

2 – Ink spots dipped in hot tallow with be removed after washing the garment.

3 – If a broom is dipped in hot soap suds, it will wear longer.

4 – One part oil of lavender to one pail of water, placed in an atomizer and sprinkled freely about the room, will be found an excellent means for keeping flies out of the room.

5 – Hot alum water is the best insect destroyer known.

6 – To prevent dust from rising when sweeping, sprinkle the broom with kerosene oil.

7 – Use sour milk and salt to brighten brass.

8 – To remove grass stains from wash goods, spread the soiled parts with molasses and let stand five or ten minutes before putting article in the water.

9 – Apply a hot iron on a blotter or brown paper to any tallow or grease spot on your carpet or dress.

10 – Cough cure: 2 ounces paregoric, 2 ounces glycerine, 2 ounces syrup squill, 2 ounces syrup tolu and 2 ounces syrup anise. For adults: 1 teaspoon three or four times a day. For children: 1/2 teaspoon three or four times a day.

No cook book would be complete without a section devoted to weights, measurements and substitutions. In addition, CAROLINA CUISINE includes in this section useful hints for cooking, cleaning and household management. Many of the suggestions have come from personal experience, some have been handed down from mother to daughter for generations and all are presented with a wish to make the career of homemaker a little easier.

COOKING TIPS

CAKES

1 — Soften sugar in warm oven for 10 to 15 minutes.

2 — Quicker creaming of butter and sugar: add about three tablespoons of the liquid in the recipe.

3 — Grease the bottoms, but never the sides of the cake pans.

4 — Cake won't stick to the plate, if you spread a little flour on the top.

5 — To keep cakes fresh: put half an apple in the container.

6 — A pinch of salt added to the sugar in making icings will prevent graining.

7 — Ingredients should be at room temperature.

8 — Stir a half package of chocolate chips into your seven-minute frosting while it is still hot. It will turn out creamy and taste wonderful.

COOKING TIPS

PRESERVING

1 — Add 2 tablespoons vinegar when canning strawberries to retain the red color.

2 — You can make jelly much clearer and more attractive by straining the fruit and juice through a flour sifter.

3 — Dip a silver fork into the boiling jelly; and if it fills in between all the tines of the fork, the jelly is done.

4 — Scald pears for canning, as you do tomatoes, and the skins will slip off.

VEGETABLES

1 — Broccoli — to shorten the cooking time, make a few gashes through the stem ends, then cook as usual.

2 — To freshen wilted greens: douse quickly in hot and then ice water, with a little vinegar added.

3 — Cut down odor of cabbage when cooking by adding a little vinegar to cooking water.

4 — To remove excessive taste of salt: while cooking, add 1 teaspoon each of vinegar and sugar, or in soup a few slices of raw potato.

COOKING TIPS

MEATS AND POULTRY

1 – To hurry a meat loaf, put the mixture into well buttered muffin tins to bake at 450 degrees for 15 to 18 minutes.

2 – Rub chicken with lemon juice to tenderize and remove odors.

3 – Ham may be basted with the syrup drained from pickled peaches.

4 – Sprinkle salt in frying pan before frying meat to prevent fat from splashing.

5 – Freeze hamburger patties individually in tin foil. To remove, run warm water over foil – patties slip out easily and may be cooked frozen.

6 – To prevent frying fish odor, put a piece of orange skin on the side of a stove burner.

PIES AND PASTRIES

1 – Pie crust: Add sesame seed to pie crust when rolling it out. Sesame seed can also be used in tiny party biscuits.

2 – Roll pastry between two sheets of wax paper. When the top paper is peeled off, the pastry may be easily turned into a pie pan and the other paper removed.

3 – Use tapioca instead of flour for thickening in fruit pies.

4 – Set pies and cobblers on a rack to cool and the bottom crust will not be soggy.

5 – For a prettier pie shell, chill for thirty minutes, then bake.

MISCELLANEOUS COOKING TIPS

1 — Herbs and Spices: Do not store over the range or near heat. They lose their savor quickly.

2 — Frozen Punch Ring: To make a clear frozen ring, boil water, then cool and freeze.

3 — Grease or oil the pot in which you intend to melt chocolate. This will prevent the chocolate from sticking.

4 — Add raw rice to a salt shaker to keep the salt from sticking.

5 — When cutting marshmallows or candied fruits, dip scissors in confectioners sugar or hot water.

6 — To tint coconut: add food coloring to one tablespoon water until you get the color you want. Put coconut in jar, add colored water, cap jar, shake. Drain on paper towel.

7 — To shell pecans: cover with boiling water for a few minutes, drain, crack on the ends. The sides will break and the meat comes out in perfect halves.

8 — Add 1 teaspoon of salt to water to keep egg white from escaping a cracked shell when being boiled.

9 — To measure molasses: grease measuring cup.

10 — To preserve egg yolks in refrigerator cover with cold water.

11 — Coconut grates easily if you freeze it first.

12 — To prepare oranges for a fruit salad or cup: cover unpeeled orange with boiling water and let stand about 5 minutes. When you peel them, the white will come off with the rind.

TERMS USED IN COOKING

1 – Au Gratin: Creamed food covered with browned crumbs or cheese.

2 – Barbecue: To roast meat slowly on a spit over coals, or in the oven, basting frequently with a highly seasoned sauce.

3 – Baste: To moisten foods during cooking with pan drippings, water, or special sauce to prevent drying or add flavor.

4 – Blanch: To partially cook or to remove skins by briefly immersing food in boiling water or steam.

5 – Braise: To cook meat by moist heat. The meat is browned and then simmered in a small amount of liquid in a covered utensil.

6 – Caramelize: To melt sugar slowly over low heat until it becomes brown in color.

7 – Cream: To work shortening and sugar by pressing the spoon against the side of the bowl until the mixture is fluffy and creamy.

8 – Dredge: To cover food completely with flour, crumbs, etc.

9 – Fillet: Cuts of meat or fish which are boneless or from which bones have been removed.

10 – Flake: To break into small pieces, usually with a fork.

11 – Fricassee: To cook by braising, usually applied to fowl or rabbit.

12 – Garnish: To decorate with small pieces of colorful food.

13 – Glaze: To coat with a thin sugar syrup cooked to crack stage.

14 – Marinate: To allow a food to stand in a liquid – usually French dressing or a mixture of oil and vinegar – to soften or add flavor.

15 — Mince: To cut into very fine pieces.

16 — Pan Broil: To cook uncovered in a hot frying pan, pouring off fat as it accumulates.

17 — Parboil: To boil in water until partially cooked.

18 — Pare: To cut away outer covering, as potato or apple.

19 — Pit: To remove pits or stones from fruits.

20 — Puree: Fruits or vegetables which have been pressed through a food press or sieve.

21 — Sauté: To cook or brown in a small amount of fat.

22 — Scald: To bring to a temperature just below the boiling point.

23 — Scallop: To bake a mixture of food and sauce topped with crumbs in a casserole in the oven.

24 — Score: To cut narrow grooves or gashes part way through the outer surface of food.

25 — Sear: To brown quickly by intense heat, in a hot oven or pan.

26 — Simmer: To cook slowly over very low heat, at a temperature of about 185 degrees.

27 — Skewer: To fasten meat or fowl with metal or wood pins to help hold its shape.

28 — Steep: To extract flavor by immersing in water just below boiling, as to steep tea.

29 — Truss: To tie fowl or other meat with metal or wooden pins to hold shape during cooking.

WEIGHTS AND MEASURES

3 teaspoons	1 tablespoon
4 tablespoons	1/4 cup
5 1/2 tablespoons	1/3 cup
16 tablespoons	1 cup
2 tablespoons	1 liquid ounce
1 cup	1/2 pint
4 cups	1 quart
4 quarts	1 gallon
8 quarts	1 peck
4 pecks	1 bushel
16 ounces	1 pound

SUBSTITUTIONS

1/2 cup cocoa plus 1/2 tablespoon margarine	= 1 ounce square chocolate
3/4 cup honey minus part of liquid	= 1 cup sugar
1/2 cup evaporated milk plus 1/2 cup water	= 1 cup fresh milk
1/4 cup dried milk plus 1 cup water	= 1 cup fresh milk
1 1/2 tablespoons flour	= 1 tablespoon cornstarch
1 cup sifted all-purpose flour minus 2 tablespoons	= 1 cup sifted cake flour
1 cup sour milk plus 1/4 teaspoon soda	= 1 cup milk
1 tablespoon very cold water added to 1 egg white	= 2 egg whites

DRY INGREDIENTS

4 cups sifted all purpose flour	1 pound
4 1/2 cups sifted cake flour	1 pound
6 cups oatmeal	1 pound
2 1/3 cups rice	1 pound
2 1/4 cups granulated sugar	1 pound
3 1/2 cups confectioners sugar	1 pound
2 cups dried beans	1 pound
2 1/4 cups firmly packed brown sugar	1 pound
2 1/2 cups seedless raisins	1 15-ounce package
1 cup chopped nuts	1/4 pound
15 marshmallows	1/4 pound
7 coarsley crumbled salted crackers	1 cup
9 finely crumbled salted crackers	1 cup
9 coarsley crumbled graham crackers	1 cup
11 finely crumbled graham crackers	1 cup

LIQUID INGREDIENTS

8 1/2 ounces milk	1 cup
12 ounces molasses	1 cup
Juice of 1 orange	6 to 8 tablespoons
Juice of 1 lemon	3 tablespoons
8 average eggs	1 cup
8 to 10 egg whites	1 cup
12 to 14 egg yolks	1 cup

INDEX

313

314

317